Domestic Abuse: All Sides

M. WEBB

PublishAmerica
Baltimore

© 2005 by M. Webb.

All rights reserved. No part of this book may be reproduced, stored in a retrieval system or transmitted in any form or by any means without the prior written permission of the publishers, except by a reviewer who may quote brief passages in a review to be printed in a newspaper, magazine or journal.

At the specific preference of the author, PublishAmerica allowed this work to remain exactly as the author intended, verbatim, without editorial input.

Any resemblance to actual places or persons living or dead is purely coincidental.

First printing

ISBN: 1-4137-8727-4
PUBLISHED BY PUBLISHAMERICA, LLLP
www.publishamerica.com
Baltimore

Printed in the United States of America

DEDICATED TO:

* MY CHILDREN
* MY BROTHER
* MY SISTER IN LAW
* MY STEP FATHER

ACKNOWLEDGMENTS:

* TO MY CHILDREN - I LOVE YOU
* TO MY BROTHER - (WHO HAS ALWAYS STOOD BY ME), HIS WIFE AND MY STEPFATHER - AT LEAST THE THREE OF YOU TRIED!
* TO MY DAD, MOM AND SISTER
* TO MY STEPMOTHER AND STEPSISTER
* TO MIKE M.
* TO GAIL K.
* TO MY GRANDPARENTS, GREAT AUNT, AUNTS, UNCLES & COUSINS
* TO MY PUBLISHER - I AM GRATEFUL
* TO WOMEN'S SHELTERS
* TO ALL THE VICTIMS OF DOMESTIC VIOLENCE

Domestic Abuse:
All Sides

CHILDREN'S STORIES

This is a collection of stories about children who have lived with abuse. They saw their mothers being abused. Some have been abused themselves, by their fathers, stepfathers or their mothers' boyfriends. These children witnessed their mothers being abused and sometimes even worse.

Some of them have gone through the courts with their mothers. Others have been forced to go into hiding with their mothers to escape their abusers, having to leave their families and friends behind, because of these men.

No one hears about them, because their stories are never told.

Some of them have dealt with it, while others seem to have been unable to cope. Some of them have grown stronger because of it and still others haven't been able to move forward. A few have not survived the abuse.

Some of their stories are truly horrible. Our legal system has to do something to protect these women and their children. Visitation is something that needs to be re-evaluated. Not everyone should have the right to visitation, it should be based on an individual evaluation of each and every case.

Unfortunately these kids are often played by the father against the mother, because a woman's weakness is her children.

These are their accounts of what has happened inside their homes. Let's listen this time.

RYAN

My name is Ryan and I'm ten-years-old. When I was smaller my dad used to hit my mom a lot. I used to hear her screaming, but I was too afraid of my dad to come out of my room. I wanted to help my mom, but I knew that my dad would hurt me.

One day when I got a little older I did come out of my room. I saw my mom sitting on the floor with her hands above her head. I also saw my dad swinging his fists at her. He kept hitting her whenever he could. I yelled for him to stop and he turned around and punched me in the head. Then he yelled at me to go back to my room, which I did.

Later my dad went outside and after I heard his car drive away, I again came out of my room. My mom was sitting on the floor crying. She looked up at me and I saw that she had red welts all over her face. I was real scared and I felt really bad for her. I went over to her and she hugged me, telling me that she was okay. This happened a lot of times, too many times.

TODD

My name is Todd and I'm eight-years-old. My mom and her boyfriend used to fight all the time. I used to hear him tell her that he was going to kill her.

One day, they were really going at it and my mom yelled for me to call the cops. I grabbed the phone, then Paul came over to me and pulled the phone out of my hand. He hit me in the head with it, and then he threw it at my mom, hitting her with it.

JESSICA

I'm Jessica and I'm twelve-years-old. My dad used to beat on my mom. My mom and the police finally made him leave. I hated it when my dad lived with us. I used to stay in my room and cry, while he would yell and hit my mom in the other room.

One day after he had been kicked out, he came back to our apartment. My mom was in the shower and my dad went into the bathroom. He stabbed her a lot of times.

I found her when I came home from school that day, I will never forget it.

Now I live with my grandma.

My dad's in jail, where he belongs. I visit my mom at her grave all the time. I really do miss her a lot and I wish that she was still here with me. My grandma tries, but it's just not the same as having my mom around.

ANNA

My name is Anna and I am six-years-old. My daddy hit my mommy and he would made her cry. My mommy and I moved into my Aunt Lisa's house. Now my daddy leaves us alone.

I'm happy now, because my mommy doesn't cry or get hurt anymore.

LORI

I'm Lori and I'm fourteen-years-old. My mom had a boyfriend who was a real jerk. He used to hit her a lot.

One day I came home from school and I saw him sitting on top of my mom, choking her. I ran over to him and started pounding him on the back. He let go of my mom and pushed me away from him. This gave my mom a chance to get up. He grabbed me by the hair with one hand and punched me in the stomach.

My mom ran over and hit him. He let go of my hair and then he went after her again. I grabbed a pan, and hit him on the back of the head with it. He let go of my mom and fell to the floor. He didn't move at all. I thought that I had killed him! My mom went over to the phone to call the cops.

I remember seeing blood all over the floor, it was coming from his head. My mom came up to me, and she held me while we waited for the cops to get there. When they finally came, they told me that he wasn't dead. But I had cut his head up pretty bad. My mom made him leave after that.

Her new boyfriend Bob is really nice. They have been together for two years now, and we are all really happy.

BRANDON

My name is Brandon and I am sixteen-years-old. I don't have a girlfriend and I don't have any friends. My dad used to hit my mom a lot, we finally got tired of it and we moved out. My mom filed for a divorce and for custody of me.

One day my dad came to pick me up, he was acting very weird. He kept saying that if he couldn't have me, that my mom couldn't have me either. I was nine at the time, and my dad was really scaring me.

We went back to my old house, my dad still lived there. It was a mess, there were dirty dishes and clothes everywhere. He told me that we were going to have a cookout in the backyard. That sounded pretty cool, so I waited for him out back.

When he finally came around the corner of the house, I saw that he had a can of lighter fluid in his hand. He opened the can and started to spray it on me, it went all over me. It even went into my eyes and it burned real bad. I couldn't understand what he was doing.

Then he threw a match at me. Man, did that hurt! I caught on fire, my clothes were melting to my skin. I guess that a neighbor called the police, when they heard me screaming.

I don't remember much, except for a lot of doctors appointments and being in a lot of pain. The doctors said that I had third degree burns over 95% of my body. They say that I'm lucky to be alive, I don't call it lucky.

I scare people when I walk by them, they stare at me and sometimes they call me names. Kids are the worst, I hear them laughing at me and saying awful things. Some people just stare at me with a horrible look on their faces.

My mom still calls me her perfect boy, but I don't feel perfect. I know that I am ugly. I have no friends. No one talks to me in school, the kids are all mean to me. Either that, or they ignore me completely.

I didn't do anything! It's not my fault that I look like this.

My dad is in prison for what he did to me and I hope that he stays in there forever.

My mom has been great. When I get depressed, she kicks me in the butt. Not really, but she makes me feel better. I don't understand why my dad did that to me. My mom says he was upset with her for leaving him. But I still don't understand why my dad did such an awful thing to me.

Sometimes I think that I'd be better off dead. Sometimes I really do wish that I had died that day.

UNKNOWN

My name is Sam now and I'm eleven-years-old. I used to have a different name, so did my mom. We had to get away from my dad, because he used to hurt my mom real bad. When my mom told him that she was going to leave, he told her that she couldn't take me with her. He told her that if she tried to take me, that he'd kill the both of us. I was really scared of him and so was my mom. Sometimes my dad could be real mean, especially when he was drinking.

One day my mom told me that we were going to go to a shelter, to get away from him. At first I was mad at her. She had made me leave my house and all of my friends behind. But then I was glad, because my dad wouldn't hurt her anymore.

The shelter was pretty bad. We had to share a room with a woman and her two daughters. We had to stay with people that we didn't even know and that was pretty weird. My mom kept telling me that it was just for a while.

The women at the shelter were real nice. They helped us to get away from my dad. They gave my mom some money and told her where we should go.

We have our own apartment now and I have new friends. I miss my old friends, but I am pretty happy here. My mom has a job and some friends, too.

It's pretty nice here, but it sure gets cold in the winter.

I can't tell anyone where I used to live or what my name used to be, but that's okay. I don't mind that part of it, I even like my new name now.

NICOLETTE

My name is Nicolette and I am sixteen-years-old. My dad used to beat on my mom a lot. Quite a few times my mom had to go to the hospital for stitches, or because she had a broken bone. He was a real jerk, but he used to be okay before he lost his job. After he was fired, he was miserable to be around. I hated to be at home when he was there.

My mom worked nights to pay the bills. My dad used to come into my room and tell me that I had to be the woman of the house, while she was at work. I hated it, I hated him. I hated my mom for having to work and for leaving me alone with him.

I was eight-years-old when he first started coming into my room. He told me not to tell my mom or anyone else. He told me that he'd beat me like he did my mom, if I ever told anyone. I was really afraid of him.

During the day he'd work on an old beat up car, that was in our garage. Once my mom left for work, he'd come into the house and down the hall to my room. He would always smell like grease and beer. To this day I can't stand those two smells.

I would try to pretend that I was sleeping, but he didn't care. He'd tell me that it was time for me to wake up and make daddy happy. Sometimes I had to touch him or he would touch me.

When I turned ten he started to have sex with me. When I was eleven he started to hit me, sometimes even during sex.

At twelve I ran away from home. I don't know if my parents are still together or not. I haven't talked to either one of them in almost five years. I don't know if they are dead or alive. I know that I will never go back there, I can't.

I am a dancer in a nightclub now, and I make pretty good money. They even think that I'm eighteen, I guess that I look older. I share an apartment with a friend of mine from the club, she is a dancer too. She's only nineteen, but she has helped me a lot more than either one of my parents ever did. Katie watches out for me at the club, too. She is like a big sister to me.

I'm happy to be away from my dad, but sometimes I miss my mom. I hope that she got away from him, and that she is okay.

UNKNOWN

My name is Jenny now and I am seventeen-years-old. We took off from my dad when I was twelve. My dad used to beat on me, my little brother, Billy, and our mom.

One night after my dad passed out, we left. My mom had been saving money for quite a while. She finally had enough put away to buy two bus tickets. Billy took turns sitting on our lap, so he rode for free.

I remember that the bus ride took forever. It seemed like every time I would fall asleep, the bus would stop and then I would wake up. My mom was nervous each time the bus stopped, she was so afraid that my dad would be there, to bring us back home.

We must have looked pretty bad off, a woman with a black eye, sitting with her two bruised kids. A young woman came over to my mom at one of the stops. They talked together, quietly for a few minutes. Then my mom told us we were going to go spend the night in a shelter. We followed the woman down a couple of streets, until we stopped outside a really big house. You couldn't even tell it was a shelter, it looked like all of the other houses that lined the street.

Inside the shelter was pretty nice. We went into one of the bedrooms and waited, while mom talked to a couple of the women. I got myself and Billy ready for bed. Later my mom came into the room. She said that they were going to help us to leave my dad. My mom also told us, that we were going to get new names.

For the next few days we stayed in the shelter, waiting for everything to be set up for us. My mom talked with the other women who lived there. Billy and I played with the other kids in the shelter.

On our fourth day at the shelter, my mom came running into our room. She was real excited, when she told us that we were leaving the next morning. I was happy, but kind of scared too. I had just gotten used to being in the shelter.

We were going to get back on another bus. We had one way tickets to go a few states away. We were going to stay in a shelter there, until my mom could get a job. Then she could save up money for an apartment for us. We were going to live in our own place, I couldn't wait. Billy and I were so excited that night, we both had a hard time getting to sleep.

The next day we left, and a few months later we moved into an apartment. It wasn't the best or nicest place, but it was ours. It was safe and my dad wasn't going to hurt us anymore.

That was five years ago. Now I have my license and a job. The best part is that we haven't seen my dad.

I haven't told anyone about my past. Not my friends and not even my boyfriend, Brian.

We are all very happy now, especially my mom.

My brother is thirteen and he has lots of friends, he is even on the baseball team.

BILLY

My name was Billy and I am thirteen-years-old. I was eight when my mom, my sister and I left my dad.

I remember my dad hitting me, my sister and my mom a lot. He was always mad. First he'd start yelling, then he'd start hitting and punching us. My mom always got it the worst, because she would try to stop him from hurting us. If my sister mouthed off, oh man, she got it real bad.

I tried to make him proud of me, I wanted him to be happy. But no matter what I did, he'd get mad and tell me that I wasn't good enough to be his son. He'd tell me that I was a loser and that I wasn't any good at sports. He said that I was just like one of the girls.

Well, I'm not his son now. We left one night on a bus and we never went back. I'm glad that we did. I had to change my name, but I got to pick my new one, so that was cool!

At first we stayed in this huge house with a lot of other people. We even had to share a room with a lady and her kids. Then we went to another house for a while.

Now we have our own apartment. It's pretty small, but my mom fixed it up real nice. I'm not allowed to tell anyone my old name and I can't talk about before, but that's okay. I'd rather forget about it all anyway. I do like my new school and my new friends.

We still watch out for my dad, but I hope that he never looks for us or finds us. I'm glad that we left him.

MARIE

My name is Marie. I'm eleven-years-old. I saw my dad stab my mom and now we live with my grandma. My mom and I live with my grandma, because it is too hard for my mom to live with just me. My mom has to stay in a wheelchair all of the time, except for when she goes to bed. She got stabbed in the back and the doctors say that she'll never walk again.

When I was nine we moved into a shelter. There were a lot of women and kids there. My dad used to hit my mom a lot and that is why we moved out. I was happier at the shelter, I hated it when my dad got mean. The people in the shelter were real nice and we ended up staying there for a long time.

After a while my mom got a job, she seemed happy. It was summertime, so I stayed at the day care in the shelter. There were a lot of other kids there and I made some friends.

One day my mom and I had gone downtown, to go shopping for some new shoes. While we were at the bus stop waiting for the bus to come, I heard my mom quietly say, 'Oh no.' I looked around and that's when I saw my dad, running towards us. My mom and dad talked for a few minutes and I heard my mom keep telling him 'no.' I also heard her tell him, that we weren't going to go back with him.

My dad got real mad and he hit her right there on the sidewalk. My mom yelled for me to go get help. We were the only ones waiting for the bus, so I ran up to the first doorway I saw. I turned around and looked back at my mom. My dad had pushed her down onto the ground and he was sitting on top of her. She was laying on her stomach and he was stabbing her with a knife in the back. I started screaming, I screamed as loud as I could.

Someone from inside the store came out and quickly dragged me inside, then they called the cops. When the police finally came, they pulled my dad off of my mom. The whole time, he just kept stabbing her. He wouldn't stop stabbing her with that knife. My mom didn't move. There was a lot of blood on her and on the ground around her.

I ran out of the store calling for my mom, I knelt down on the ground next to her. I kept talking to her, telling her that help was coming and to please not die.

The ambulance took us to the hospital and I kept asking them if my mom was going to be okay. No one ever answered me. One of the cops called my grandma. I felt better when I saw her. I ran to her outstretched arms and we both cried. We waited for a while, then after she had talked to the doctor we went back to her house.

Everyday grandma and I went to the hospital to see my mom. She was in a coma for a long time, then finally one day she woke up. Grandma and I were so happy!

The doctors did lots of tests on my mom and they told us that she would never be able to walk again, that she was always going to be in a wheelchair.

I like living at grandma's house. My mom and I still do things together. But there are also a lot of things she can't do now, that she used to be able to.

My mom still has tubes that she's hooked up to and she is on all kinds of medicines, but at least she didn't die.

My dad is in jail and will be for a long time. I hate him, I hate him for what he did.

I'm never getting married!

STACY

I'm Amanda now, but my name used to be Stacy. We left my house when I was eight-years-old. My dad always beat on my mom and sometimes he'd hit me too. The police were constantly coming to our apartment and then they would take my dad away with them. My dad would stay gone for a while, but he'd always come back. Things would be good for a while, then he'd get mean again.

Sometimes my mom and I would leave, we'd stay in a shelter. It was okay, but I missed my room and my things back at home. Then we'd end up going back home again, because my dad would find us or my mom would run out of money.

I hated him when he was mean, which was almost all of the time. My mom was always sad, she never seemed happy.

One night my dad took a gun out of his jacket pocket. He told my mom that he was going to kill us all, if my mom ever tried to leave him again. He put the gun up to her head and my mom started to cry. He just kept yelling at her. When he finally did stop and put the gun down, it was starting to get light outside.

When my dad fell asleep, we left. We went back to the shelter. The women there helped me and my mom to finally be able leave my dad.

That was six years ago and we haven't seen my dad at all since we left. We have our own apartment and even new names. We feel pretty safe now.

MARGARET

I'm Margaret and I am twelve-years-old. My mom married my stepfather when I was eleven, but I never liked him. When he and my mom would fight it was usually about me. My mom would let me go over to my friends house or watch tv. He'd get mad, because he always wanted me to do other things, like hand him tools out in the garage. That was so boring.

Sometimes they would really go at it, then he'd end up hitting her. When I'd yell at him to stop, he'd push me or hit me too. This would really get my mom mad. She'd start yelling at him and he'd hit her again, then he'd leave for a while.

One night he didn't leave, he just kept yelling at her and telling her that I was just a spoiled brat. He pushed my mom down the stairs and she hit her arm pretty hard. I ran down to help her. He grabbed me by the back of the neck and he told me to stay out of it. He said that all I did was cause problems for them. He said they would be happy if I weren't around.

He let me go, then he walked back over to my mom and he kicked her. My mom slowly got up, holding onto her arm. She yelled for me to go call the cops. Then she told him to get out of our house, she said that he had hurt us for long enough.

When I started to go back upstairs to call the cops, he tripped me. I hit my head on one of the stairs and cut my forehead. When I got up I could feel the blood running down the side of my face. My mom pushed past him to help me up the stairs. She called an ambulance and held a towel on my head, while we waited for them to show up. He kept walking back and forth saying that everything was my fault. This wouldn't have happened if I wasn't always trying to get in the middle of them.

The police and an ambulance both came. The police arrested him and me and my mom were taken to the hospital. My mom had a broken arm and I had to get twenty four stitches on my head.

After that my mom divorced him and we haven't seen him since.

LUCY

Lucy was a pretty fifteen-year-old girl. She did good in school and had a lot of friends. But at home, well, at home she walked on eggshells. Her dad drank a lot and used many different kinds of illegal drugs.

Her mom had to work nights during the week, but during the day and on weekends it was usually okay at their house. At night, with her mom gone and her dad drinking, it was miserable to be around. Lucy hated to be left alone with her dad.

When they were all home he'd start by yelling at Lucy and her mom, then if he was in a really bad mood he'd hit them both. The worst was when her mother worked, because it was just her at home with him. All of his anger was directed at her.

One night when her mom was working, Lucy had her friend Jen over. The girls were working on a science paper together which was due the next day. Lucy tried really hard to get the paper done before her dad got home, but they had taken longer than Lucy realized. The girls heard a car pull up outside and Lucy quickly looked up at the clock. She realized that her dad was home from work and she got scared.

Jen asked her friend if she could use her phone to call her mother. The girls went out into the kitchen. Lucy looked at the door and saw her dad standing there.

"Why aren't the dishes done?" he asked her.

"We've been trying to get a paper done for school, it's due tomorrow. I'll do them soon, I promise." Lucy told him, hoping that he wouldn't embarrass her by starting anything in front of her friend.

"Yeah right, your probably just sitting around talking about boys. All that'll do is get you pregnant!" he yelled at her.

"Dad, please!" Lucy pleaded, wishing now that they had done their paper over at Jen's house.

"Isn't that right?" he asked Jen. "You girls were talking about boys."

"We were doing our paper, just like Lucy said." Jen said quietly. Not sure what to do, she looked over at Lucy.

"You are a whore, just like your mother!" he said, slapping Lucy hard across the face.

Jen backed up towards the door very frightened. She had never experienced anything like this before.

"Go home, Jen ! Leave!" Lucy yelled at her friend, knowing that things were going to get worse. She didn't want him to say anything to Jen.

DOMESTIC ABUSE: ALL SIDES

Jen opened the door and looked over at Lucy. "I'll go get help," she said, as she started to back out of the doorway.

He hit Lucy again. Jen quickly ran away from Lucy's house and headed for the house next door.

"Mr. Campbell! Call the cops. Hurry, please!" she yelled, banging on the neighbors door.

By this time, Lucy's father had hit her a few more times, causing her to lose her balance. Lucy fell and hit her head on the corner of the counter.

Lucy died instantly and her father is now in jail.

JULIE

I'm eleven-years-old and my name was Julie. My dad used to beat on me and my mom a lot. He used to always say that women were good for one thing. He would do other things to me.

My mom used to be a nurse at the hospital, but now she is a waitress. She can't do what she used to do, because if she did my dad could find us very easily. She really misses being a nurse, but she says that she'd rather have us be safe. Sometimes at night I can hear her crying. I think it is because she misses being a nurse.

At school I can't tell anyone where I really moved from. We made up a place that we used to live. We even made up a whole new past. My mom says that I have to forget what really happened to us. We go to counseling together at the women's shelter, sometimes it helps. I'm just glad that my mom and I are okay now.

My dad used to touch me when my mom was at work. We went to court and I told the judge. He said that I shouldn't lie to help out my mom! He didn't believe me. When we got home, my dad really went crazy! He told us that if we ever pulled a stunt like that again, he'd kill the both of us.

The next day I didn't go to school and my mom didn't go to work. Instead we packed up all of our things and went to the women's shelter. They helped us out a lot. They listened to us and they believed us. I don't know why that judge didn't believe me, I didn't lie about anything.

It took the shelter about a week, but they helped us to move and everything.

Now my name is Karen.

BOBBY

My name is Bobby and I'm sixteen-years-old, I am also on probation.

I saw my dad beat on my mom a lot. I used to try to stop him, but when I did he'd hit me too. My mom would fall to the floor and cry. My dad would just keep yelling at her to shut up. Sometimes he'd kick her or choke her.

No one ever knew what went on in my house. My mom was quiet and she had no friends, so she never told anyone. My dad sure wasn't going to tell his buddies that he hit me and my mom.

When I got into the fifth grade, one of the sixth graders used to hassle me. One day I got really sick of it and hit him. I didn't just hit him once though, I kept on hitting him. I had to be pulled off of him by one of the teachers at school. My parents were called to the school the next day, because the kid's dad said that I had broken his son's nose.

I got into a lot of fights, I started to get a reputation for not putting up with any crap. I didn't care how big that other kid was either. If they gave me any shit, I'd pound them. I was always in the Principal's Office or the Guidance Counselors Office, and my parents were called to the school a lot.

No one could figure out why I was so angry, my parents sure weren't going to volunteer any information about why I had become so violent.

When I turned fifteen I got my first girlfriend, her name was Janie. She was okay, I guess. We went out for about a year. We fought a lot though, because she was always running her mouth. I had to tell her to shut up. If she didn't shut her mouth, I'd twist her arm or I'd shove her to make her be quiet.

One day when we were at the mall, Janie told me that she wanted to talk to me outside. We walked out into the parking lot, that's when she told me that she wanted to break up with me. I asked her why and she told me that she wanted to go out with Tommy Walker. I couldn't believe what she was telling me, Tommy Walker! I hated Tommy Walker, he thought that he was so perfect in school. I had beaten him up last year.

I slapped her across the face. That was when she told me, she had already spent the last few days with Tommy. That really pissed me off, I started to pound on her. I kept hitting her and hitting her. She fell down and I started to punch her.

I don't know how long that I hit her and punched her, but after a while a security guard pulled me off of her. She just lay there on the pavement, not moving at all and I got really scared. I thought that I had killed her, I hoped that I'd killed her. I was so mad at her for cheating on me. She went to the hospital and I went to jail. I was released later into my parents custody, because I was still a minor.

Janie turned out to be okay, after a while. My parents said that they couldn't understand why I hurt people. Why did they think that I hurt people?

I went to court soon after that. The judge told me that I had to get counseling, do community service and he also put me on probation.

Janie got a restraining order against me and I haven't seen her since we went to court.

I have been going to counseling and my parents have been coming too. My counselor thinks that my anger stems from my home life. Apparently, witnessing my dad beat up on my mom affected me more than I had thought. My mom and my dad are actually trying to work things out between them.

My community service is cleaning up the garbage on the side of the roads. It's hard, but the hardest part of all of this is my counseling. I realize now that I could have killed Janie. I'm glad that I didn't, although I had wanted to at the time. My counselor told me that I should write a letter of apology to Janie, I'm working on it now. That is really hard!

BOB

My name used to be Bob and I used to have blond hair. I'm Andrew now and I have dark brown hair. I am also twelve-years-old. My dad is a cop, he looks like a cop and he acts like a cop. Sometimes he'd come home from work and be in a really ugly mood.

Everything that my mom did he thought was wrong, I really think that he hated her. He'd throw food at her, call her names, slap her, punch her and even kick her. But the time that really scared me, was when he took out his gun and held it up to her head. I thought for sure he was going to shoot her, but he laughed and then he put his gun away.

I was ten-years-old when we finally left him. My dad really wasn't much of a father anyway. I wanted him to come to my basketball and soccer games, but he was always too busy with his girlfriend Wendy. He didn't think that I knew about her, but I did. I knew about Sara and Laura too. I never told my mom about any of them, because I didn't want to hurt her anymore than he already had.

It seemed like all my dad ever did was yell at me and my mom or hit her. I never thought that he liked either one of us very much, he used to tell me that I was just like my mother. He called me a little sissy. He said that I was such a disappointment to him and that he was embarrassed to call me his son.

He got pretty busy for a while. They put him back on the midnight to eight shift. He slept during the day and didn't bother me or my mom much. It sure was nice while it lasted. No one yelled at us or hurt my mom.

One afternoon when I came home from school my dad was screaming, yelling and hitting my mom. She was sitting down on the floor holding her hands above her head trying to ward off his blows.

"Leave her alone." I yelled at him.

"Get out of here!" he told me, taking off his belt and hitting me with it. I ran from the room, I knew that I couldn't call or ask anyone for help, because the cops always protect each other. When we had called them in the past, they hadn't helped us at all. My dad had gotten really mad and it was worse for us.

I hid around the corner and listened to my dad yell at my mom. I looked into the room and saw my dad pick up his gun from the table, then he put it up to the side of my mom's head.

"If you ever threaten to leave me again, I'll kill you." he told her.

"I won't." My mom said to him, looking real scared.

"I would hunt you down and kill you. I'll kill the brat too." he told her.

"Do you hear me?"

"Yes, please put your gun away." My mom begged him, starting to cry.

My dad hit her across the face with his hand. Then he did put away his gun.

"Bobby, get in here." My dad yelled to me.

I went into the room and he told me to help my mom make dinner, so he could get to work on time. I helped my mom get up. When we got out into the kitchen, I asked her if she was okay. She hugged me and told me that everything was going to be okay.

My mom threw a quick dinner together and then my dad left for work. I was happy to see him go, but was real surprised after he'd left by what happened next. My mom got a few bags of our stuff together and told me that we were leaving. We went out to the car and drove away.

We drove for a while and then stopped outside a house. It looked like every other house on the street. I later found out that it was a women's shelter. Two of the women left in our car, so that my dad wouldn't find it near where we were staying.

My mom talked to the women there. Later she told me that we were going to stay for a few weeks in the shelter. That was okay with me, at least that way my dad wouldn't hurt my mom for a few weeks!

A few weeks later, we left the shelter. The women there helped us to become different people. That way my dad would never hurt me or my mom again. My mom has a job now and we are both very happy. My mom smiles and laughs now too. She hasn't done that in a very long time.

TIFFANY

Tiffany was a happy, pretty little two-year-old girl. Luckily she didn't understand a lot of what was going on in our home at the time. I am her sister Dawn. I'm sixteen and I did see what was happening inside our house.

My mom and dad got divorced when I was eight and then my mom got remarried to Phil, Tiffany's father.

Phil used to beat up my mom a lot. My mom got pregnant with Tiffany and Phil seemed happy. He was actually nice to the both of us, for a while.

Once Tiffany was born he was back to his same old miserable self. One day he was getting the grill ready and Tiffany was just learning to walk. She was starting to grab hold of things to steady herself. She tried to grab onto the grill and he told her that she'd get burned. He told her that it was hot, then he took her hand and forced it onto the grill. Tiffany started screaming and crying.

"I guess she won't do that again." Phil said, laughing as she held her hand out.

I couldn't believe that he had done that. My mom was so mad at him, she scooped Tiffany up. Then brought her into the house to put ice on her hand.

Another time Tiff was trying to climb up the stairs. Phil told her 'no' and then he pushed her backwards. She lost her balance and she fell down the stairs. She hit her head pretty hard on the floor. My mom asked him if he was crazy. He slapped my mom and told her that Tiff was only on the third step! He said that it was better that it happened on the third step, rather than at the top of the stairs. He just kept on doing stupid stuff, I don't know what his problem was.

We lived in a townhouse apartment. Our livingroom and kitchen were on the second floor. There were only two bedrooms and they were on the third floor. Tiff and I shared one of the bedrooms.

We had ledges on the inside of the windows that my mom used to put her plants on. Phil used to dump his warm beer into her plants, eventually they all died and my mom couldn't figure out why.

Tiff used to climb up on the ledge in the livingroom, to look out of the window. She would watch the people walk by on the sidewalk. Mom and I used to tell her 'no.' Then we would put her back down onto the floor.

One day Tiff tried climbing up onto the ledge when Phil was in the livingroom. He told her 'no,' and then he pushed her hard. All of a sudden the screen popped off and Tiff toppled out of the window. She fell out the window, onto the concrete sidewalk.

I ran over to the window, screaming. I saw Tiff's little body on the sidewalk below our window. There was a pool of blood around her head. Mom and I quickly ran downstairs and a neighbor called 911.

Phil came downstairs a few seconds later. He was still holding his beer in his hand. Phil said, "I didn't know that she'd fall out."

My mom lost it and she started screaming at Phil. He punched my mom in the face and told her if she had taught Tiff to listen, it wouldn't have happened. He hit my mom again and again, until one of the men outside pulled him off of her.

The ambulance and the police came. Later the police questioned all of us about what had happened.

There were no charges pressed against Phil for the death of my sister. The cops said that it was an accident.

Tiffany had fallen head first. She'd died as soon as she had hit the sidewalk.

My mom did throw Phil out later that same day. She also divorced him.

AMBER

I'm Amber and I'm ten-years-old. My dad used to hurt my mom all the time. He'd hit her and he'd throw things at her. Sometimes he'd punch her and even kick her.

We left a few times, but he always found us and then we'd have to go back home with him. My dad used to tell my mom that she could never do anything right. My mom was kind of heavy. He'd tell her that she was just a fat pig and that no man would ever want her. He said that's why he was stuck with her, because no one else would ever want her.

One day my mom left me at my Aunt Lisa's house for the day. She was gone the whole day and when she came back to get me, it was almost dinnertime. I told her that we better hurry home and fix dinner, before my dad got mad at her. My mom told me that everything was going to be okay. She told me that my dad wasn't going to hurt her anymore.

Boy, did I want to believe her, but she had told me that before. She held up a piece of paper and told me that it was going to stop my dad. I didn't understand how a piece of paper was going to stop my dad once he got going, but I really wanted to believe her this time.

When we got home my mom went right over to the phone, instead of starting to cook dinner. Man, I knew that my dad was going to be real mad at her. She went to the door and put a chair in front of it. I watched her as she wedged it up under the door knob. I couldn't figure out what she was doing.

Then my mom walked over to the window, she looked outside and waved to someone. I went over to stand next to her and saw a police car out in front of our house. I watched as my dad drove into our driveway. I saw the cops get out of their car and walk over to my dad. One of the cops handed my dad a piece of paper. He looked at it and I could see that he was getting real mad, as he read what it said.

They talked to my dad for a few minutes, then one of the cops walked up to our door. My mom moved the chair away and she opened the door. The cop told her that my dad wanted to get some of his things. He told my mom that they would come inside with him, so that nothing would happen to us. My mom said okay and the cop waved to the other cop, signaling for him to come inside.

My dad and the two cops came into our house. When my dad walked by my mom, he gave her a real mean look. He went into the bedroom and got some of his things, while the cops talked with my mom.

I watched my dad as he went into the bathroom and then out into the kitchen. He had a funny look on his face as he moved through our house.

All of a sudden my dad ran up to my mom, holding a knife and he stabbed her. The police looked at each other, as I stood there watching my dad. He kept stabbing the knife into her. I started screaming for him to stop, but he didn't listen to me.

Finally the cops moved and pulled my dad away from my mom. He dropped the knife and I saw that it was covered with blood. I ran over to my mom as she fell onto the carpet, moaning.

Once they had handcuffed my dad, one of the cops came over to where I was sitting next to my mom on the floor. He knelt down next to me as he called for an ambulance. Then he tried to pull me away from my mom.

"No!" I yelled at him. I looked over at my dad, "I hate you." I told him, as I started to cry.

Blood was coming out of my mom's nose and mouth. The off white carpet under her, was turning red from her blood. The cop stood up, when he heard the ambulance's siren stop out in front of our house. He went over to stand by the door and he opened it when they got to the step.

Once they were inside, the same cop came over to me and put his arm around me. He tried to comfort me, while I watched the ambulance guys trying to help my mom. One of the guys from the ambulance looked up at the cop and shook his head.

I knew that my mom was dead. The cop asked me if I had a family member that lived close by, that they could call. I told him about my Aunt Lisa. He asked me for her phone number and then he called her. He talked to her for a few minutes, then he hung up the phone.

"Your aunt is on her way," he told me, with a sad look on his face.

The other cop took my dad out to the police car in front of our house. More cops showed up and the ambulance left with my mom. I waited for my Aunt Lisa to come, while I sat down on the couch. I couldn't believe that my mom was dead and that my dad had killed her. I didn't know what was going to happen to me now, I felt so alone.

When my aunt finally got there, I could tell that she had been crying. I could see tears on her cheek and her makeup was all messed up. The cop talked to her for a few minutes and then she started to yell at him.

"Why weren't you watching him? How could you just stand there and let this happen?" she started to cry again. The cop put his arm around her. "And in front of my niece, she saw the whole thing!"

I went over to her and she put her arms around me.

"I guess it's just you and me," she said, kissing me on the top of my head. "Let's get some of your things and we'll go back to my house." We went into my bedroom and gathered together some of my clothes and toys.

We left my house and I never went back there again. I'm sure that my aunt went back there, because one day all of my stuff was at her house.

I live with her now. I love my aunt, but I really miss my mom.

I hope that my dad never gets out of prison. Ever.

CRYSTAL

My name is Crystal, I'm twenty-three-years-old and I'm married to a horrible, terrible man. My husband is twenty-four-years-old and he hits me, a lot. I've tried to figure out how my life turned out this way. The only thing that I can come up with, is that I used to see my dad beat on my mom a lot of the time. I guess that I thought it was kind of normal.

That's how I grew up. Almost every night my dad would find something that he could get angry about. I really think that he enjoyed having that kind of power over my mother. She would curl up into a ball on the floor and try to cover her head. My dad would kick her, he'd even spit on her and tell her how disgusting she was. He was a real jerk to her.

My dad didn't drink or anything he was just a miserable man. He said that women were there for one reason and for only one reason.

I found it hard to believe that when my mom was in high school, she was runner up for Prom Queen. My mom was actually a very pretty and happy person at one time. Then my dad just beat her down, until her self esteem was completely gone. Now she is just a shell of the person she once was.

All my mom ever did was cook, clean and take care of me and my dad. That was her whole life.

My mom met my dad when she was a senior in high school, then she got pregnant with me. My mom had to quit school. I guess that's when things changed for her, for the worse.

My mom always wore drab looking house dresses, so that my dad couldn't accuse her of dressing up to get the attention of any guys. I could still see some of her prettiness, but my mom looked drab and worn out. She tried to cover up her good looks. Instead of my dad being flattered by her beauty, as he once had been, he now seemed to hate and resent it.

I remember hearing my mom cry at night, almost every night. I used to wonder if he really loved her at all. It looked as if he hated her. Everything that she did seemed to annoy him.

Why didn't my mom just leave him? I could never figure it out. I used to think to myself at night while lying in my bed, that I would never put up with that. No man was ever going to treat me the way my dad treated my mom. I told myself that I was a lot stronger than my mother was. And look at me now!

Here I am with a husband who beats on me. Now I understand why my mom never left. Where would she go? Where would I go? I have no money and nowhere that I can go. I'm too embarrassed to tell anyone that my husband hits me. I feel so alone. My husband may not be much of a man, but he is right about one thing, he does provide for me.

KATE

Kate was a pretty blond six-year-old, who was caught up in the middle of her mothers abusive relationship. Her mother, Jackie was engaged to Billy. Billy seemed to have a hard time finding and holding onto jobs. So, Jackie had to use her waitress money to support the entire household. Some weeks the money just didn't seem to stretch very far.

Billy would get really upset when their wasn't enough money for his beer. Jackie and Billy would fight a lot. Sometimes he would hit her. When he was drinking, he would almost always hit her.

Jackie would waitress in the restaurant during the day. She would cocktail waitress in the lounge, which was on the bottom floor of the restaurant, on weekends. Her neighbor, Mrs. King, would watch little Kate, while Jackie was worked.

Billy and Jackie had a huge fight on a Friday morning. That day she had to work a double shift, plus work in the lounge that night. The fight hadn't been worked out by the time she had left for work. She told him that she was tired of fighting with him. She said that her and Kate were going to move out on Monday, which was her day off. This made Billy furious. Jackie was afraid to leave him that day because he was so unpredictable, but she had to go to work.

Apparently, that evening at around 7 p.m. Billy went over to Mrs. King's apartment, to pick up Kate. He told Mrs. King that they were going to see a movie. She thought that it was a nice idea and had told Billy so.

Billy tried calling Jackie at work earlier, but she had been short with him. She told him that she wasn't going to change her mind. She said that she and Kate were leaving him, because things just weren't working out between the two of them. Besides, he needed to get his head together, get a job and hold onto it. She couldn't go on supporting the three of them. She also told him that all the fighting wasn't good for Kate.

In the background Billy heard a man start talking to Jackie, he got very upset. He accused her of fooling around on him. Jackie told him that she had to go. She said that she'd talk to him later, when she got home. Then she hung up the phone on him.

At 2:30 a.m. Jackie got home and she saw that Billy was gone. Good, she thought, when she noticed that all of his things were gone too. She got ready for bed and went to sleep. On Friday and Saturday nights Kate slept over at Mrs. King's, so that Jackie didn't have to worry about picking her up so late at night.

DOMESTIC ABUSE: ALL SIDES

At 7 a.m. Jackie went to Mrs. King's apartment, to pick up Kate. Mrs. King told her that Billy picked up Kate the night before, to take her to a movie.

Jackie ran upstairs to her apartment. She went into Kate's room and found a lot of her things were also missing. There was no note, no nothing.

"Oh God, please let her be okay," she prayed, silently.

Jackie called the hospitals, no Billy or Kate. Then she called the police. A while later, the police came over and took a missing persons report. Within a short amount of time, they had issued a warrant for Billy's arrest, on the charge of kidnaping.

It's been three years and they still haven't found Kate or Billy. Jackie prays everyday that her innocent little Kate is safe. She also says a prayer asking if she isn't okay, that she didn't suffer at all.

BRITNEY

My name is Britney. My mom and dad used to fight all of the time. I am twelve-years-old and I live with my aunt. When my parents would fight my dad would hit my mom, a lot.

One day, my mom told my dad that she was leaving him and taking me with her. He told her that he was never going to let her go. He started to get real mad at her. He said that he would kill us all, before he'd ever let her leave him.

My mom told him that he was crazy. She said that he was talking crazy and scaring her. I watched as my dad got up and went into the bedroom.

"Stand near the phone, baby." My mom told me quietly and I did as I was told. I wondered what my dad was going to do next. I didn't have to wait long to find out.

My dad came back out and stood next to my mom. "Do you want to leave me?" he asked her.

"I have to. You keep hurting me," she told him.

"So, you've made up your mind and you are leaving me, right?" he asked her again.

"Yes, I am. We are both leaving." My mom said to him.

"Did you forget about the 'til death do us part'?" he asked her, as he held up his gun for her to see.

My mom screamed when he aimed the gun at her. I stood there and watched him shoot my mom. I couldn't move. I tried to run. My brain screamed at me to run, but I just couldn't. It was like my feet were glued to the floor.

My dad turned to me, as my mom fell to the floor. He smiled and aimed the gun at me. Suddenly I felt an awful pain in my side and I fell to the floor. That's all that I remember.

When I woke up, I was in the hospital. My aunt was sitting by my hospital bed, holding onto my hand. The cops came to talk to me while I was there. They told us that my dad had shot himself, after he had shot me. I guess he had thought that I was dead, too. They said that my mom and dad had both died, before they'd arrived at the hospital.

I had been shot on my right side, just under my arm. I'm glad that he thought I was dead, but I do miss my mom. I think about her everyday.

I know one thing for sure, I'm never going to get married.

TONY

I'm Tony and I am twenty-one-years-old. I'm in prison for murder. I killed my girlfriend and I've been in here for three years, so far.

I was eighteen, actually I had just turned eighteen a few days before I killed her. I don't really remember a lot of what happened that day. I know that I caught her cheating on me and I lost it. I just completely lost it. I do remember punching her the first time, but I was told that I kept punching her and I didn't stop.

I do remember thinking about how my dad used to beat on my mom. He did it all the time, because he thought she had cheated on him. I knew that my girlfriend had cheated on me, she'd admitted it to me. My mom was afraid to even talk to my dad, because she didn't know if he would hit her or not.

People had to pull me off of my girlfriend. Some of my friends told me, that she had been moving a little when the ambulance came that day. But three days later, she died from a blood clot in her brain. I caused her death.

My girlfriend was seventeen. We had been going out for only four months. Four months, and now everything is so messed up. I will never have a life and neither will she. I took that away from the both of us.

Her family will never see what she could have become or any of the children that she may have had in the future. I also messed things up for both of our families. I killed her, because I caught her kissing another guy. I killed her, because she told me she had cheated on me. Man, do I regret it! I wish I could take back that day. I'd give anything to go back to that day. I wish that I could change the way that things had turned out.

I do go to counseling now. At first I didn't want to, but now I'm finding out that it's really helping.

I could blame this all on my dad. I could say that I did it because that's all that I knew. It's how I grew up, that it was my destiny. But then I wouldn't be taking the blame. I'd be trying to shift it to someone else. I did it and I knew better. I am an adult and I was held accountable for my actions, as I should have been.

Susie, Mr. and Mrs. Hamner, I am truly sorry.

BRIAN

I'm Brian and I just turned fourteen-years-old. Every week, for as long as I can remember, my father would hit my mom. Each and every Friday night, he'd come home drunk. I don't remember when it all started, but I do remember it always being that way.

We would leave our house, then after a while we'd go back home. My father would always talk my mom into moving back in. He used to tell her that I needed a father. My mom would feel bad. Then we'd move back to our house.

When I was smaller I would try to help my mom, but my father would just push me away. So I started to stay out of it. I felt bad that I couldn't help my mom.

But as I grew older, I would tell my dad to leave her alone. Sometimes he would leave her alone. Sometimes he'd push me away and tell me to stay out of it. He'd say that it was none of my business.

I never saw my mother do anything that deserved a beating. My father was just a mean and stupid drunk.

One night when I was thirteen, I came home from a basketball game. We'd lost the game and I was in a bad mood. My father was screaming and yelling, as usual. I could hear my mom crying and pleading with him. She kept asking him to stop hitting her and to leave her alone.

When I opened the door, I saw my father on top of my mother. He was punching her in the head. I ran in and told him to get off of her. He yelled at me to get out. I tried to pull him off of her, but he hit me in the stomach pretty hard.

"Get off her!" I yelled at him again. He ignored me and started to choke her.

I grabbed the closest thing to me, which was my hockey stick sitting in the corner of the room. I swung it at my father. I hit him in the back of the head. He fell forward and hit his head on the edge of the coffee table.

Then he fell on top of my mother and didn't move. I reached over and dragged him off of her. She sat up slowly. She was still crying and I hugged her, as we looked over at my father. I looked at my mom and saw that she looked really scared. I reached over and shook my dad, but he didn't move. My mom got up and called 911. I kept telling my dad to get up, but he didn't.

When the ambulance came, they told us that my dad was dead. The police asked us some questions. We had to go to court and they decided that it was an accidental death, because I was just trying to protect my mom.

My mom works now and is pretty happy. I don't miss my father at all. I am sorry that he's dead, but I'm glad that he's gone.

PAIGE

My name was Paige. I'm sixteen-years-old and I used to hate to go home. My step dad used to be such a jerk. If my mom said something that he didn't like, he'd pop her in the mouth. My mom didn't even have to do or say anything wrong. If he had a bad day, he'd come home and be miserable to the both of us.

My real dad died when I was eleven. When I turned fourteen, my mom met the jerk. I never liked Jim. Half the time he didn't work and when he did, he'd take all of his money and blow it at the dog track. He'd spend the day at the track and lose more than he won. Then he'd get mad and be a real jerk.

He didn't care which one of us that he hit. He'd hit my mom, he'd hit me and he'd hit my little brother, Ben. My mom tried to get him to stop, but when he got mad there wasn't anything that you could do. Everyone just tried to stay out of his way, most of the time.

The cops used to come to our house a lot. Sometimes they'd take him away with them and other times he'd stay. He'd look at my mom when the police were there and say to her real quiet, 'Did I do anything, babe?' Most of the time she would put her head down and mumble 'no', not daring to look up at anyone.

Jim was a con man. He conned my mom, he conned Ben and he even conned the cops. He tried to con me, but I hated him. I never believed anything that he said.

We left a few times and stayed with friends. But he'd find out where we were. After a while he'd come to bring us all back home.

One night he went crazy on my mom. She had us all run outside to try to get away from him. We ran down the street in the dark, but Jim ran out to the road and he saw us.

He jumped into his car and tried to run us down. He swerved the car and almost hit Ben and me, we managed to jump out of his way. Then he saw my mom running the other way. She was trying to get him away from us. He drove the car towards her, I guess that somehow he hit her with the bumper. We saw her as she flew up into the air and then fell to the ground. Ben and I both screamed.

Jim drove off down the road, probably thinking that he'd killed her. Ben and I ran quickly over to my mom. She didn't move at all. I told Ben to go get help and I stayed with her, hoping that the jerk wouldn't come back.

Finally Ben came running back over to us. He told me that an ambulance was on it's way. A few minutes later we heard the sirens, my mom still hadn't moved. When the ambulance got there, they loaded up my mom and took her to the hospital. Mrs. Todd, our neighbor, drove us to the hospital. When we got there Mrs. Todd talked to the police. Then they asked me and Ben what had happened. The police told us that Jim was going to be in jail, because of what he had done to all of us.

The doctor talked to Mrs. Todd and then he talked to us. He told us that our mom had to stay in the hospital for a while. I asked him if she was going to be okay, but the doctor said that he wasn't sure yet. He told us that they were going to do everything they could for my mom.

One of the cops told Mrs. Todd that he was going to call Children's Services to come and get us. Mrs. Todd told him we could go home with her and call our grandmother to come get us. Boy, am I glad that Mrs. Todd was there for us.

We went to our house and called our grandmother. We also grabbed a few of our things. Then we went over to Mrs. Todd's house to wait for our grandmother to pick us up. My grandmother said that she wouldn't be there until the next day. She lived a few hours away from us and she wanted to stop in to see my mom before she came to get us. Mrs. Todd told her that she would be glad to watch us until she got there and to take her time.

Later we saw Jim pull into our driveway and Mrs. Todd called the cops. We had the pleasure of seeing the cops take Jim away in handcuffs.

A while later, Mrs. Todd told me and Ben to go to bed in her bedroom, while she slept on the couch. In the morning when we woke up, our grandma was sitting in the kitchen talking with Mrs. Todd.

As soon as she saw us, she gave us a big hug. She told us that our mom was going to be okay. She said that when our mom hit the ground, she jarred her brain. It caused some swelling, but it had gone down during the night. She would have to stay in the hospital for a few more days. Mrs. Todd told our grandma we could stay with her for a few days, while our grandma went back and forth to the hospital to see our mom.

Finally, one day my mom came home. Ben and I were so happy that she was okay. Our grandma stayed with us for a while after that. We all had to go to court to testify against Jim.

Jim is in jail now and he'll be there for a long time. Mom and Jim are divorced now, too. Mom says that she'll never let him come back. He keeps trying to call her, but my mom doesn't accept the collect calls from the jail.

KIM

My name is Kim and I'm fourteen-years-old now. My dad wasn't a very nice man. He used to get real mad, he'd hit me and my mom a lot. Timmy, my little brother hardly ever got hit. Timmy was 'his little man.' He was five years old when my dad left.

As far back as I can remember, my dad had always hit my mom. Finally she got tired of it and threw him out. Well, actually the cops told him to leave. Then my parents got a divorce. My dad didn't want it, but my mom did.

She told me that she was tired of being hit by my dad. She said that she wanted us all to have a better life. She said that she owed it to us to try to give us a better life. Things had to be better than the life that we had with him.

The judge gave my mom custody of us and my dad got visitation every other weekend. Sometimes my dad would show up and sometimes he wouldn't. We never knew if he was coming or not, which was pretty hard on Timmy.

When their divorce was almost final, my dad kept pleading with my mom to take him back. She kept telling him 'no way.' My dad told her that she'd be sorry, I was seven years old at the time.

One day my dad came to pick us up. He said that we were going to go camping. Timmy was pretty excited about it, I didn't really want to go camping. I hated the idea of sleeping outside, with all those bugs. My mom sent us with extra clothes, like my dad had asked her to. She told me that I would more than likely have a good time.

We drove for such a long time, Timmy and I both fell asleep in the car. When we woke up, it was dark outside. We drove some more, then my dad stopped the car in front of an ugly colored green house. He told us to be good for a few minutes and that he'd be right back.

A few minutes later, my dad came out with a woman who had red hair. He told us that her name was Cindy.

"We are going to stay here with my friend Cindy, for a while," he'd told us.

"What about camping?" Timmy asked, sounding disappointed.

"Next time, sport," my dad said.

"For how long? And what about mom? Does mom know?" I asked him.

"Kim, we will talk about it soon. I've got to talk to Cindy for a few minutes first," he told me, turning towards Cindy.

We went into the house and watched tv, while my dad and Cindy talked in the other room. A while later Cindy went outside, got inside my dad's car and drove away. When Cindy came back, she was driving a different car.

When we had stayed in that house for a few days, I asked my dad when we could go back home. I really missed my mom and I knew that she had to be worried about us.

"Kim, your mom had a bad accident. She is dead, baby. I'm really sorry." My dad told me, sadly.

"No! I don't believe you. Mom's not dead! Why are you lying to us?" I asked him.

"She is dead, did you hear me Timmy? Your mom is dead?" my dad said again.

"Yes, I heard you dad." Timmy said, beginning to cry.

I put my arm around Timmy, I didn't believe my dad. But why would he lie? Deep down I knew that my mom was still alive. I knew for some reason that he was lying to us, but I didn't know why. I knew if I asked him too many questions, my dad would get mad and start hitting me, so I kept quiet.

Cindy was pretty nice to me and Timmy. But she wasn't my mom, I missed my mom terribly. Timmy did, too. Cindy was nicer to us than our own dad was.

We stayed in that house for a while, then we moved to an apartment. I don't really know how long we were there in that house, but it seemed like we were there for a long time.

Cindy worked nights and my dad worked during the day. I didn't go to school and neither did Timmy. My dad told us that we had to call Cindy 'mom.' I didn't want to, so I didn't. But my dad slapped me when I didn't, so I ended up calling her 'mom.'

One day Cindy colored my hair red and then she cut it real short. She colored Timmy's a dark brown color like my dad's. I hated my hair red! I missed my blond curls. Dad said that he liked our hair the way that Cindy had fixed it.

When I was ten, I begged my dad to let me go to school with the other kids. He said that I couldn't go. He would buy me little workbooks at the grocery store and tell me I could pretend I was in school. Timmy was eight then, so my dad also got him some workbooks.

I didn't read very well and I wasn't very good at math, either. Timmy couldn't read at all. Cindy would try to teach us, when she had the time. She was actually pretty nice to us. When my dad would get mad and hit us, she'd hold us for a while, until we stopped crying. I felt better when Cindy would hold us, but I still missed my mom.

When I was thirteen, I told my dad that I wanted to see my mom's grave and he told me no. I begged and pleaded with him, but he still told me no. I got so mad at him. I told him that I wouldn't believe him, until I could see it for myself. 'No', he told me again. I argued with him for a few more minutes and he punched me in the face. Cindy jumped up and yelled at him to leave me alone. He turned around and slapped her. This was the same way that he used to act with my mom.

"Why can't we go to school?" I asked him. "Why can't we go outside?" I yelled at him. "Why can't we have any friends?"

My dad yelled at me to shut up and he hit me again. "Because someone might see you." He yelled back at me, really getting angry at that point.

But I kept going, even though I knew I was making him mad. "So what if someone see's us?" I asked him. "What difference does it make?"

Cindy told my dad that it was enough. He turned to her and smacked her hard in the face. "Shut up!" he yelled at her."These are my kids, you just shut your mouth up."

Cindy put her arm around me and we sat down on the couch. She rubbed my back as we sat there together, both of us afraid of my dad.

"You are not going outside. Do not question me, ever! If you think that your lives are so bad now…just disobey me and see how bad they can get." He said to me, before he walked out of the apartment.

"You kids stay here and be good. I'll be back soon." Cindy told us, a few minutes after he'd gone.

We watched tv for a while. Finally a little later, Cindy came back.

"Timmy, Kim, get your stuff together and put it in a bag. Hurry!" Cindy told us, rushing around the room.

"Why? Where are we going?" I asked her.

"I'll tell you everything, as soon as we are safely inside the car. For god's sake, let's hurry," she said to us.

Timmy and I ran into the room that we shared. We put our clothes and the few other things we had into a bag.

"Come on!" Cindy yelled from the other room, nervously.

We hurried into the living room carrying the bag with all of our things. We followed Cindy out of the apartment and raced over to the car.

"Get in, get in!" Cindy said, trying to get us to move faster.

We climbed into the car, then she started to drive away. Once we had been driving for a while, Cindy seemed to relax a little. When we had first gotten into the car, she kept looking in all of the mirrors and she acted very nervous.

"Where are we going?" I asked her, finally getting tired of waiting for her to tell us.

"We've got to get away from your dad, before he hurts us all real bad." Cindy said.

"He used to hurt our mom a lot, too. Almost like today, but it used to get much worse." I told her.

"Yes, I had heard that, but your dad told me it wasn't true. He told me that your mom wanted to take you kids away from him. I felt bad for your dad and I believed him. I guess that I loved him," she said, sadly looking at me in the mirror.

"So where are we going?" I asked her.

"To see your mom." Cindy told me, looking in the mirror again.

"At the cemetery?" I asked.

"No. Your mom isn't dead. I couldn't tell you, because your dad said that he would kill me. I love you kids, just like you were my very own. I'm really sorry." Cindy said, starting to cry.

"Our mom is alive? I know the way my dad is. I know you had no choice. But my mom is really alive?" I asked, hardly daring to believe what she was telling us.

"Yes, I talked to her earlier today. She's going to meet us, when we get you nearer to your home." Cindy said, trying to smile at me. I could tell that she was very nervous.

"You'll go to jail, won't you?" asked Timmy. "For taking us away from our mom."

"Probably." Cindy said.

"I don't want you to get into any trouble." Timmy said. "I love you."

"I love you, too. I'm really sorry," she said, to the both of us.

"I don't want you to go to jail. I know why you had to do it, my dad made you. What will happen to him?" I asked her.

"He did kidnap you both, he'll probably go to jail." Cindy said. "You both are going back to your mother, where you really belong."

We drove all that day and when it got dark out, we pulled into a motel. In the morning after Cindy used the phone, we got into the car and drove some more. Finally, we pulled over into a shopping center and parked outside of a Sear's store.

Cindy told us to stay inside the car. She got out and walked over to a blue Toyota. She leaned inside the passenger side window and talked to someone for a few minutes. Then she stood up and we watched as the driver's side door slowly opened. Timmy and I both leaned forward, trying to see who was going to get out of the car. A very pretty blond woman climbed out of the car. She was wearing jeans and a t shirt. It was Mom!

"Oh my god!" I whispered, holding onto Timmy's hand. "It's mom!"
"Is it really mom?" asked Timmy, trying to get a better look.
"Yes!" I said, excitedly.

Cindy and my mom walked over to the car we were waiting in. I was so excited that I could hardly sit still. Cindy motioned for us to get out of the car. I swung open the door and ran straight into my mother's outstretched arms, Timmy quickly followed me. We were all laughing and crying at the same time.

"I can't believe that I am holding the both of you! After all these years, is it really you?" my mom asked, through her tears. "My babies, oh, my babies are finally back where they belong. I've missed you both so much."

Mom looked over at Cindy, "Thank you so much for bringing them back to me." My mom said to Cindy, as she gently pulled away from us. She put her arms out for Cindy. They hugged each other and talked for a few minutes. I saw that both of them were crying.

Cindy looked over at us and held her arms out. We went over to her and hugged her. Cindy had been our 'mother' for almost seven years. I told her that I loved her and started to cry.

"Here's the address to where Tim is staying." Cindy said, handing my mom a piece of paper. "I guess that you should call the cops. You probably better call them before he leaves." She said, wiping away the tears that were still running down her face.

"Cindy was real good to us. She took care of us and tried to protect us from dad. Please don't call the cops on her." I pleaded with my mom.

"Is this true?" Mom asked, looking from me to Timmy.

"She took care of us and she even taught me how to read." Timmy said. "She did try to stop dad from hurting us. He hurt her, too."

"Please let her go, mom." I begged my mother.

Mom looked towards Cindy, "Tim made you do things that you didn't want to do, huh?" Cindy nodded her head. "I know. Tim can be a very forceful man. He will make you sorry, if you don't do the things that he wants you to do, I remember all to well. Why don't you take off, before I call the cops on Tim." My mom told Cindy, with a smile. "Go ahead."

Cindy looked at my mom with a surprised expression on her face. "Are you sure?" she asked my mom.

"You aren't a threat to anyone. You were under Tim's influence. You were just as much a victim as we were. You go, I'll call the cops and hopefully they will get Tim before he takes off."

Cindy hugged my mom, "Thank you." Cindy whispered to her.

"Good luck." my mom told her.

Cindy hugged me and Timmy, "I will always love the both of you and I'll miss you terribly."

We watched her get into her car and drive away. After she left my mom called the cops and gave them my dad's address. My dad was arrested for kidnaping us and now he is in prison.

All the years that I was living with my dad, I missed a lot without having my mom around. I am and always will be grateful to Cindy. I hope that Cindy is okay and happy, wherever she is. I am glad that I'm with my mom again. I missed her so much. I always knew my mom was really alive. I knew that my dad had lied to us.

At first it was kind of weird living with my mom. We really don't know each other anymore, but my mom's really cool. We are trying to get to know each other, all over again. I still don't understand how my dad could tell us that my mom was dead. That was really mean and hateful of him.

My dad keeps asking the judge if he can see Timmy and me. The judge keeps telling him no. If the judge ever decides to tell him yes, I am going to tell him no!

DEBBIE

My name is Debbie and now I am fourteen-years-old. My dad used to hurt my mom a lot. He used to hurt me, too. When I was ten-years-old my mom and I moved out of our house. We moved into a women's shelter. We stayed in that shelter for over a year. I didn't like it there. We had to share a room with a bunch of other people, but it was good because my dad didn't hurt either one of us.

My mom had to get a restraining order against my dad, because he kept telling her that he was going to kill us. My mom and I went to court a lot of times. I wanted to tell the judge what my dad was like, but he didn't want to listen to me. He told my mom that he wasn't going to listen to a brainwashed kid.

I wasn't going to lie. I was going to tell him the truth about the things that my dad had done to me and to my mom. I didn't want to have visitation with him either, I was afraid of him. I especially didn't want to be alone with him.

The judge said that I had to do the visitations. I knew what my dad was like, but the judge didn't. Yeah, I was only ten years old, but I had lived with him. My mom pleaded with the judge not to allow the visitations, but he wouldn't listen to her. He told my mom that because he was my father, he had certain rights.

Every time my dad would go to court, he'd be dressed in a suit and he acted real quiet and nice. I knew that he wasn't really like that, it was all just a show for the judge. I didn't like the judge at all, he didn't care about me or my mom.

When I would come back from my forced visitations with my dad, I almost always had bruises on my arms and legs. My mom would get really mad, but she felt like there was no one that would listen to us.

We would go back into court and my mom would beg the judge to stop the visitation. The judge would tell my mom that she was wasting his time and the taxpayers money. He told her that he was convinced she was the one bruising me, to stop my dad's entitled visitations. What a dumb judge!

My mom was getting tired of this, so we stopped the visits. My dad went into court and had my mom put in contempt of court. She still didn't make me go to the visitations and that stupid judge arrested her. He made my mom stay in jail for three days.

During that three days I had to stay with my dad. He was real mad that we were causing all these problems for him. He yelled at me, because he thought people at his work would find out about everything. He hit me a lot in those three days. It seemed like those three days lasted forever.

When my mom was released from jail, I went back to live with her. I was really happy. I had missed her a lot. I told my mom what those three days had been like for me and my mom was furious. She went back into court and asked the judge to please let me speak and to listen this time.

The judge told my mom that she had better stop creating problems. He said if she kept it up, he was going to give my dad custody of me, instead of her. He told her that he didn't appreciate the fact, she was trying to stand in the way of my dad's court appointed visitation rights.

How could a judge be that stupid? We left court and went back to the shelter. My mom and I talked to the women there and they decided to help us.

Now I am Kirsten and we don't have to deal with my dad anymore.

HANNAH

My name is Hannah and I'm twelve-years-old now. My dad lived with us, but he wasn't ever home very much. When he was at home, he was mean to us. He would throw things at me and my mom, he'd even call us names. But the worst, was when he used to hit us. Sometimes he'd hit us for stupid things, like if we walked between him and the tv. If dinner was late or if my mom spent too much money on groceries, he'd hit her.

I hated living with him. You never knew when he would haul off and belt you. Our house was always real quiet. We didn't make much noise, because my dad always had a headache. When he would get a headache, he was real mean.

One day, my mom told him that she'd had enough and that he needed some help. He got mad and punched her in the head. My mom dropped down to her knees. She told my dad that she was leaving him and taking me with her. My dad asked her if she meant it. My mom said that yes, she did mean it this time.

My dad went out into the kitchen and came back holding a knife in his hand. He grabbed me and held onto me real tight.

"You are not taking my Hannah with you." He said, stabbing the knife into my stomach. It hurt, it hurt so bad! My mom screamed and I felt my legs go weak under me, but my dad was holding me up, so I didn't fall down. I started to cry when I saw all of the blood. I was really scared, I thought that I was going to die.

"Look what you've done!" My mom screamed at him.

My dad looked down at all the blood that had started to cover my shirt and pants. "Oh my god. I'm so sorry baby, but I have to keep your mom with me. I can't let her leave." He said to me, with a crazy look on his face.

When my mom saw him raise the knife to stab me again, she tried to pull me away from him. She tried to grab his arm, but my dad pushed her away. He stabbed me again. Oh, the pain that I felt!

That's all that I remember, about that night. My mom told me that the cops came and arrested my dad. I know that I was rushed in for emergency surgery. The knife had barely missed some of my major organs.

I am okay now, but I will never forgive my dad for what he tried to do to me that night.

My mom and I have moved away since then. We have never gone to the jail to visit my dad.

LORI

My name is Lori and I was ten-years-old the last time my mom tried to leave my dad. He used to beat on my mom a lot, at least a few times a month. We'd left him before, but he'd always talk her into coming back. Sometimes my mom would feel sad or lonely and end up going back to him on her own. We didn't have any place to go or any money, so we had to go back to him eventually.

My dad would be okay for a while after we'd come back, but it wouldn't take him long to start hurting her again.

The last time that we had tried to leave, my dad had been beating on my mom for almost the whole day. She said that she was done, that we were going to go stay at a shelter. My mom grabbed me by my hand and we headed for the door.

My dad ran over and grabbed my mom by the hair, pulling her back away from the door. She yelled for me to run, to get away from him. But I couldn't move, I just stood there. I watched my dad take a knife from the counter and slice it across my mom's throat! My mom made some gurgling noises, then her eyes rolled up into her head.

I screamed and ran next door for help. Our neighbor called the police and they arrested my dad. My mom was dead by the time anyone had gotten there to help us.

I live with my aunt and uncle now.

TONY

My name is Tony and I am sixteen-years-old. I was twelve when my mom had a loser for a boyfriend. He was mean to my mom. He was always yelling at her and hitting her. When I would try to stop him, he would push me or hit me. I begged my mom to leave him, but when she got laid off from her job she had no money of her own. The loser was paying all of the rent, so we couldn't afford to go anywhere else.

I found things to do, to get out of the house. I was on the baseball team at the Community Center, I loved playing baseball and I was good at it.

One afternoon I came home from practice and I saw Andy sitting on top of my mom, he was choking her. I saw my mom trying to pull his hands away from her throat. She was also trying to kick him.

I held up my bat, then I went behind him and swung it with all of my might. I hit him right on the side of the head. Andy fell to the floor landing next to my mom.

My mom sat up gasping and trying to catch her breath. She looked over at Andy and motioned for me to come next to her. I dropped my bat, which had a little blood smeared on it and sank down into her outstretched arms. She hugged me for a few minutes, telling me how sorry she was. I helped her to stand up and together we went over to the phone to call the police.

Andy was dead by the time they arrived and we told the police what had happened. We did end up having to go to court and the judge ruled it as self-defense, because I was trying to protect my mom. I have been going to counseling since then. It has helped me to deal with what happened and what I did.

Today I have a girlfriend and we get along great. My mom has gotten remarried and Tom is a really great guy. He treats my mom real good and she deserves it.

I feel bad that I have killed someone, but I'm happy that my mom is safe now.

EMILY

My name is Emily and I am eighteen-years-old. I couldn't wait to get out of my parents house, so I got pregnant when I was fifteen. Now I have two kids and a third one is on the way.

My dad was a very violent man, he used to beat up my mother pretty bad. At least a couple of times a month, she'd get a really bad beating. If he was in a real bad mood, I'd also get beat. I hated my dad. I don't know why my mom didn't leave him. Maybe she thought that in some way she deserved the things he did to her. One day she told me that when she was younger, she used to see her dad hit her mom.

When I was fifteen, my dad found out that I was pregnant and he went crazy. I'm surprised that I didn't lose my baby, with the beating that I got! I was forced to marry the man who had gotten me pregnant, which was a family friend. He was thirty five at the time. My husband, Henry and my dad worked together, they still do.

Henry is pretty good to me, except for when I get him mad. He tells me that I'll learn to be a good wife someday. I've burned more food than I haven't, I admit that I'm not a very good cook. I came to Henry not knowing anything, I didn't know how to cook or how to clean.

I am not in love with my husband, but I am grateful to him for taking me out of my father's house. Henry is a very good father, he loves his boys and he loves me. He calls me his pretty little trophy. We don't have much money, so I don't think that I'll be able to have any more babies. Henry says that I'll have to get fixed, because it's cheaper than having another one.

My mom enjoys being a grandmother, my father even has fun with my boys. But they sure are a handful. They are both in diapers. I don't have lots of time to keep the house clean, having to take care of my little ones. That gets my Henry mad, but he only hits me once in a while.

DIANE

My name is Diane and I am fourteen-years-old. When I was younger, I used to hear my father hitting my mother and I often heard her crying. I remember the first time that I actually saw him hit my mother. She looked up and saw me watching, she seemed embarrassed. My dad got mad and yelled at me to go away or he'd hit me, too.

I don't remember him hitting her everyday, but he did hit her a lot. My mom never smiled and she never seemed happy.

As I got older their fights happened much more frequently. My dad didn't just slap her anymore, he'd haul off and punch her. I remember one time when my mom was doing the dishes, for some reason my dad got mad at her and he put her face down into the sink filled with soapy water. He held her there for what seemed like a very long time. When he finally let her up, she was choking and gasping for air.

Another time that my dad got mad at my mom, she was cooking dinner and he held her hand above the flame on the stove. She got a pretty bad burn on her hand. All because he wanted her to cook something else.

It didn't seem like it took very much for my dad to get mad at her. He'd be nice one minute and real nasty the next. Sometimes I don't even know if he knew why he was mad. It seemed like my poor mom just couldn't make him happy.

When I was thirteen it seemed like my dad was mad more times than not. He wasn't just mad at my mom, he'd get mad at me too. I know that sometimes I'd do bad things, but I wasn't bad all of the time. He started punching my mom and throwing things at her. If he happened to hit her with something he had thrown, he'd yell out 'strike' and laugh. He didn't punch me or throw things at me, but he did slap me across the face and start calling me lots of real bad names.

One afternoon my dad was in a real foul mood. He was yelling at my mom and then he started hitting her. I walked into the room and he punched me in the head. He told me to mind my own business. I fell to the floor and my mother came over to help me get up. She put her arm around me and we started to walk out of the room. All of a sudden, my dad picked up the cordless phone and threw it hard at my mother.

I heard a sickening thud and felt my mom's arm slide off my back, as she slipped to the floor next to me. I heard my dad yell 'strike' and start to laugh. I looked down at my mom, the cordless phone was laying next to her. He had thrown it and hit her in the head with it. She didn't move and it didn't look to me like she was breathing.

I picked the phone up from off the floor and quickly dialed 911. The ambulance came and took my mom away to the hospital. The police came and took my dad away with them. We didn't have any other family, so I was placed in a foster home.

My mom died later that night, at the hospital. My dad is in prison, for the murder of my mother.

They didn't even let me see my mom in the hospital. I never got a chance to say good bye to her and I didn't get to tell her that I loved her.

TROY

My name is Troy and I am in prison for killing my dad. I did it to protect my mom, but I did it when he was passed out in his chair. If I had done it when he was beating on her, I wouldn't be in here now. But, I was a coward just like my dad. I've been in here for four years. Next month I will turn twenty-one-years-old.

My dad used to beat on my mom quite often. I felt so bad when I would see her crying. She seemed like she was always crying and I felt so helpless. My dad was a big guy and I admit that I was afraid of him.

My dad lost his job, so my mom had to get a job in a restaurant. I don't remember my dad ever looking for a job after he got fired. He was always either sitting in his chair in front of the tv or standing over my mom, swinging his fists at her.

A while later, my mom got a raise at work and she was real proud of herself. This was the first job that she'd had in seventeen years. Sometimes, I'd go to the restaurant to see her while she was working. She seemed like a completely different person. She was confident, happy, smiling and joking around with the people that she worked with. At home she was sad, she never smiled and she was always quiet. I liked the person that she was when she was at work. I wanted her to be happy. My dad said that even with the raise, she still wasn't making very much money.

One day I found out that I had been awarded a scholarship to go to college in the fall. My mom was real happy and so proud of me. She told everyone at work that her baby was going to college. She said that I was going to make something out of myself. My dad told me I was too stupid to go to college. He told me that I was dumb and lazy, just like my mother. The funny thing was, who was the person that got fired? Who was the former mechanic that sat around and drank all day? Who was the man that sat in his chair and controlled the tv remote day and night? It wasn't me or my mom.

One afternoon I came home from hanging out with my buddies and my dad was going after my mom. She was curled up on the floor and he was kicking her. He kept kicking her and pushing her face down onto the floor. I ran up behind him and shoved him as hard as I could. My dad staggered a little and then turned around. He punched me in the face and I fell back. His attention was on me and my mom was able to sit up. My dad went back over to sit in his chair, in front of the tv.

My mom was crying and holding onto her side. I asked her if she wanted to go to the hospital and she told me no. My dad called me a little sissy and a mama's boy, as I helped my mother into her bedroom. She wanted to lay down. I went into my room and thought about ways that I could stop all of this. I wanted my mom not to have to deal with the beatings anymore. I could hear her in her bedroom crying softly. That's when I decided what I was going to do.

I waited in my room until I didn't hear my mom crying anymore. Then I waited until I could hear my dad snoring. I went out into the garage, got the shovel out and brought it back into the house. Then I went into the living room and stood in front of my dad. I watched him as he sat in his chair drooling and snoring. It made me sick to think of all of the pain that he'd caused my mom through the years.

I raised the shovel high above my father's head and swung it down as hard as I could. I heard a loud crunching sound that turned my stomach, blood gushed from my dad's head. It was running down onto his shirt. I dropped the shovel and I ran from the room. I vomited in the bathroom, then I went to get the phone. I called the police, trying not to cry.

While I waited for the police to come, I went into my mom's room and woke her up. After I told her what I had done, she started to cry and I felt real bad for her. I had wanted to stop her pain, not be the cause of it! I'd killed my dad to stop her pain and had just ended up creating more pain for her. I didn't think about what she would go through when they carted me off to jail, or the pain that she would feel in the courtroom when the judge sentenced me.

The judge found me guilty of murder, because I had planned it. My attorney told me that if I hadn't planned it and had killed him while I was trying to protect my mom or myself, it would have turned out differently. It probably would have been ruled self-defense and I would have been released.

My mom and I could have lied and said that with all of her bruises it had been self-defense, but we didn't. The judge was fair. I got eight years in prison, which is not a long time. It sure feels like a long time though! The judge did look at my mom's bruises and he also listened to both of our stories. That's why he only gave me eight years, instead of life in prison.

I really blew it! I could have gone to a real college and now I have to take college classes in prison....it's not the same.

My mom comes every week to see me and she still tells everyone at work that I am taking college classes! She tells me that she loves me and that she is proud of me.

DONNA

My name is Donna and I am twelve-years-old. My dad used to beat up my mom all of the time. A few times it was so bad that my mom had to go to the hospital. My dad would also do things to me, he would touch me in ways that he shouldn't have. I was afraid to tell anyone and I was embarrassed, because I knew that it was wrong. I was also afraid of him, I hated it when he would touch me. He told me that if I ever told my mom, he would beat the both of us.

One day my dad beat her up really bad and then he drove her to the Emergency Room. He dropped her off outside of the hospital and we drove away. I asked him why we had left her and where we were going. My dad told me that we were going to go home. I didn't want to just leave my mom there, but I had no choice. I didn't know how bad she was hurt or anything, I was really worried about her.

We stopped at a hardware store on the way home. My dad ran into the store and told me to wait for him in the car. When we got home, my dad changed all the locks in the house. I asked him why and he told me that my mom had lost her set of keys. He told me that she couldn't remember where she had lost them, so it was safer to just change the locks.

The next day my mom called and I heard my dad tell her not to call again. I wanted my mom, I really missed her. My dad made me sleep in his bed with him and he told me that I was going to take my mom's place from now on.

A few days later, a taxi pulled up in front of our house and I watched as my mom got out. She came up the walkway and tried to unlock the door with her keys. But my dad had changed the locks, so her keys didn't work anymore. She looked scared and started pounding on the door. My dad stood by the door for a few minutes, then he slowly opened it.

He blocked the door and wouldn't let her come in. My mom asked him if she could please come in and he told her no. She begged him, but he wouldn't move away from the door. He told her that she had abandoned us. He also told her that he had gone to court. My dad said he had custody of me. I didn't want to stay with my dad, I didn't want to take my mothers place anymore. I wanted to sleep back in my own room.

I started to scream for my mom to come in. My dad turned around and he hit me across the face. He slammed the door shut on my mom. She stayed out there sitting on the front step and cried for a while, then she slowly walked away. I thought she was going to leave me forever. I ran into my room and I cried for the rest of the day. That night I had to go back into my father's bedroom.

DOMESTIC ABUSE: ALL SIDES

On Monday I went to school. While I was standing in line waiting for the bus after school, I saw my mom. Oh man, I was so happy to see her! I quickly ran over to her and she told me that she had come to take me away with her. She told me that we couldn't get any of our things out of the house. We had to leave right away. I told her, I wanted to be with her and that I didn't care about my things.

We went to a women's shelter, where my mom and I both talked to the women there. My mom was shocked when I told them about having to take my mom's place in my dad's bed. Rhonda, one of the women who worked there, told my mom that she could go to jail for kidnaping me since my dad had custody. My mom said she didn't care. She said there was no way that I was ever going to go back to my dad.

It's been two months since then and I'm still really scared that my dad will find us. Rhonda said that a judge probably wouldn't believe us about my dad. She said that he would think that my mom made me lie.

I'm not lying, my dad really did do things to me. My mom never told me to lie. If I had lied, my mom would have grounded me.

Next week we will be leaving here. I don't know where we will be going, but I sure hope that it's far, far away from my dad.

ANGEL

My name is Angel and I am sixteen-years-old now. My mom and I have been in and out of women's shelters for many years. My dad would beat her up, then we'd leave and go into a shelter. My mom would try to stay away. She'd try to get a job and make a life for us, but she'd never had a job her whole life. It was real hard for her to find anyone who would hire her. It wasn't fair. My mom would go out early every morning and come back real depressed. Then after a while, we'd end up going back home to my dad.

My mom said that she was too weak and she couldn't survive without my dad. My mom tried to get along without him, but she didn't believe in herself enough. It probably would have been easier for my mom, if she just had herself to worry about and not me too.

The last time that we went home my dad just lost it, he beat her up and kept kicking her. I yelled at him to stop, I begged for him to stop.

"Okay, Angel, I'll stop kicking mommy." He said, with a strange look on his face.

Then he went into the kitchen. When he came back out, he was holding a knife. He went over to my mom and cut her across the stomach, he cut her pretty deep. I ran over to my mother and tried to hold onto her stomach, to stop the bleeding. Her stomach just kept opening up under my hands. Her intestines slipped out through the gaping hole. I tried to push them back inside of her and hold them in. I didn't know what else to do.

My dad stood next to me, watching for a few minutes. He kicked my mom again and then he moved the knife across his wrist, slicing it. I saw blood start oozing out of his cut. I was afraid to let go of my mom's stomach, but I did manage to reach for the phone with my other hand and I dialed 911.

By the time the ambulance got there, both of my parents were dead.

I have been on my own since I was fifteen-years-old. I ran away, so that I wouldn't have to live in a foster home. I didn't have any other family that I could stay with.

KRISTEN

Kristen was small for a six-year-old girl. She had brown hair and brown eyes. She loved to be with her mom. They would go to the playground, the park and the library together. Kristen also liked to play with other kids. She was a very happy, outgoing little girl.

She was too young to remember her dad hitting her mom. Although she seemed to be afraid of her dad and she did shy away from men, especially when they were loud.

Kathi was a good mother and she enjoyed doing things with her daughter. Kathi and her husband, Troy were divorced. Kathi had custody of the couples daughter. Troy had visitation rights for every other weekend. Kathi pleaded with the judge not to allow visitation, because Troy had threatened to hurt Kristen repeatedly. But the judge wouldn't listen, even when Kathi produced notes that Troy had written threatening both of their lives.

One day Kristen and Kathi were at the playground. Kristen asked her mom if she could go play with a group of preschoolers, over by the fence. Kathi told her that she could and watched as her daughter approached the group of kids. Kristen sat down with them and they all began to play together. They weren't very far from Kathi, so she picked up her book and started to read. Occasionally she would glance over in Kristen's direction.

One time Kathi looked up and didn't see her daughter. She put her book down and stood up to get a better look around the playground. Panicking, she ran over to the group of kids that her daughter had been playing with.

She frantically asked them if they'd seen where Kristen had gone. Two of the kids pointed over to the parking lot. Kathi asked them how she could have gotten onto the other side of the fence. One of the kids said that a man had called to her. When she went over to him, he had picked her up over the fence.

Kathi ran from the playground and out into the parking lot as fast as her shaking legs would carry her. She was slightly relieved when she saw Kristen standing next to Troy. She called to her daughter. Troy told Kristen to go on over to her mother, as he got into his car. Kathi called to her daughter again and watched as Kristen slowly walked away from her dad.

Kristen was half way through the parking lot, when Kathi heard Troy gun his engine. She saw Troy drive straight for their daughter and hit her with his car. She screamed and ran over to help her daughter.

She knelt beside Kristen's still little body, pulling her daughter onto her lap and gently rocking her. Blood covered the pavement and Kathi noticed that one of her daughter's shoes had fallen off, it lay a few feet away from them.

An ambulance came and rushed them to the Emergency Room. Kathi waited nervously in the waiting room and after a while the doctor came in to talk to her. He told her that her daughter had died. He said that they hadn't been able to stop the bleeding inside of her body, all of her major organs had just shut down from the trauma.

Troy is in prison now. Kathi visits a small headstone in the cemetery on the other side of the park. It is the same park that she used to bring Kristen to play.

Kristen is missed very much.

MARC

Marc was nine-years-old the last time that his mother saw him. Marc Sr. had visitation for the weekend. Donna had an uneasy feeling that she just couldn't seem to shake, the day that her ex husband came to pick up their son. But because of the court order, she had to comply.

She watched as her son waved goodbye to her from the passenger seat of his father's car, on Friday afternoon. She was very concerned and couldn't figure out why.

On Sunday evening, little Marc still hadn't gotten home. He was supposed to be home by 3:00 that afternoon. 'Where was he?' she wondered.

She got into her car and drove over to her ex husbands apartment. Donna knocked at the door, then she tried the doorknob and found that the door was locked. She went around to the side of the apartment and saw that one of the windows was opened a little. Donna pushed up the window and climbed inside.

What she saw shocked her. The place was completely empty. No furniture, no clothes and no Marc Jr.

Donna ran out of the apartment and stopped when she saw a pay phone in the courtyard. She quickly snatched up the phone, called the police and reported her missing son.

There is a warrant out on Marc Sr. for kidnaping Donna's son. Marc Jr. will be fourteen in January.

ANDY

Andy was seven-years-old. Tony and Amanda, his parents, fought constantly. Tony used to hit Amanda when he would get mad at her. They could get into some pretty loud yelling matches.

One day Amanda told Tony to leave. She told him that she just didn't want to be hurt by him anymore. Tony got real mad and told her that he wasn't about to leave. Amanda said fine, then she would be the one who was going to leave. He got really upset with her and he hit her.

She grabbed Andy's hand and together they left the apartment. They started to walk down the road and within a few minutes, Amanda heard a car coming pretty fast behind them. She turned around and saw that the car was being driven by Tony. He was driving straight towards her and Andy. She quickly pushed Andy over to the side of the road, thinking that Tony was coming after her.

Tony surprised her by turning the speeding car towards Andy. Amanda screamed as she watched the car run over her son. Tony backed the car up, running Andy over again. Then he sped away. Amanda ran over to her child, she could see right away that he was dead.

The police caught up to Tony two days later. He is now in prison.

Amanda has been trying to move forward with her life, but she says that the emptiness she feels inside will never go away.

JAMI

My name is Jami and I am eighteen-years-old. I ran away from home when I was thirteen and I've been living on my own for five years now. I've lived off the streets and I can scrounge food from just about anywhere.

I left home because my stepfather used to beat on me and my mom. My stepbrother, Rob, used to molest me, he was fifteen at the time. I miss my mom, but there is no way that I'll ever go back there.

I had two kids that I sold. I know that it sounds real bad, but I couldn't afford to take care of any kid right now. Not with my life the way it is. I don't have a home or any money. I had two boys, one when I was fifteen and the other when I was seventeen. I got $300.00 for my first one and $500.00 for the second.

I had my boys outside in an alley next to a trash bin. I cut the cord myself and everything. I had to, I was all alone when I had them both. I guess that they are healthy, I didn't go to the doctors at all when I was pregnant. I didn't even know that I was pregnant for a long time, because my periods haven't been regular since I left home. Sometimes I go for months without getting my period.

I know the guy who gave me the money for my kids, sort of. I had to pay him $200.00 for selling each of my kids for me. After all, he found the people to buy them. I don't want to get pregnant again, but if I do I'll deal with it. Tyrell knows a lot of people that want to buy babies, some of them pay more than the others.

I hope that my mom is okay, maybe she finally left him.

SAMANTHA

My name was Samantha and I'm sixteen-years-old. My dad is a cop and my mom stayed at home, because he didn't want her to work. My mom did a lot of charity stuff though. She helped teach people how to read at the library, and she was always ready to volunteer anywhere that she was needed.

My dad would work during the day, then go to a bar after his shift. By the time he would finally get home, he was pretty well toasted. If we did anything that he didn't like, he'd hit us or point his gun around the room. He used to tell my mom that he was going to kill us all.

My mom tried to work things out with him, but you just couldn't talk to him or reason with him at all…ever. Especially when he had been drinking.

My dad came home real drunk one night and threw our dinner right off of the table. All the plates and food flew onto the walls and fell onto the floor. Then he grabbed my mom by the hair and told her to clean it up. He was mad because my mom had cooked him pork chops with leftover vegetables. My dad hated leftover vegetables.

I watched as my dad drag my mom's face through the food on the floor. I yelled for him to stop, that's when he pulled out his gun. He pointed it at my mom and told me he was going to kill her. Then he told me that he was going to kill all of us.

He let go of my mom and started walking towards me. I started to run when I saw him point the gun at me. I heard a pop, then a whizzing sound went right past my head. My dad had shot the gun at me! This was crazy!

My mom screamed at him to put the gun down. He turned around and pointed it at my mom. He smiled and pretended he was going to shoot it. My mom and I both screamed at him to stop. My dad laughed, put his gun away and then he walked out to his truck.

After my mom heard him drive away, she told me to hurry and grab some of my things. We both went into our rooms and came out a few minutes later, each with a bag of stuff.

"Quick, go out to the car." My mom yelled to me, as she reached for her car keys.

I ran out to the car and my mom followed me. We drove to the bus station, got out of the car and took a bus into the city. Once we got there, my mom made a phone call. We waited in a small diner for someone to come and pick us up.

A while later, a woman in a van drove up and parked outside of the diner.

DOMESTIC ABUSE: ALL SIDES

She came inside, ordered a coffee and sat down with us. The woman and my mom talked for a few minutes. Then we left with her. The woman drove us to a shelter downtown, it was really just a big house. We stayed there for two weeks and then we left on a bus.

I have a new name now and so does my mom. My mom has a job in a motel and we stay in one of the rooms for free. It's not much, but my dad doesn't bother us and he hasn't found us. We don't know for sure if he is even looking for us, but we hope not.

My mom is afraid that he may end up finding us, so we are very careful about everything that we do.

I hope that he never finds us. It's nice to feel sort of safe.

JUDI

My name is Judi and I am sixteen-years-old. My dad would hurt my mom when he'd get really drunk. My mom would always tell him that she was going to leave. He'd just laugh at her. He would tell her to go ahead and leave him, he also said she'd be back.

My mom used to tell me that I was pretty enough to be a model. This year I won 'Miss Tomato.' That is a beauty pageant that we have here. I won the title, which made my mom really happy. She said that I was going to make something of myself and get out of this town someday. She always told me not to settle for any of the guys in our town. She said that they had no dreams, no ambition and nothing to offer me. My dad even surprised us by saying he was proud of me, the day I was crowned.

One day my mom and dad were fighting. He yelled at her, saying that I always came first to her. He asked her, 'What she would do if her little beauty queen wasn't a beauty anymore?' My mom told him that he was talking crazy. He said that I was going to end up just like her, pregnant at sixteen, no education and not worth anything.

My mom surprised us all when she yelled at him to shut up. My dad grabbed me by my hair and pulled out his pocket knife. I could smell the booze on his breath.

"You want to see your beauty queen now?" He asked my mom, holding the knife up to the side of my face.

"Leave her alone!" My mom screamed at him.

My dad took his pocket knife and cut me across my cheek. The cut went from just under my eye, all the way down to my chin. I screamed and put my hand up to my face. I could feel the blood running down my face and through my fingers. My dad let go of me and my mom came over with a towel. Blood was gushing from my cut and my mom held the towel tightly to the side of my face.

When she realized how deep it was, we hurried out to the car and she drove us to the hospital. I needed 67 stitches to close up my face. I also had to turn my crown over to Miss Runner Up. I guess that I will probably never leave this town, I'm too ugly now. I have a huge scar. It goes from below my eye, all the way down to my chin.

The doctors say I'm very lucky that I didn't lose my eye. I'm the one who has to look at my face in the mirror everyday and I really don't feel very lucky.

My dad has disappeared, no one has seen him since he cut me. He just up and left us. I don't want to see him ever again, but I do want them to catch him and put him into jail. My mom had to get a job in town at the feed store. My mom has been real depressed, I know that she's real disappointed because I'll never be a model and never make it out of this town. I guess I will end up just like my dad said I would, worth nothing.

JOANIE

My name was Joanie and I am fifteen-years-old. My mom and her boyfriend didn't get along at all. He used to hit her and a few times he punched her in the face. My mom had a few of her teeth knocked out by him. She has a couple of crowns on her teeth now.

One night, Hector grabbed me and punched me in the back. All because there were a few dirty dishes in the sink. I was waiting to wash them until after we'd had dinner. When he punched me, my mom told him to leave me alone. Then she hit him with a pan on the side of the head.

He got real mad and punched my mom in the face. Her nose started to bleed really bad. Hector grabbed my mom by her hair and started to pound her face onto the floor. Blood was all over the place. I jumped on his back and tried to pull him off of her. I started pounding him on the back and on the head. He just wouldn't loosen the grip that he had on my mom. He kept hitting her face onto the floor and it was making such a sickening, thudding sound.

I jumped off of him and ran to the phone. When he heard me start talking, he realized that I was calling the cops. That's when he let go of my mom. He started to come after me, telling me that he was going to kill me. I ran around the sofa and he tried to catch me. I noticed that he had blood running down his face, from where my mom had hit him with the pan.

I heard sirens in the distance. He must have heard them too, because he looked at me and told me he'd be back to finish the job. He walked over to my mother, who wasn't moving and kicked her twice. Then he ran out of the house.

I went over to my mom and she moaned a little when I touched her. He had left the door opened when he ran out and the police walked in. They had their guns in their hands. One of them came over to my mom and the other one called for an ambulance.

I told them what had happened and another couple of cops came. They searched the area for Hector, but they never found him.

The ambulance brought my mom to the hospital, where she ended up staying for two months. I stayed with my mom's friend Barbara, at her apartment for the two months. During that whole time the police still hadn't found Hector. They told us that he was wanted for assault and for attempted murder.

When my mom was released from the hospital we were finally able to go home. Our landlady was going to let us catch up on our rent, because she felt bad about what had happened. She said that it wouldn't be right if we lost our home, along with what had happened.

Once we had been home for a few days, we started to get threatening phone calls from Hector. He kept telling us that he was going to come back and finish the job. He said that he was going to kill the both of us. He told my mom he was going to kill me first. He said he was going to make my mom watch, as he tortured me.

We left our apartment and went into a shelter. The women there told my mom that we wouldn't be safe unless we left the area, which we did do, with their help. They also told us they were going to work something out with our landlady, because she had been so understanding.

My mom and I have new names now and a new place to live. Barbara told my mom that they still hadn't found Hector.

TIFFANI

My name is Tiffani and I'm sixteen-years-old. My mom was the manager of a motel and we lived in the apartment behind the office. Our apartment was huge and it was really nice inside.

When my mom and dad got married, they had moved away from this town. When I was twelve, my parents got a divorce. My mom and I moved back here, to where she had grown up.

My mom used to go out on Wednesday nights, to play in a pool tournament. She loved to play pool and she was pretty good at it. I used to bring my homework and walkman along. I'd sit at one of the tables while she played.

That's where she met Mark, an old friend of hers. She knew Mark from school and when she saw him playing on a different pool league, she walked over to him. They started to talk and seemed to hit it off. For the next few weeks, Mark and my mom saw a lot of each other.

One day Mark told us, he was getting evicted from his apartment. My mom suggested that he move into our apartment with us. She even hired him as the maintenance man for the motel.

Things went okay for a while. My mom worked in the office during the day and Mark helped her out, by doing repairs and keeping the yard looking neat. They would go to their pool tournaments at night and other nights they would just go out. Sometimes I'd go with them and sometimes I'd stay home. I did notice that my mom started to drink a lot more than she used to. She used to drink occasionally when she went out, but now it was almost every night.

Mark got so that he wouldn't make any repairs at the motel anymore. My mom had to do them herself or else fire Mark, which she didn't want to do. So mom and I would unplug toilets or do whatever needed to be done, because she didn't want Mark to leave. My mom was a pretty heavy woman and didn't think that she'd be able to find anyone else. She wasn't fat, she was just big.

Mark started going out during the day and he'd go out at night, without my mom. She would get mad and yell at him. She told him that he had to do his job or he was going to get fired. He used to just laugh at her. He'd tell her that she was crazy and that she wasn't going to fire him. He told her that she was lucky to have him, because no one else would want a fat slob like her.

Then came the time, Mark didn't come home for three days. My mom was real worried and very mad. On Thursday night, we went out looking for him.

We drove to one of the bars he went to and saw his car in the parking lot.

My mom told me to wait outside in the car, of course I didn't. I followed her inside. Mark was sitting at the bar with his arm around a red-haired woman. I watched my mom walk over to him and she asked him what was going on. He looked up at my mom and told her to leave him alone. He told her to go back home.

"I'll go home," my mom told him. "I'll pack your things for you, pick them up in the morning." She said, as she turned away from him. He jumped up off of the bar stool and grabbed her by the arm.

"I'm not moving out," he told her. "Why would I give up free rent? Are you stupid?"

"You are moving out and your fired!" My mom told him, trying to pull her arm away from him.

Mark grabbed my mom by the hair and dragged her over to the pool table. "I will be home later. It is my home," he said to her.

"Mark, I'll call the cops if you show up." My mom said to him, looking pretty scared.

Mark picked up a pool ball and smashed my mom in the head with it. I saw the bartender pick up the phone, I knew that she was calling the cops.

"Please, leave my mom alone Mark!" I yelled at him.

Mark picked up a pool stick and he let go of my mom. He walked up to me and hit me across the chest with it. Then he went back over to my mom and hit her with it. The pool stick broke in two, as he hit her a few times.

The breath was knocked out of me for a few minutes, I didn't know what to do. I know that I fell down to my knees, on the dirty barroom floor.

Just then, the cops showed up. They threw Mark against a table and took him away in handcuffs.

My mom and I were brought to the hospital. My mom had to get stitches across her forehead. I was okay, but really sore for a couple of days.

A few days later, my mom and I packed Mark's clothes. We dropped them off at the bar he hung out at.

He is still in jail for assaulting us.

JEFF

My name is Jeff and I'm fifteen-years-old. I lived with my dad, because my real mom was in jail for robbery. I didn't see her for a long time, well, for over three years. My dad got a new girlfriend and her name was Val. We moved in with her for a while.

She was pretty nice to me and my dad, but I didn't feel right being there. She worked and my dad didn't. She was a teacher at my school, I know, it sounds pretty weird.

My dad told me not to tell her that he'd been in jail before. But when my dad started to treat her bad, I wanted to tell her. I knew that if I told her, she would throw out my dad. I would have had to go live in a foster home again, so I said nothing.

Val helped me to do my school work. I'd fallen behind in school, from doing the 'foster home shuffle.' She took the time and explained things to me. She never yelled or called me stupid either. I wanted to do something with my life. I didn't want to be in and out of jail, like my parents had always been, for as long as I could remember.

I really wanted to talk to Val about my dad, because she really seemed to believe in me. No one had ever believed in me before. No one have ever cared about me before. The people in the foster homes told me that I would end up just like my parents. They'd tell me that I was nothing but a loser, that I was just a paycheck to them.

My dad was always trying to work one scam or another. Val didn't know what was going on, but I did. My dad had started breaking into houses again, I knew he was. He'd start bringing expensive things home and then he'd hide them from Val. He would sell them or pawn them a few days later. I heard him talking to his contacts on the phone. Val actually thought that he was calling about jobs.

One day she came home from work early and caught my dad with a few of his ex-convict friends. They were sitting around a bunch of stolen stuff, right there in her livingroom. She asked my dad what was going on and he lied to her, as usual. But she didn't believe him this time and she told him to leave. He sat there and he told her that he wasn't going to go anywhere.

She went to the phone and she told him that if he wasn't going to leave, she was going to call the cops. He got up real slow from the chair that he had been sitting in and walked towards her. He looked at her real mean, then he slapped her hard across the face. I got mad at my dad. I knew that he was going to ruin everything. He reached out to hit her again and I ran up behind him, pushing him away from her. His friends said that they didn't want any part of this and they quickly left.

My dad started to come towards me. That's when I noticed Val on the phone, calling the cops. My dad hit me so hard, I saw white spots. I fell back against the wall and my dad went over to Val. He started slapping her again and again.

I looked out the window, just in time to see a cop car pull up out front. Two officers got out of the car and ran up to the door. Val screamed as she fell down. My dad had hit her again. I quickly ran over to the door and opened it for the cops.

They rushed over to my dad and pulled him away from Val, then they handcuffed him. He was real mad at me. He said to me as he walked out the door with the cops, that I wasn't his son anymore.

Val and I told the cops what we knew, which really wasn't all that much. The cops took out all of the stolen stuff and put it into the trunk of the police car. When they came back inside, they asked Val if she wanted them to bring me to Protective Services. Val told them no. She said that I was going to be staying with her, she would call Protective Services in the morning and take care of the arrangements.

After the cops and my dad left, Val and I sat down and had a long talk. I told her everything and she wasn't even mad at me. She told me that I had done a very brave thing, standing up to my dad like I had. She said that she'd be honored if I'd stay with her.

She also told me that she believed in me and would do her best to help me as much as possible. She then asked me if I wanted to live with her. I told her yes, I did want to live with her.

The next morning Val and I went to Protective Services and soon after that we went to court. At first, I just lived with her as a foster kid. It's been two years since all of that happened and Val is in the process of adopting me. I love living with her. I play on the basketball team and I am doing really good in school. It helps to have a teacher for a mom!

We haven't heard from my dad or real mom, but the court issued a stay away order. It is in effect indefinitely, against the both of them. So they can't ever come around either one of us.

I've decided that I am going to be a social worker, when I get out of school. I want to help kids make something of themselves and help them to make the right choices. Val gave me a chance and I want to do the same thing for other kids.

I don't know where I would be now if I didn't have Val. I will always be grateful to her, my mom.

ISAAC

My name is Isaac and now I am fifteen-years-old. My dad used to beat up my mom. He's knocked out some of her teeth and he's broken some of her bones. One time, he even busted her jaw and she had to have her jaw wired shut.

We'd always leave him and go to a woman's shelter for a while. Then my mom would start to feel real bad. She would get depressed, because she couldn't get a job. Eventually, we'd go back to live with my dad.

He'd be okay for a while, then he'd start beating on her again. When I turned twelve, the shelters wouldn't let me go in anymore. They said that I was too big and that I'd make some of the women that stayed there feel uncomfortable.

So my mom really felt trapped. She had to stay with my dad, she had no choice. My mom had no money and no where else that she could go. He knew that and he would torment me and my mom more than ever.

I felt helpless, I didn't know how to help my mom. I'd hit my dad or push him, trying to make him stop hurting her, but he'd just get madder and hurt her more. He'd punch me whenever I would try to help her out.

One night, I woke up to hear them fighting and I heard my mom keep pleading, 'No, please, no.'

I got out of bed and went into the other room. I saw that my dad was holding a knife up to my mom's throat. I yelled for him to put the knife down.

He told me if I didn't shut up and go back to bed, he'd kill her right there in front of me. I took a step towards him, hoping to grab the knife away from him. Suddenly he sliced it across her throat. I backed up as my mother screamed in pain, but her cut didn't look that deep.

"Dad, let mom go." I pleaded with him, trying real hard not to sound as scared as I really was.

"No, your mom says that she wants to break up our family. She said that she wants to leave me," he told me, sounding like a little kid. "I can't allow that, son."

"Let her go and we'll all sit down and talk about it." I begged him, trying to convince him to trust me and put the knife down.

"I can't let your mom leave. You don't want to leave with your mother do you, Isaac?" he asked me.

"No.' I said, willing to say anything to try to calm him down. I saw blood coming from my mom's throat.

"You don't want to leave the same way that your mother is going to leave, do you?" he asked me.

"No." I said, not really understanding what he was saying.

"You won't be able to go with me either, son," he said to me.

"Why not? Where are you going?" I asked him, still very confused.

"I'm not going to jail, that's for sure." he said, looking down at my mother.

"Why would you go to jail, dad?" I asked him.

"I love you son." My dad told me, as he pulled the knife across my mothers throat again. This time I could see that it was a much deeper cut. He let her fall to the floor, then he took the knife and plunged it deep into his own chest.

I didn't know what to do, it had all happened so fast. I had no idea that he was going to do that. There was nothing I could have done to stop him. I ran to the phone and dialed 911. Then I ran back over to my mom. I picked up her hand and held it tightly in mine, so that she would know I was there for her. By the time that anyone got there, both of my parents were dead.

I've lived in four foster homes, since it happened six months ago. I still don't know why he did it, the whole thing makes no sense.

SYLVIA

My name is Sylvia and I am fourteen-years-old. When I was seven years old, my mom let her boyfriend move in with us. I didn't like him, he was pretty mean to me. My mom worked at a grocery store during the day and he didn't work at all. I don't know where my mom met him. Maybe at the grocery store, she never told me and I never asked.

Ruben, her boyfriend, used to drink and do drugs. I saw him do them during the day, when my mom was working. He would drive her to work and then he'd take her car for the day. During the day he would watch me, sort of. He'd leave me home a lot, while he went driving around with his friends.

When he was at home with me, people would come over and drink. They did drugs and some of them even had guns. Ruben would yell at me to go out into the backyard when his friends would come over. It was boring outside, I hated being thrown out there. I was hot, while they all sat inside with the air conditioner on.

A couple of times, when some girls would come over, he would make me go out into the backyard. He told me not to tell my mom. He told me he'd shoot her with one of those guns that I'd seen him and his friends with.

I was afraid of Ruben and he was a real jerk. He and his friends would sit in our house and eat all of the food that my mom bought. My mom had no idea what went on during the day, while she was at work and I couldn't tell her.

Ruben started going out at night, sometimes he wouldn't get home until early in the morning. My mom would get mad. He'd take her car and she needed it to get to work. My mom and Ruben started to fight a lot. I was glad and I hoped that she would make him leave, but she didn't. He stayed. They argued a lot, but she didn't throw him out. I couldn't figure out why not.

Ruben started doing drugs while I was in the house with him. I knew that he had been doing them before, but now I actually saw him using them. Ruben and his friends would tie things around their arms, it looked like a little rubber tube and then heat something up. I watched them fill up their needles and inject the stuff into their arms. I know now, that it was heroin. I didn't know what it was at the time, but I did see the effect it had on them.

One afternoon I came out of my bedroom and asked Ruben if I could go over to the neighbors and play. Mr. and Mrs. Smith's grandchildren were visiting, besides I was really bored over at my house. He told me no, because I hadn't gone to bed on time the night before.

"Please." I begged him.

He swung his hand out and slapped me across the face. "No," he told me again. I started to cry. The slap had really hurt and there were a lot of people there. I was embarrassed and I ran back into my room. I stayed in there waiting for my mom to come home. I could hear Ruben and his friends, laughing in the other room.

Later he came into my room and lay on the bed with me. He told me that I was getting to be such a pretty girl, then he started to rub my leg with his hand. It made me feel very uncomfortable.

After dinner that night, Ruben went out as usual. I finally had a chance to talk to my mom. I told her that he had slapped me earlier that day and she got pretty mad at him. We sat next to each other on the couch and watched tv. Then after a while, my mom told me that it was time for me to go to bed.

Later that night, I woke up to hear people screaming and yelling. I quietly came out of my room and saw that it was my mom and Ruben. I watched as Ruben pulled her out of the house by her hair. They were arguing about her car. I ran to the front window and watched them.

He still had her by the hair as he slammed her face into the windshield. Then he pulled her head up, by holding onto a handful of her hair. He shoved her face back down, onto the hood of the car.

When he finally let her go, she slid down the car onto the driveway. I could see that blood was streaked all over the windshield and on the hood of the car.

I started to run over to my mom, but Ruben scooped me up. I screamed for my mom. I saw that she was leaning against the tire with her head down. I thought she was dead.

Ruben opened the car door and pushed me inside. I started to cry, because I was real scared. He slapped me and told me to keep my mouth shut. I just sat on the front seat with tears running down my face. Ruben went back over to my mom and pushed her away from the car. He threw a beer can out into our yard and started the car up. I screamed again for my mom, she shook her head slowly and looked around. He started to back the car up and that's when my mom realized what was happening. She called my name and yelled for him to stop the car.

My mom got up and started pounding on the car. Ruben put the car in gear and we drove off. He ran over my mom's foot as he was driving away. My mom screamed for him to stop. I saw the Smiths' outside light come on.

As we drove off, Ruben kept yelling at me to shut up. He told me he'd shoot me. I turned around in the front seat and looked back at my mom. I didn't know if I would ever see her again.

Ruben drove for a long time and I fell asleep in the car. When I woke up it was light outside and I was lying down across the front seat. I didn't see Ruben anywhere. I was trying to get my bearings and decide what I was going to do next. I didn't know where I was, but I did notice that all of the houses were run down and scary looking. I was scared, hungry, cold and I really wanted my mom.

I decided to get out of the car, but as soon as I opened the door someone on one of the porches called Ruben's name. Just then, the door to one of the houses flew open and Ruben came running out.

"Get back inside the car!" he yelled at me.

"No!" I said, as I got out of the car and started to run down the sidewalk. Ruben caught up to me and grabbed me by the hair. He slapped me a few times, before I was able to bite him on the hand. I bit down as hard as I could. He punched me, after looking down at his hand. He saw that I had made him bleed.

While he tried to wrap his hand in his shirt, I ran off into someone's yard. I climbed the fence and ran through another backyard, climbed another fence and found myself on a sidewalk. I was afraid that Ruben was going to follow me and I was afraid of this neighborhood. I just wanted to go home and be with my mother again.

I kept walking and walking, I didn't know where I was going. I hoped that I was heading home, but I didn't even know where I was. I got tired and scared, then I started to cry. I sat down on the grass in someone's front yard. After a few minutes, an older woman came over to me. She asked me if I was okay. She held out her hand to me, which I took and I followed her into her house, even though I knew that I shouldn't.

She brought me into her kitchen and told me to sit down. She gave me some lemonade and cookies. Then she asked me some questions. While I ate the cookies, she called the police.

When the cops came, I thanked the woman for helping me. The cops took me to the police station. I waited in a room for a while and then a cop took me by the hand. We went out into the parking lot and got into one of the police cars. Neither one of us talked very much, as we drove down the road. Pretty soon he stopped the car. I leaned forward and looked out of the front window, I saw my house! The cop opened his door, then he came around the side of the car and opened the door for me. I jumped out and ran towards my front door, but before I made it, my mom opened up the door. I jumped into her arms and the both of us started crying.

I noticed that she had a cast on her foot. She told me that it happened when Ruben had run over her foot with the car. Mr. and Mrs. Smith came over and we all hugged and cried.

The cop asked me and my mom a lot of questions and then he left. I was so tired and worn out from everything that had happened. I took a bath, then I went into my mom's bed and fell asleep laying next to her. My mom told me that she held me the whole night.

About a week later, the cop came back and told my mom that they had arrested Ruben. When my mom went back to work, the Smith's started to babysit for me. Ruben was put into jail.

THOSE THEY LEFT BEHIND

These are stories about the friends and families who have lost loved ones. They have lost their daughters, grandchildren, nieces, friends and sometimes entire families. Some have been forced to leave their abusers by going into hiding. Others haven't been as lucky, they died at the hands of their abusers.

These people that are left behind tell heartbreaking stories of their losses and grief.

Our legal system needs to change to protect these women and the women who are trying to protect their children from the abuse and the abuser.

JANIE

My name is Georgia, my daughter's name was Janie. She met Phil, dated him for a while and married him shortly after that. I never liked him. I felt he had beady little eyes and he was also a very sneaky person.

One day I caught him going through my purse, he denied it and then later said that he was looking for a pen. Janie believed him, I knew better though, I had seen him.

A few weeks later, Janie came over to my house for a visit. She had bruises on her face and her throat. I asked her what had happened and she told me that Phil had hit her and tried to choke her. I pleaded with her to leave him, but she told me he was never going to do it again. She told me that she was pregnant.

Pregnant! I was so excited, my first grandchild! But I was also afraid for her.

Later that afternoon while we were talking at my house, she told me he had gotten upset when she told him that she was pregnant. I was worried for her safety, but she assured me he had just been shocked by the news.

When she left to go home I was really worried. I worried about her and my grandchild. I put away my knitting at ten o'clock and went in to bed. I just couldn't shake the feeling I had that something was wrong.

I woke up when I heard a banging at my front door. I crawled out of bed and fumbled around in the dark for my robe. I went to the door, looked out the peephole and saw two cops standing there on my step. I opened the door and let them inside my house.

They told me they had responded to a domestic call earlier that night. When they arrived at my daughter's apartment, they'd found her dead. They told me that Phil had been arrested for her murder.

"What happened?" I remembered asking them, through my tears.

They told me that a neighbor had called after hearing my daughter screaming. Phil had stabbed her in the chest and the stomach, numerous times.

My daughter and my grandchild were both dead. That monster took my baby away from me, both of my babies.

I went to all of the court hearings and finally found a little peace when they gave him fifty years in prison. They found him guilty on two counts of murder.

I miss my daughter every day and I often wonder about my unborn grandchild. I would give anything to have my daughter and her baby back with me.

KIM

My sister was forced to leave us all behind, when she had to run away from her husband. He would beat her up a lot and sometimes he even kicked her. No one in our family knew what to do to help her. We would beg her to leave him and she actually did for a while. Then he'd find her and bring her back home.

We called the cops on him a few times, but he'd somehow convince her not to press charges. I knew that she was afraid of him. He told her over and over that he was going to kill her. Sometimes he would tell her that he was going to kill us, if she ever left him again.

Our parents were old, they had me when they were in their late forty's and they had her two years after me. They are almost eighty years old and not in that great of health anymore. My sister Kim and I tried to keep a lot of things from them. They didn't know everything that happened, so it was hard for them to understand why she had to leave the way that she did.

I helped her to leave that day, it was the same day that she had been released from the hospital. The night before he had roughed her up real bad. The emergency room doctor had called me. When I saw her that night, I was so shocked. I hardly recognized my own sister, her face was so bruised and swollen.

Both of her eyes were almost totally swollen shut. Her lip had been stitched back up, from where he had kicked her and split it open. Big chunks of her hair had been ripped out, leaving empty bloody, bald patches all over her head. But worse than all of that, was the big cut that ran across her face. He had taken a knife and cut her up pretty bad. She had forty two stitches, that seemed like such a large amount for someone's face. The doctors told me they had put in extra stitches to reduce the scarring.

When my sister was finally able to talk to me, I convinced her to leave him. I told her that the next time she might be dead.

I called a woman's shelter and brought my sister there the next day. The hospital had kept her overnight for observation. A woman at the shelter told my sister that she could stay there for two months, maybe longer.

The women who stayed at the shelter were not supposed to tell anyone where the shelter was located. When I was there, I saw a woman get picked up in front of the shelter by a man. Later that night, that same woman told my sister that she was seeing her abuser again. She told my sister that he was the one who had picked her up earlier that day. So much for a safe house! After hearing that, I knew it was just a matter of time before my sister was found.

Everything went semi smoothly for about two and a half weeks. Although, during that time my brother in law did threaten my parents. He told them if they didn't tell him where my sister was, he was going to kill them. He also came to the restaurant where I worked and harassed me. A few nights I was even followed home by him.

I got a phone call from my sister late one night, I knew from the sound of her voice that he had found her. She sounded frantic. She cried when she told me about how he had been pounding at the shelter's door. Then about how he'd run out onto the sidewalk and screamed for her. He kept yelling that he was going to kill her.

The women in the shelter heard him and they were very concerned. They told my sister that they could help her to get away from him. They told her they could help her to get a new name and a new life away from him, but she would never be able to contact anyone here again.

They also told my sister that we could relay messages back and forth through them, but that direct contact had to be avoided at all costs or else it could jeopardize her safety. I told her that I thought that it was a good idea, I felt she should do what they told her.

I was terrified that he would end up killing my sister, eventually. I would rather not have my sister around and know that she was okay, than to have her stay here and wonder if she would be alive the next day.

I told her I would stop by the next day to say goodbye to her. I said I'd bring some of her things with me. I went to my bank and withdrew some money to help her out. Then I stopped at my parents house and told them what was going to happen, so that they could say goodbye to her.

The next day I brought our mom and dad to the shelter to see my sister for the last time. We all cried many tears that day. Our parents tried to understand what was going on, but they just couldn't.

As we were leaving I told my sister I loved her and how I would miss her terribly, but I knew that she would be better off. I know it wouldn't have taken much to convince her to stay, but that would have been unfair and selfish.

We do get letters from her and I write back to my sister. I drop the letters that we write and pick up the letters from my sister at the shelter every two weeks. I miss her so much and wish that we could be together again. She has a new name and a whole new life now. She seems happy and that's all that I want for her.

My parents ask about her all the time. My brother in law comes around and still bothers us, but we can honestly say that we don't know where she is. That way we will never accidently tell him.

I'm thankful that the shelter has been able to keep my sister safe. I really do hate my brother in law for tearing apart our family.

JULIE

My name is Tom and my sisters name is Julie. About five years ago she got married for the second time. Her first husband had died in a car accident, after they had been married for almost twenty years.

Julie had no kids and was very lonely after Todd died. She met Victor and she seemed happy...for a while.

At first Victor seemed to treat her really good, so no one said too much when they announced that they were going to get married.

Our parents were in their seventies when Julie and Victor got married. Things went okay for a while, until one day Julie came over to my house pretty upset. She had a black eye and bruises up and down both of her arms.

I tried to convince her to leave him, but she told me he was sorry and that he had apologized to her. He promised her that it wouldn't happen again...but it did. It kept on happening, one time she had to get stitches. Another time she had broken ribs and yet another time he went after her with a knife and cut her up pretty badly.

Julie left him and went into a shelter. The women there told her that she should leave him, because he was going to end up killing her. She called me from the shelter and we arranged to meet the next day.

My heart sank when Julie told me that she was going to leave. She told me that the women in the shelter were going to help her to get away from him.

I knew that it was the best thing for her to do, I knew that it was the only thing for her to do. Julie said that she would never be able to contact any of us, because Victor could easily find her that way.

"When are you leaving?" I asked her.

"In two days," she told me, sadly.

"What about your things? What are you going to do about money?" I asked.

"I'm going to become a whole new person. I'll be able to work and actually have a safe life. But I will miss you all terribly." Julie said, beginning to cry.

"I'll miss you too, but I want you to be safe. At least I'll know that you are okay." I told her.

I hugged my sister for the last time that day. I think about her every day and I wonder how she is doing.

Since the time she left, our parents have both died. I wish that I had my sister with me to help me deal with things. Together we could have made the funeral arrangements for our parents. I can't even tell her that our parents have died, because I don't know how to get in touch with her.

I really resent Victor because he destroyed our family. He should have been the one that had to leave, not Julie.

KELLI

My name is Sonya and my daughters name was Kelli. Kelli was a junior in high school. She was a quiet girl and she did very well with her studies.

Kelli had just gotten her license and had a part time job at the mall after school and on weekends. I told her that she could keep the job as long as it didn't interfere with her school work.

Once she had been working for about a month, I noticed that she seemed to become withdrawn. She had always been a pretty happy girl, but something was different about her besides the obvious. She never smiled anymore and when I asked her what was going on she wouldn't make eye contact with me. She would keep insisting that everything was okay.

One day I waited outside the mall for her to get out of work. I was convinced that the problem was there. I watched as my daughter walked out of the side doorway followed by a slightly older boy. They stopped by a car, it seemed as though they were arguing. I watched in horror as the boy slapped my daughter across the face. Before I could react she got into the car with him.

I followed them as they drove away, but unfortunately I lost his car. I drove around for quite a while and still I was unable to find them.

I drove back to the mall and parked next to my daughters car, to wait for her. I guess that I must have fallen asleep, because the next thing I knew it was light outside.

My daughters car was still parked there next to mine, she had never come back for her car! I started my car and drove back home to see if she had gone there instead.

I raced through the entire house calling out her name, but she wasn't there. I called the police, because the mall didn't open for a few more hours and I thought maybe they could get some answers.

Two officers came over to our house and wrote up a report. I found out later that day that the boy who had been with my daughter worked in the mall at a music store. One of the officers told me that they had taken the boy in for questioning.

Four agonizing days later, the same two officers came back over to my house. I knew that they were there with bad news.

They told me that they had found my daughters body in a wooded area near the mall, not far from where I had lost his car. She had been strangled and her body had been left in the woods. The boy was arrested for my daughter's murder, but he never gave any reason as to why he killed her. I have never been able to have any closure, I wish that I knew why he had felt that he needed to kill her.

It came out later on in the trial that they had been dating. I also heard that he had been very jealous.

PAM

My daughter in law, Pam, was the most wonderful person. She gave me two beautiful grandchildren. My son and Pam used to argue quite a bit. I know this, because they used to live with me.

Jimmy did some drugs and he used to drink occasionally. When he was drugged up is when he used to turn into a miserable man, he was just like his father.

I watched Pam go from being a happy girl who loved life, to a depressed and afraid person. It was a terrible thing to watch and I was powerless to do anything to help her.

You see, my son would beat on Pam. He'd beat on his two baby girls and he'd even hit me. I was afraid of my son, we were all afraid of him.

One night he picked up a knife and waved it around the room, he threatened us all with it. Then he picked up my youngest granddaughter and held the knife up to that poor baby's chest.

No one moved, we were all too frightened to do anything. Pam yelled at him to leave little Amanda alone. She went over to him and kept shouting at him.

Jimmy dropped Amanda and she fell onto the floor. Then he turned to Pam and plunged the knife deep into her chest. I watched in horror as Pam slowly slid down to the floor. My granddaughters were screaming and crying.

I was watching Jimmy afraid that he would go after one of the girls next. He looked down at Pam and then he dropped the knife. Jimmy walked out of the house and sat down on the front step.

I ran over to Pam and I told her to hold on. Then I dialed 911 and waited for them to show up.

Jimmy was still sitting on the step when the police came. They arrested my son and took my daughter in law to the hospital. Pam died in the ambulance on the way to the hospital.

Now I live with my two grand babies who seem to be doing pretty well, considering everything that has happened to them.

LISA

My Aunt Lisa was really cool, we used to do all kinds of things together. She was only five years older than I was, so we were pretty close.

One day when we were at the mall she met a guy named Randy. They talked for a while and then she gave him our phone number. My aunt was eighteen-years-old and she lived with us. My grandparents lived with us too, because their house had burned down a few months earlier. But it worked out okay, because we all got along really well.

A few days later, Randy called her and they went out to dinner. They saw each other every couple of days, for a few months.

One day my aunt didn't come home after going out with him. We looked everywhere for her and then my grandparents called the police.

The police questioned Randy. Even though they knew that he had done something to her, they couldn't do anything to him without finding her first. With no body they couldn't press any charges against him, that's what they told us.

That happened six years ago and the police still haven't found my aunt. We all miss her terribly. It's awful not knowing what happened to her.

Randy is still their number one suspect, but until they can either find her body or he confesses, they told us that there is nothing that they can do.

We all know that Randy killed her, but what can we can do? I wish that we knew where she was so that we could at least stop wondering.

CINDY

My name is Dana and my mothers name was Cindy. We moved from California to Kentucky, after my mom and dad got a divorce. I hated it in Kentucky, I missed all of my friends back home in California. My grandmother wasn't doing very well, that's why we moved back to Kentucky, I was fifteen at the time.

My mom started to go out with a guy that I absolutely couldn't stand. He was such a jerk. They dated for a few months. About that same time my mom told me that he was starting to tell her things she could and couldn't do. I knew that he was a jerk! My mom told me she was going to tell him that she didn't want to see him anymore.

A few days later he came over to our house. My mom went outside to talk to him and I watched them from the window, as they argued. It looked to me like Ken was crying and I almost felt sorry for him.

I watched when my mom turned away from him and started to walk back towards the house.

"Cindy, please. I want to give something to you." I heard him call out to her.

My mom turned back to Ken as he reached into his car.

Very quickly, he turned and lunged towards my mother. I saw a gleam that came from the knife he was holding.

I screamed and ran out onto the front lawn, as my mother fell to the ground. Ken yelled at her and stabbed her again, then he jumped into his car and sped away.

A neighbor ran outside, after hearing what was going on. She told me that she was going to call for help.

I held my mother's head in my lap, I stroked her hair as she died in my arms. I kept telling her that I loved her, I don't know if she heard me or not. The whole time I held her, she never even opened her eyes.

The police and ambulance came a while later. The guys in the ambulance told me that my mother was dead. Then the police questioned me about what had happened.

A few hours later, the police told me and my grandmother that they had arrested Ken.

It's been two years since my mom died and I miss her very much.

UNKNOWN

My daughter and her two children left us, so that they could be safe. Her husband used to hurt her and sexually molest her two daughters.

She had no choice, but to leave. The courts didn't help them or protect them and the police couldn't. The police could only do so much, without approval from the courts.

My daughter went into a shelter and it was there that she found the help that she needed. They helped her to get away.

Since she has been gone, her husband has made my life miserable. He has broken into my house, he's stolen my phone bills and my mail…it has been unbelievable.

I am heartbroken to have lost my daughter and granddaughters, but I am very happy that they are safe.

ANNIE

Our daughter died at the hands of her husband Tom. Annie was separated and had filed for a divorce from Tom. He used to drink too much and then he'd hit our Annie.

After living with this for two years, she finally decided that he wasn't going to change. She moved back in with us and that's when the trouble really began.

My wife would answer the phone and Tom would threaten her. Tom would pull up into our driveway and blare the horn at 2:30 in the morning. Sometimes he would just get out of his car and bang on our front door. He was such a menace and the neighbors were not real happy, either.

One day Annie was outside weeding the garden with my wife and Tom pulled up into our driveway. He aimed a gun at Annie and he shot her.

I ran outside when I heard the gunshot. I saw my wife leaning over Annie's body, screaming out her name. I saw Tom's car speeding off down the road.

I quickly went back into the house and called for help. Our daughter lived for three days, after she had been shot in the head. She never regained consciousness.

We buried our only child a week after she had been shot.

Tom is in prison, but it doesn't ease our pain at all.

KARLA

My sister Karla was eighteen-years-old, when her twenty-year-old boyfriend Brandon beat her to death with a baseball bat. They had only been going out for a few months. Brandon was very jealous of her and he seemed like he wanted her all to himself. He didn't like any of her friends or any of her family around.

At first Karla had been flattered by the attention that he gave her, but eventually his possessiveness is what drove her away from him.

On the night that he murdered her, she had told me that she was going to break up with him. He met her at a restaurant that night and they had dinner, that much we know. Beyond that, we can only guess what actually happened. But sometime between the time that they ate and five the next morning he had killed her.

The police found the bat, complete with his fingerprints. It was next to her car which had been left in a used car dealers parking lot. There wasn't much of her left for us to identify, the police did manage to find some of her teeth on the front seat of her car. When they compared them to her dental records, they knew they had a match.

I only hope that death came quickly for her. I couldn't stand the thought of her suffering through all of that. Her death was a horrible and senseless act.

To this day they still haven't found Brandon. We buried my sister four days after her eighteenth birthday.

ZOE

Zoe was my best friend and we went to the same high school. We even had a lot of the same classes together.

A guy named Tom started to hang out at our school. He would sit on his motorcycle in the parking lot. Everyone thought that he was so cool. He was cute and you could tell that he had an 'I don't care attitude.' Anyway, I caught Zoe checking him out one day.

"I'm going to go out with him." Zoe said to me, keeping her eyes on Tom as we walked by.

I laughed at her and said, 'Yeah right.' We were both sixteen years old and he had to be at least in his twenties.

Every morning he sat on his motorcycle and talked to some of the kids at our school. He was also there every afternoon.

One morning Zoe and I walked past him and suddenly she stopped right in front of him. She smiled and said hi to him. I couldn't believe she had done that. He looked up at her and gave her this gorgeous smile, then he said hi back to her.

I pulled her by the arm trying to get her to leave, but she just stood there.

"Can I have a ride on your bike sometime?" she asked him, I felt my mouth drop open.

"Today, after school," he told her, with his perfect smile.

"Okay." Zoe said to him, as she started to finally walk away with me.

"Are you crazy?" I asked her, when we were out of his earshot.

"What?" she asked me, innocently.

"He's way older than us, you can't go with him on his motorcycle." I told her.

"Why not? He's so cute." Zoe said.

"Did you not see the ring on his left finger? I think he's married. What if he has kids?" I said. I couldn't believe that we were having this conversation.

"I'll find out, won't I?" she said to me, as we hurried off to class.

Through the whole day, all that she could talk about was Tom. On her notebook she kept writing, 'Tom and Zoe.' She was beginning to drive me crazy.

After school, she dragged me over to where Tom always parked his bike. Tom saw her and motioned for her to go to him. Zoe ran over to him and I stood there. I watched them for a few minutes, then I left to catch the bus.

At about seven o'clock, Zoe's mother called me and asked if I knew where Zoe was. I lied to her and said that Zoe had told me she was going to go to the library.

The next day on the bus Zoe was holding a seat for me. I asked her what had happened the night before. I told her that I had to lie to her mother.

Zoe said that they had driven around for a while on his motorcycle.

"So, what about the ring? Is he married?" I asked my friend.

"Yeah. But we didn't do anything. Anyway, he doesn't love her. They only got married because she got pregnant." Zoe whispered to me.

"Is he still married? How many kids do they have?" I asked her.

"Yeah, he's still married and no kids yet. She's seven months pregnant." Zoe said.

"Stay away from him, he's just trouble." I warned Zoe. "He just got married."

Of course she didn't listen to me and for months she would take off with him every day after school. Her mom had no idea what was going on and I found myself lying to her a lot. I hated the whole situation.

Zoe was so sure they loved each other. No matter how hard I tried to convince her that they weren't in love, she wouldn't listen to anything I said.

One morning on the bus, Zoe told me that she was pregnant and that she was going to tell Tom that morning. I had thought that she was still a virgin, she had never said a word to me.

"His wife just had the baby, didn't she?" I asked in shock, feeling like I never really knew Zoe.

"Yeah, a boy. But he doesn't think that it's his. Anyway, he loves me and he doesn't love her." Zoe said. "I'm going to tell him before school. I just can't wait. I'm so excited! I want you to be with me so that I can prove to you how much we really love each other."

"How do you know he won't say that your baby isn't his?" I asked her.

"He won't say that, because he loves me," she told me, happily.

I hated to see her acting so stupidly. Once we got to school I noticed that Tom was talking to a girl. Zoe saw it too and got pretty upset. She marched right over to him and announced that she was pregnant. The timing wasn't the best.

I swear that Tom's face turned beet red. "What?" he asked her.

Zoe repeated what she had said and he very slowly got up off of his bike. He stood right in front of her and slapped her hard across the face. Then he twisted her arm around and told her to get rid of it.

"No I won't!" Zoe yelled at him. He slapped her again and to my surprise she threatened him, "I'll tell your wife about us."

"I'll kill you." Tom growled at her, then he let go of her arm and slapped her again. "Think about it," he said to her before she ran off towards the building, holding onto her cheek.

I looked over at Tom again, before I ran off after my friend. I saw a few of the kids turn to watch us. The look on his face is something that I will always remember. He scared me so much that day. I sometimes see him with that same expression in my dreams.

Once I caught up to Zoe, we went into the girls' room. We stayed there for the entire first period. I tried to comfort my friend, but all she did was cry.

"I'm going to go back out there to talk to him. Maybe he got mad because there were other people around. Yeah, that kind of news I should have told him when we were alone together." Zoe told me, wiping her eyes.

"No, I saw his face. You need to stay away from him. I'm afraid of him." I said to Zoe.

"You don't know him like I do," she said to me, blowing her nose. "He'll be fine. I just surprised him."

"Please don't go out there." I begged her.

"You worry too much," she said, taking me by the hand. "Look, walk me over to the door and I'll be back before school is over, I promise."

We walked down the hall and up the stairs to the door. I looked out of the window and saw that Tom was still there, leaning back on his motorcycle, while he smoked a cigarette. A shiver went down my back and I looked over at Zoe.

"Please don't go. Stay here with me." I begged her.

"I'll be okay. Cover for me and don't tell anyone." She said, as she went out the door.

I stood there looking out the window at the both of them, I saw Zoe run up to Tom. I watched them, as he threw his cigarette down and Zoe hugged him. Then she climbed onto the back of his bike and they drove away. I went to the rest of my classes and I kept expecting to see Zoe all day. I was afraid for her and I just couldn't seem to concentrate on any of my classes.

By the time school was over, I was a nervous wreck. I went out to the parking lot and I saw Tom in his usual spot, but I didn't see Zoe anywhere. I walked over to him and saw that he was talking to the same girl, who he had been talking to earlier that day.

"Where's Zoe?" I demanded.

"I haven't seen her, since earlier this morning." He said staring at me, waiting to see if I said anything else.

"I saw her leave with you at nine thirty." I told him, trying not to show how nervous I was.

"Sorry, your wrong. When school started I left to get some breakfast, alone. I didn't see her at all." He told me, glaring at me.

I wasn't sure what to do, so I left and ran to catch my bus. When I got home I called Zoe's house, no one answered. I kept calling over there all afternoon.

At seven thirty Zoe's mother called me and asked if I'd seen Zoe. I told her that I had been trying to call all afternoon. We hung up the phone and I nervously told my dad what had happened. Together we went over to Zoe's house, where I told her mom, everything. I'm sorry if I broke a confidence to Zoe, but I was so worried about her.

By nine o'clock, the police had come and gone. My dad and I were still at Zoe's house. I was up in her room crying and my dad was in the livingroom with Zoe's mom. They were both very upset and trying to make some kind of sense out of the whole thing.

I knew where Zoe kept her diary and I took it out. We shared everything, so I didn't think that she would mind. I only read between the days that Zoe had met Tom and that day. What I read shocked me, Zoe wrote that on numerous occasions, Tom had hit her. Once he had even punched her on the head. Why hadn't she ever told me? Why did she keep so many secrets from me?

I read and read, while tears flowed down my cheeks. She had really thought she loved him, but she had also been terribly afraid of him.

She wrote about how she wished she could tell me everything, but that she was embarrassed.

I slowly put her diary down beside me on the bed and I cried. I knew that I had to show Zoe's mom. It was ten thirty and still Zoe hadn't come home or even called. I was sure that something bad had happened to her. Zoe wouldn't have put her mother through this, no matter what. I knew Tom had done something to her. I went down the stairs, holding Zoe's diary tightly in my hands.

"I think that you should read this, Mrs. Campbell." I told her, handing her the small book. I went out into the kitchen to make her a cup of tea, while my dad stayed with her.

"Did you know this boy Tom?" Mrs. Campbell asked me, when I came back into the livingroom.

"Not really, I knew who he was. I never talked to him until today." I told her.

"We'd better call the police back over here." My dad said, going over to the phone. He had just picked it up, when there was a knock at the door. My dad put the phone back down and he went to answer the door. I walked over to stand by Zoe's mom and I took her hand, feeling that we were both going to need each other.

DOMESTIC ABUSE: ALL SIDES

Two police officers walked into the livingroom. I could tell by the looks on their faces, they had bad news.

"God, no!" Mrs. Campbell screamed, sensing what was about to happen.

"I'm sorry," one of them said.

"Where? How?" she asked them, as she just fell back onto the couch.

"We found her at the rifle range, it's a popular hang out in town for the kids. She appears to have been strangled." The other officer told us.

My dad went over to Mrs. Campbell and he sat down next to her, putting his arm around her. "I'm so sorry, Cassie." He said to her, as a tear rolled down his cheek.

I couldn't believe it. My best friend was dead. "Did you find Tom?" I somehow managed to ask them.

"Tom Hill? He drives a motorcycle?" the first officer asked me.

I nodded my head, I hadn't even known his last name, until I'd read it in Zoe's diary.

"We have him in custody now. He has confessed to your friends murder. He will be going away for quite a while." The cop said, trying to reassure Mrs. Campbell.

The days that followed remain hazy in my mind. I vaguely remember going to Zoe's funeral and to Tom's trial.

It has been three years since Zoe died and I still miss her everyday. It's really weird how things have turned out, because Mrs. Campbell and my dad got married two years ago. I know that Zoe would have been pleased, because we had always wished that we were sisters.

Zoe's mom sold her house and moved in with us. She and my dad seem happy. I really feel as though I have lost my sister.

DARLENE

My name is Terry and my cousin Darlene had to leave because of her husband. His name was Sam and he treated her terribly bad.

As soon as they got married, he didn't let her see any of her friends or family. He always wanted her to stay home or to be with him, he didn't want to share her. He wouldn't even let her see her own mother. She used to call me all the time and cry because he was so miserable to her. It was almost like he kept her locked up in a tower.

Darlene was a very pretty girl and at the prom in high school, she had been voted Prom Queen.

Darlene and Sam didn't have any kids, which is a very good thing. I remember her calling me more than once, crying into the phone that he had beaten her up again. I kept telling her to leave him, but she was afraid to.

One day, she called me up and asked me to come and get her. I quickly drove over to her apartment, not quite sure what to expect. I was shocked by what I saw, her face was all swollen and bruised. Under and around both of her eyes was black and her lip was split open.

"What happened?" I asked her.

"I burned dinner, I was taking the clothes off the clothes line and it took me a little longer than I thought it would. I accidently burned the roast," she said, trying to pull her hair back into a pony tail.

"He did this, because you burnt some meat?" I asked her, disgusted.

She nodded her head and I noticed caked up blood in her hair. When I took a closer look, I saw that she had a pretty deep cut on her scalp and that the blood had matted into her hair.

"I'm getting you out of here." I told her. "Do you want to bring anything with you?"

Darlene pointed to two bags, that were hidden behind the couch. I quickly grabbed them and she followed me out to my car. As we drove away, I tried to think of where I could bring her, so that she could be safe.

"I'm driving you to the shelter. You should be safe there. If I brought you to my house or your mother's...those would be the first two places that he would look for you. We can't afford to let him find you." I told her.

I drove to a payphone and I called the shelter. They gave me directions and I got back into the car. I was very worried about Darlene, the gash on her head looked real deep. Luckily we were only a few blocks away from the shelter, when I had called them. I saw the house up ahead and I pulled into the driveway.

"Here we are." I told my cousin. "Let's leave your bags in the car for now and see if we have to sign you up or what we have to do first."

"Okay." Darlene said, getting out of the car and following me over to the side door.

There was an intercom by the door with a few buttons on it. I pressed the buzzer and I could hear a humming, echoing through the house, announcing our arrival. I heard a voice over the speaker, asking who was there.

"Terry and Darlene. I called a few minutes ago." I told the voice, that came from the small box.

I heard a key turn and a few bolts sliding, then the door opened to reveal a dark haired woman. "Come in, I'm Mary Ann and you talked to me on the phone. Oh my, we need to take a look at you, baby." She said, as she looked Darlene over.

We followed her into the house and down a hallway.

"Come in here, the light is much brighter." Mary Ann told us, motioning for us to go into the room. It looked like a doctor's examination room. "Jump up on the table, baby." She told Darlene, as she closed the door behind us.

Mary Ann looked Darlene over and wrote down some notes on a piece of paper as we talked. "Kathie!" Mary Ann opened the door and yelled out, to someone in the hallway. "Call Dr. Brian." Then she took some Polaroid pictures of Darlene's injuries. She told us that it was a good idea to keep some kind of a visual record of things.

"A doctor that makes house calls?" I asked her.

"We need to have one, sometimes the Emergency Room can be a dangerous place. Not only for the women who go there, but for the innocent people just trying to help them. Especially for a woman trying to get medical attention, after she's been beaten. It's normally the first place that a man will look, when he knows that he has hurt the woman. It could present a very dangerous situation for many people. The man is very angry at that point and innocent people could get hurt. We try to cover all the bases." Mary Ann said to us. "We are going to have you stay here for a while. You'll be safe, I promise."

"The men don't find the women here?" I asked her.

"Sometimes, but the police are often very quick to respond. We don't take any chances, we simply can't afford to. We have police officers constantly patrolling the area," she told us. "What does your husband do for work?"

"He is a computer programmer. He always tells me that he can find out anything about anyone, on the computer. He told me that if I ever left him, he could track me down within a couple of hours." Darlene told Mary Ann.

"Not necessarily." Mary Ann said, smiling at us. "We have our ways.

Most of the time the men don't find the women that we help, unless they somehow slip up and don't do as we tell them."

"But some do? Some of them are found?" I asked her.

"The women have to take precautions and be on guard all of the time. Sometimes they forget that, especially as time passes. They begin to feel too safe and comfortable." Mary Ann said to us.

There was a knock at the door and a very handsome man walked into the room. "Hi, I'm Dr. Brian," he told us, looking over at Darlene. "It looks like you could use a little help."

"Please." Darlene said softly, as a tear slid down her cheek.

I noticed that Mary Ann and Dr. Brian looked at each other and nodded. While Dr. Brian examined Darlene, we told them about Sam and how he treated Darlene. Dr. Brian put stitches in Darlene's head and her bottom lip.

"Don't worry, there shouldn't be too much of a scar." He told her when he was done.

"This is really a great service that you offer." I told them both.

"He really did a number on you. This isn't the first time is it?" Dr. Brian asked Darlene.

"No." Darlene said, looking down at her hands. "It's happened before."

"You do realize that this isn't the last time this will happen, if you go back to him." Dr. Brian told Darlene.

"I know." Darlene said, agreeing with him.

"We can help you to leave here and find safety. You can and will be able to live a safe and comfortable life, if you are willing to listen to us." Dr. Brian said to her.

"I will, I don't want to go back to him, ever. I'm sick of being hurt. I'll do whatever you say." Darlene told them, reaching for my hand.

Together we listened to all that they had to say. When they were done talking, we asked them a few questions. It was decided that Darlene was going to stay in the shelter for a few days, while Mary Ann and Dr. Brian arranged everything.

When I got home later on that night, I kept getting phone calls from Sam. All night long he continued to call me and I continued to tell him that I had no idea where Darlene was.

Within the week all of the arrangements had been set into place. I met Darlene at the shelter to say good bye to her. I knew that I would never be able to see my cousin again after that day.

We spent the whole day together, crying and talking. Later that night as I left the shelter, I knew that I was going to miss Darlene terribly. But I also needed to know that she was going to be safe.

In the months after Darlene left, Sam kept coming around and bothering me. I could honestly tell him that I didn't know where she was and I knew that I would never accidently let it slip. Occasionally he still comes around, but no where near as often as he did when she first left.

I pray every night that Darlene is safe and doing well. I really miss her and I hate the fact that Sam got away with all of those years of abusing her.

KAREN

Karen was my only daughter and she is no longer with me. My son in law killed her and all four of their children. Today I am so lost without them, my life feels like it has no meaning anymore.

Kenny, my son in law is in prison. I don't ever go to visit him, even though he continues to write me letters asking me to come see him. I just can't seem to forgive him, no matter how hard I try to. I know the Lord wants me to forgive him, I just can't.

I feel such a sense of loss. I still can't believe within a few minutes that man took a gun and wiped out my entire family. His mother tells me she also feels such a sense of loss, but at least she can still see her son.

SUSIE

Susie was my sixteen-year-old daughter and she had a dream of becoming a model. She was a very pretty girl, she was tall and thin. She had long brown hair and brown eyes.

Everyone always commented on how beautiful she was. She had lots of friends and she did very well in school. Susie was also on both the basketball and the swim team.

She never got into any trouble...until she started dating Tommy. He looked like trouble and he turned out to be just that. They had a very strange relationship and they fought constantly.

One afternoon while he was at our house, they started to argue. I saw him slap her across the face and that's when I told him to get out of my house.

Once he left, I asked my daughter if he had ever hit her before. Susie admitted to me that yes, he had hit her more than a few times. I was very upset by what she had told me.

"How can you let him hurt you?" I asked her.

"He says that he loves me," was Susie's response.

"Please, think about this. If he loved you, he wouldn't hurt you. He has a problem sweetheart. You deserve better than this, what about your dreams of becoming a model?" I asked her.

"I'm really not that pretty, mom." Susie said, sadly. "Tommy says that he has been out with girls that were way prettier than me."

"Are you kidding me? You've already had offers come in. You deserve better than this. If he can't treat you right, leave him." I said to her.

Susie gave me a big hug. "Your right. Thanks, mom. I'm gonna tell him tonight at the game. Can you pick me up at 9:00?" Susie asked me.

"I have to deliver the food for the Carson's dinner party, then I'll try to catch the last half of the game. If it takes me longer at the Carson's, I'll be there by 9:00." I told her. "Can you help me load this stuff into the van?" I asked her, pointing to the trays of food on the counter.

I was a caterer and my business was finally beginning to take off. Susie and I loaded up the van and then I dropped her off at her friend Janie's house. The girls were going to shoot a few hoops first and then go to the game.

I delivered my trays to the Carson's and got everything all set up. I gave instructions to a few of the girls, that I had hired to serve at the party.

By the time I arrived at the high school, the second half of the game had already begun. I looked around the gym for Susie, but I didn't see her anywhere. I did see Janie and I waved to her, I saw her look around the room.

I thought that she looked upset, so I made my way over to the sidelines.

A few minutes later Janie ran up to me.

"Where is Susie?" I asked her.

"The last time I saw her was just before half time. Tommy was waiting for her over by the door. She hasn't gotten back yet and neither has he. We sure could use her now!" Janie said to me, as she watched the rest of the team.

"I'll go outside and see if I can find her." I said to Janie. I could tell that she was pretty upset, which made me upset.

I left the gymnasium and went out to the parking lot. I didn't see Susie anywhere and I didn't see Tommy either. I started to walk through the parking lot, looking inside some of the cars. As I walked around the second row of parked cars, I saw a pair of shoes. I quickly ran to the side of the car and that's when I saw my baby girl. I dropped to my knees and I noticed the knife sticking out of her chest.

"Baby, can you hear me?" I asked her, while I brushed the hair from her face.

"Mommy?" It came out as a faint whisper, more like a tiny exhale.

"Oh my god, Susie! What happened?" I asked her. I noticed a puddle of blood on the ground beside her.

"Tommy said…he said…I could never…leave him." Susie whispered.

"Hold on, baby." I said to my daughter. "Help!" I yelled out, trying to get someone's attention. "Please help us!"

Susie coughed softly a few times. "I love…you, mommy." Susie said to me, as she let out a tiny shudder in my arms.

"No!" I screamed out, feeling like my heart was being ripped out of my chest. "No!"

I cried in that parking lot, holding onto my daughter's dead body. No one came over to us until people started leaving the gym. A few people saw us there and then suddenly there were lots of people around us. Janie came running over to me and she fell down to her knees, crying with me.

Finally the police came and they talked to Janie and me, while the ambulance took away my only child. Tommy had killed Susie, because she had wanted to break up with him. What was wrong with him? How could someone do a thing like that?

Eventually they did find Tommy guilty of my daughter's murder. Right up to the end, he denied that he had killed her. He denied that he ever even saw her that night. But there were many witnesses placing him at the game.

AMANDA

Amanda was my older sister and she was married to James for about two years. They had a gorgeous little boy, who would be almost one now.

James used to beat up my sister while she was pregnant, he used to call her fat and ugly. Amanda did gain a lot of weight, but she was having a baby! He used to tell her that he didn't want to be seen with her when she was pregnant, because she was 'fat and disgusting.'

When I would go over to their apartment, he would throw food at her and tell her to eat it. He would make grunting noises, like a pig. My sister would cry, because she knew that she had gained quite a bit of weight.

During her entire pregnancy she'd gained 85 pounds. But she was in good shape, so the doctor told her that they weren't too worried about it. They said that she would probably lose it pretty quickly, which she did. She got very depressed during her pregnancy. She was also depressed after the baby was born.

I went with her to the hospital to have Jake, because James said that 'it' was her kid. I was so thrilled to be with her in the delivery room, then Jake finally made his appearance. It was such an exciting and unbelievable thing. I got to witness that baby being born.

Amanda called me two days later from the hospital. She asked me if I would come to pick her and the baby up, because they were about to be discharged. James had told her to walk home, that way she might be able to lose some of the fat.

I felt so bad for her. Here it was supposed to be such a wonderful and happy time for her and James was being a total idiot. So, I picked them up and brought them home.

From the minute that Amanda walked into that apartment, he started nagging at her. The first thing he said to her, was he asked her when the other baby was coming. He said that she was still so huge, there must be another baby in there. Amanda ran from the room in tears, holding onto little Jake.

I looked at James and told him that he was a real jerk. My sister was depressed for quite a while, but she somehow managed to find such happiness in that little boy. Jake was her whole world, especially while James got more and more verbally abusive towards her.

For some reason James got real mean and he started telling Amanda that Jake was retarded. He would call him 'the little retard.' Why would he say that about his own child? This went on for months and one day James just snapped.

Amanda and James had been arguing the whole time I'd been visiting. Suddenly James scooped Jake from Amanda's arms and he started to choke the baby. We both screamed for him to stop, but he wouldn't listen to us. I started pounding on his back and he finally loosened his grip on Jake. He threw back his arm and I caught his elbow right in the face, which caused me to fall back against the wall.

"Please, give me my baby." Amanda begged.

"Do you want the little retard?" James asked her. I noticed that Jake was extremely quiet. "Do you really want him?"

"Please," my sister pleaded, holding out her hands for Jake.

"Give him to her." I begged him.

James looked from Amanda to me then he just dropped Jake. The baby fell to the floor with a sickening thud. I realized that the baby was dead, when my sister screamed.

I don't know where it the anger came from, but all of a sudden I went right up to James and I smacked him in the head. He didn't put up any fight, as I stood there pounding on him.

My sister was rocking back and forth holding onto her son. I lightly touched her shoulder as I passed by her, on my way to the phone.

The police came and took James away, then they pried Jake from my sister's arms. I stayed with her that night. She was so devastated by everything that happened, I was afraid to leave her alone.

At around midnight, Amanda went up to bed. Before she went up the stairs, she said goodnight to me and told me that she loved me. We didn't talk much earlier that night and I figured that sleep was probably the best thing for her.

By the time I woke up the next morning it was 10:00. I put on a pot of coffee and went up to my sister's room. I knocked on the door and got no response. A shiver went up my spine, as I slowly opened the door. I softly calling out her name.

In the darkness of the room, I could make out the shape of my sister laying on the bed. I walked over to her and again softly called out her name. Once my eyes had adjusted to the darkness of the room, I noticed the bottle of pills next to the bed.

I turned on the light and saw that the bottle of pills was tipped onto it's side. In my sisters' hand, she held onto one of Jake's little sleepers.

I reached out and touched my sister's cheek, which was cold.

"No!" I screamed. I tried to feel for a pulse or any sign of life, but found none.

I reached for the phone and I dialed 911.

My sister had overdosed and she'd died sometime during the night. I blame James for her death, because I know that if he hadn't killed Jake, my sister would still be here.

James is in prison for the murder of Jake, but I find very little comfort in that. I don't want him to ever get out.

I miss my sister and Jake terribly. I would give anything to have them back with us.

FRANCHESKA

My name is Antonia and my sister Francesca was killed by her boyfriend. We were fourteen months apart and I was older. I kept telling her that her boyfriend was no good, but she was so sure that she loved him. She thought that through her love, she would be able to change him…he didn't change.

He was always so mean and sarcastic to her and to everyone else. They would argue a lot and he'd twist her arm or give her a 'Charlie horse.' At first it seemed more playful, but it steadily grew more and more violent. I saw it escalating, but our parents didn't. I'm sure that my dad would have jumped down Ted's throat, had he known. But my parents were pretty preoccupied at that time, they were having marriage problems.

I would try to talk to my sister, but she didn't listen to me. She was seventeen and she thought that she knew everything. She and I would fight because of her boyfriend. We disagreed, mostly about the way that he treated her. Francesca and I were very close before she started dating Ted. After they had been dating for a while, she seemed to become quiet and withdrawn.

One afternoon Ted and Francesca were sitting on our front steps. Our neighbor, Mario, came over to talk to her. We had known Mario for at least ten years, anyway, Ted went crazy when Mario came over. Which was really stupid, because Mario was like a brother to us and in no way was he a threat to Ted.

Ted jumped up and hit Mario. Francesca yelled at him to stop and that's when he turned on her. He called her all kinds of terrible names and then he started to choke her.

Mario yelled at Ted and I ran outside, after I heard the commotion. Mario and I both tried to pull Ted off of Francesca. We finally managed to pull him away and then he left.

About an hour later he called my sister. "Meet me in the front yard." Ted begged her.

My sister felt bad. No matter what Mario and I said to her, she still felt like she had to meet him. Finally, she agreed to talk with him and I told her that I would watch them from our livingroom window.

I saw Ted pull up outside, get out of his car and walk over to my sister. I watched helplessly, as he pulled a knife out of his pocket and stabbed her repeatedly.

My sister lay dying on our front lawn, as Ted drove away. I ran out of the house and held my sister, as she took her last few breaths.

DONNA

My name is Denise and my nieces name was Donna. She has a new name now and I don't even know it. I don't even know where she lives anymore.

She had to leave, because her husband was very abusive towards her. He was always beating on her and threatening to kill her.

The last time he beat her, she ended up in the hospital for almost two weeks. I took her to the shelter when she was released from the hospital. Within a few days, the women in the shelter had arranged everything for my niece.

Two days later she was gone. I miss her terribly, but at least I know that she is safe. She isn't allowed to call me or write to me, because that would make it easy for her husband to find her.

JANIE

Janie was a very good friend of mine, but she was murdered by her girlfriend, Darlene. They were together for three years and during that time, Darlene subjected Janie to awful abuse.

Janie was taking classes at the Community College and had quite a few friends there. Darlene didn't like that at all. She was a very controlling person and Janie was starting to get a little independent. Darlene seemed to like it better before Janie went to school. Janie stayed at home and took care of Darlene back then, she even baked cookies and brownies for her.

Eventually, Janie had wanted more and that was when she had decided to go back to school. Once there, she seemed to come out of her shell and she became a very outgoing person.

Darlene became very threatened by this and started to behave violently towards Janie. It wasn't unusual to see Janie in class with a black eye or a cut lip.

After a few months, I noticed that Janie started to become very quiet and she stayed to herself more. When I would ask her about it, she would just tell me that she and Darlene were having problems. I did sense that things were becoming more and more violent inside their home.

One day, Janie didn't come to class. That night on the news, I learned that she had been murdered by Darlene. My feeling is that Darlene felt threatened by Janie wanting to better herself.

I miss Janie terribly, she really was a good friend and a wonderful person. She certainly didn't deserve to die.

SAM

Sam and Robert met at a car show. My sister Sam and I were dragged there by my boyfriend Tommy. Robert kept smiling at Sam. It seemed as though, he was following us through the parking lot.

Eventually, he got up the courage to approach us. Sam and Robert seemed to get along pretty good. After the car show, my sister agreed to go out to dinner with him. I tried to talk her out of it, telling her that she didn't even know him, but she really wanted to go.

Tommy and I went home and a few hours later Robert dropped Sam off.

"He's pretty weird." Sam told us when she came into the house.

"I guess that you won't go back out with him again." I said, laughing.

"No way." Sam said, laughing too.

I was happy, because there had been something about him which had bothered me.

The next afternoon Robert pulled up outside of our house and honked his horn.

"Oh god, he's back." Sam said, turning away from the window.

"I'll just go tell him that your not home." I volunteered.

"No. He'll just keep coming back. I'll have to tell him that I'm just not interested." Sam told me, reaching for her white sweater.

I watched as my sister went out to his car to talk with him. I could see that he was getting very angry. What happened next was totally unexpected. Robert pulled a gun out of his jacket pocket.

I screamed to my sister as Robert raised the gun and shot her. Sam fell to the ground, as the blood quickly soaked through her white sweater.

Tommy ran out of the garage and tackled Robert. I ran out of the house and went over to my sister. I held her and waited for help to come, while Tommy held Robert down on the ground.

One of our neighbors did call for help...but not before my sister had died in my arms.

KELLY

Kelly was my baby sister and now I don't know where she is. She was forced to leave, because her husband used to beat on her. Riley threatened to kill her if she ever left him, which she finally did. He came after her a few times and the women at the shelter helped her to get away.

I hate Riley because he forced my sister to leave. No one could or would help her. Not the cops or the courts. So she had no other choice, but to leave.

I wish that I could just pick up my phone and talk to my sister.

SONIA

My daughter Sonia would have been twenty-two-years-old on her last birthday. She was beaten to death with a baseball bat, by her boyfriend.

My baby was studying to be a social worker. I never even saw it coming. I never once suspected that Troy was hurting my little girl.

After she was murdered, some of her friends from college told me that he used to hit her quite a bit. Why didn't anyone tell me that when she had been alive? Maybe she would still be alive, maybe not.

I had known Troy for four years and thought that he was a wonderful young man. I still can't believe that I couldn't tell what had been going on.

I wonder every day about what could have been for my daughter. How she would have graduated this year.

I miss her so very much.

MARTHA

Two years ago I lost my wife Martha and last year my only child, our daughter was murdered by her boyfriend. I feel like my whole world has been destroyed. People tell me that things get easier as time goes by, I don't believe that, you just cry a little less. I have to force myself to get up in the morning. I somehow manage to make it through each day, but I am left with nothing.

Two years ago my wife was killed by a drunk driver. Katie and I both had a very hard time dealing with it. About a month before Katie was killed, she met a boy named Jason. I didn't much care for him. He was a short tempered kid, who treated my little girl pretty badly.

The day before Katie died, she had told me some of the things that Jason had done to her. I couldn't believe he had done such terrible things to her. I couldn't understand why she had never said a word to me about it. That night, Katie had decided to tell Jason she didn't want to date him anymore. She wanted him to leave her alone.

The next day, my Katie did tell Jason that she didn't want to see him again and they argued. I was told by the police that witnesses saw Jason beat her to death in a parking lot, then he just walked away and left her there.

My baby died alone in the parking lot. I wish that I had been there for her.

JENNIFER

My daughter Jennifer was murdered by her girlfriend, Kerri. The girls dated for about three months and during that time Kerri was verbally and physically abusive towards my daughter. It started out with Kerri calling Jennifer names, then it steadily progressed and got worse. The next thing I knew, the police were at my door telling me that Jennifer was dead.

They told me that Kerri had run Jennifer down in her car. My daughter had been trying to run away from her.

PAM

My granddaughter, Pam was murdered by a man that she had worked with, his name was Tim. Pam's parents died in a car wreck when she was seven and after that she moved in with me. I took care of her and I even put her through business school.

When Pam turned twenty two, she got a job at a very busy computer company. She moved into a small apartment, so she could be closer to her job. She called me everyday, no matter what. After she had been working there for a few months, she told me that Tim had started to bother her. He would keep asking her out and he made inappropriate advances towards her.

One night, she told me that some of the people from work were going out to celebrate a co-workers engagement. The next day, Pam called me to tell me that Tim had followed her home and had waited outside her apartment all night. He had also followed her into work that morning.

Pam was very upset and distraught. I begged her to come home, at least for the night, but she said that she didn't want him to start bothering me. I convinced her to talk to her boss about Tim, which she agreed to do later that day.

The next day, Pam called me and told me that Tim was furious with her for telling the boss. The boss had told Tim that if he didn't stop harassing Pam, the company would be forced to fire him. That was the last time I talked to Pam.

Later that night, the police came to my door to tell me that Pam had been shot by Tim, outside of her apartment.

SONJA

Sonja is my sister and we were at one time very close. But I haven't a clue as to where she is today. She was forced to leave in order to save herself. Her husband threatened to kill her so many times, but he is a cop so she couldn't report him to anyone. The cops all stick together and they cover up a lot of 'inside things.' Usually he would hit her where no one could see the cuts or the bruises.

Sonja told me about the beatings…eventually. Although, I still don't think that I know everything. She kept a notebook detailing the beatings, dates and everything. That notebook came in handy when I brought her to the shelter.

Tanessa read through the notebook. She told the both of us that because Sonja's husband was a cop, they wouldn't be able to guarantee her safety. She told us that they could help her to get away, though.

Sonja and I talked about it for a while and in the end we agreed with Tanessa. That night my sister and I said goodbye for the last time. I felt as though a piece of my heart was being ripped from my chest, but I also knew that it was for the best.

Tanessa put Sonja on a bus and that is the last time I ever saw my sister. I think about her everyday and I miss her very much.

CARRIE

Carrie, my daughter, and Ralph were married for four years and had two beautiful little boys. I didn't find out that Ralph hit her, until the night Carrie and the boys moved in with me.

That night she told me terrible, horrible stories that just sickened me. How could I have not known? Carrie was my only child and it had always been just the two of us. I thought that we were very close. That night she told me she had wanted to tell me sooner, but she had been embarrassed.

Ralph called two times a day, for the entire two weeks they stayed with me. Finally, he wore Carrie down and she agreed to meet him at their apartment. I begged and pleaded with her not to go, but she told me that she wasn't being fair to take the boys away from Ralph. She said they were going to try to talk things through. She also told me she had no intention of ever going back to live with him, ever.

I waited until one o'clock for Carrie to come back, I guess I fell asleep on the couch. I was startled awake by the sound of knocking at my door. I saw two police officers standing on my front step and I moved aside to let them in.

"Mrs. McDonald?" one of them asked me.

"Yes." I answered, bracing myself for the worst.

"There seems to have been some kind of accident involving your daughter, Carrie." He said gently, holding onto my arm.

"A car accident?" I asked.

"No. The apartment that she was in, caught on fire," he said to me, gripping my arm a little tighter as I started to sway.

"What hospital is she at?" I asked, after a few seconds.

"No ma'am. She's not in any hospital. I'm sorry, she died in the fire." He told me, watching me closely.

"No!" I remembered screaming out, then everything in front of me turned black. When I came to, both officers were still there and I was laying on my couch.

They explained to me that there had been a fire in my daughter's apartment and that it was under investigation.

A while later, they left and I tried to sleep, because I knew that those little boys would be up early.

In the morning, a couple of other cops came back to my house. They told me that the fire chief said the fire had been deliberately set and that they had arrested Ralph.

Within an hour of being at the police station, he had confessed. He told them that he and Carrie had argued. He said that he had begged her to come back, but that she had refused. Ralph had gotten furious with her and he had hit her in the head, knocking her unconscious. Then he had poured gasoline on her and through the entire apartment. Once he was sure that the flames had engulfed everything, he left. I am thankful that the boys weren't with her, because they may not be here either.

Ralph is in prison now and I am raising Carrie's beautiful boys. Today the boys are thirteen and fifteen years old. I see so much of their mother in them. I sometimes smile and remember what a wonderful person, daughter, mother and friend that she had been. My Carrie could brighten up an entire room with her smile and now both of those boys can do exactly the same thing.

I miss Carrie and I tell her every night that the boys are doing just fine.

SALLI

My nieces name is Salli and she is paralyzed from the neck down, because of her ex boyfriend. Victor and Salli were together for two years and during that time he would hurt her, quite a bit.

I witnessed him slapping, kicking and choking her. I tried to convince her to leave him, but she wouldn't. She told me that she couldn't. For some reason, Salli felt that Victor needed her and maybe she wanted to feel needed. One day Victor was really upset and started to beat on Salli. She told me that she went outside and was going to leave him. Suddenly, he came running out after her and he started to stab her with a knife in the back and the neck.

The police showed up and took Victor away and the ambulance took Salli to the hospital. I met them there, after one of Salli's neighbors had called me. Salli was rushed in for emergency surgery.

Later it was diagnosed that Salli would never regain any feeling from the neck down. Salli would be paralyzed for the rest of her life.

Victor is in prison, but that doesn't help my niece. Salli used to smile and laugh, now she is quiet and depressed. She can't really speak, because she has a tube down her throat. There is nothing that I can do for her. No matter what they do to Victor, well, in my opinion it'll never be enough punishment for what he did to Salli. She will never have a life now, at least not like she would have had.

TANYA

My ex-wife Tanya was a wonderful woman and together we had three beautiful children. Tanya started dating Bruce, who I thought was a real jerk. It turned out that I was right.

Bruce moved into my old house with Tanya and our kids. Right from the start things didn't seem right. On weekends, the kids would to tell me things that had happened and I would get really upset. I wasn't sure what I could do to help Tanya and I didn't know if she would even want my help.

On more than one Sunday afternoon, when I would bring the kids back home, I would see bruises on Tanya's face or arms. She knew that I saw them, but neither one of us said anything about it.

One Saturday night, after seeing a movie, I pulled into my driveway. I saw Tanya sitting on my front step. I told the kids to wait in the car and I walked over to her.

"Kevin, please help me. He's going to kill me." Tanya sobbed, as she rushed into my arms. I held her for a while, as she continued to cry.

I motioned for the kids to get out of the car and to go inside. As they walked past us, I tried to give them a comforting smile.

Once they had gone inside, I led Tanya back over to the step and we both sat down. That's when I saw her face. Her eyes were almost completely closed, her lip was split and her nose appeared to lean slightly to the side.

"What did he do to you?" I asked her, horrified.

"He's high on something. I'm so afraid Kevin. I know that he is going to try to kill me. I can't go back home, but I know that he will try to find me." Tanya said, starting to cry again.

"Tonight you are going to stay here. If he comes around here, I'll call the cops on him." I told her, as I helped her up. Together we walked into my condo. We explained to the kids what had happened.

We all watched TV and a little later the kids went to bed. Tanya and I stayed up and talked some more. Then I went into my bedroom and she slept on the couch.

At around two o'clock in the morning, there was a loud crash. I quickly ran from my room and out into the hallway. That's when I heard Bruce yelling outside and I saw the curtain blowing around in my livingroom.

"I'm going to kill you Tanya, I will never let you leave me. I'll find you no matter where you go!" Bruce continued to yell from my front yard.

Tanya ran over to me.

"It's Bruce," she whispered to me.

"I know. Go call the police." I told her quietly, as I walked over to the smashed livingroom window. I saw a brick laying in the middle of the floor.

"Get out here, Tanya!" Bruce yelled again.

Tanya walked over to me and slipped her hand into mine. I could see the tears on her cheeks.

"They are on the way." Tanya whispered to me. I could feel her hand shaking in mine.

"I'm going to kill you, bitch. I'm going to kill your whole family." Bruce yelled.

We could hear the sirens in the distance, so could Bruce.

"You are gonna be sorry. I'll be back for you... if you leave I'll find you. I promise you that." Bruce yelled, before he ran to his truck and drove off.

I let go of Tanya's hand and pulled her to me. I hugged her until the police knocked at the door. We talked to the police and when they left, I taped plastic to the smashed window. Luckily the kids slept through the whole thing.

Tanya and I sat down at the table with cups of coffee and talked for hours.

"Do you think that Bruce will leave you alone?" I asked her. "Will he harass the kids?"

"I don't think that he will leave us alone." Tanya told me, as she reached for her coffee.

"Do you think that he would really hurt you and the kids?" I asked her.

"Yes. I do think that he would hurt us. Bruce doesn't like to lose...at anything." Tanya told me.

"Do you think that you would be safe at our house?" I asked her, as I thought a few things over.

"No. Not now." Tanya said, sadly.

"What would it take for you to feel safe?" I asked her.

"I'm not sure." Tanya whispered, a tear slid down her cheek.

"I think that we should call the shelter and see what they suggest we do." I said to her.

She agreed with me and together we called them. We each talked on an extension, to a woman named Denise. Denise suggested that Tanya leave the area, at least for a while.

After we got off the phone, Tanya and I again talked for a while.

What I suggested that night surprised even me.

"Why don't you leave for a while. At least you will be safe." I told her.

"I don't want to leave the kids." Tanya cried.

"Why don't you all leave. I've got some money that I can give you to help out." I offered.

"You'd let me take the kids and leave, indefinitely?" she asked me, surprised.

"I don't want to, but I feel like it would be the smartest thing to do." I told her. "Under the circumstances."

We both agreed that they would leave in the morning. I really didn't want them to go, but I needed to know that they would all be safe. Even though we were divorced, I still cared for and about Tanya.

We went to sleep for a few hours and when the kids woke up, we told them what we had decided. We drove to the bank first and then to the bus station.

Tanya and I let the kids pick where they wanted to go. We gave them a few choices and they picked a second cousin of Tanya's. I bought the tickets and then I put them on the bus.

If Tanya or the kids needed me, they were going to call me at work and I would call them from a pay phone. Neither one of us knew for how long they would be gone. At least I could still stay in touch with Tanya and my kids. I could visit them if I did it very carefully. But it wasn't going to be the same as it would have been, if they were less than ten blocks away.

I waited as the bus left and I tried very hard not to cry. I was going to miss them all so much.

When I got back in the car, I decided that I was going to stop by the house. I half expected to see Bruce there, but I went through the entire house and saw no one.

I called my brother Tom and we met at the hardware store. I got new locks for every outside door in the house and together we changed them all. I called a few guys who I knew were single and I asked them if they wanted to stay at the house for a while. Four of them agreed to stay there and keep an eye on things.

Bruce kept coming around the house and my condo. The police had arrested him for destruction of property. He went to court and they told him that he had to pay for damages, but as of today I still haven't seen a dime.

I talk to Tanya and the kids when I can, but it is still not the same. I'm hoping to be able to visit them for the holidays.

The last time I saw Bruce, he told me that he had every intention of finding Tanya.

I worry about them, but I don't think that Bruce will find them, at least I hope that he doesn't.

I lost my entire family, because of Bruce.

MELISSA

My daughter Melissa started dating Steve in college. They met at a party on campus. It was Melissa's first time away from her mother and me, she never even went away to camp.

Dolly and I first became concerned when Melissa stopped calling every week. She said that she wouldn't be able to come home for Thanksgiving and then she wasn't able to come home for Christmas.

Finally when Easter rolled around, I told her that we expected her to come home. She finally agreed.

A few days later, she called and asked if she could bring her boyfriend. "Of course." I'd told her. Her mother and I were both curious about the boy.

The day before Easter two police officers came to our house. They told us that Melissa had been murdered. Later, we found out that she had been beaten to death, by Steve.

Friends of Melissa's at the college, told us that Steve had changed her. She never wanted to do anything or go anywhere, because Steve wouldn't let her.

We found out that the day before Easter Melissa and Steve had a huge fight. He wouldn't stop hitting her.

Dolly and I were heartbroken, Melissa was our only child and we are completely lost without her.

DANNY

Danny was my only son and he was definitely a handful. His father was an alcoholic and he gambled a lot. Phil walked out on us, when Danny was twelve years old.

After twelve years of watching his daddy drink and beat on us, I guess that I should have been able to see his future, but I didn't.

After my husband left, I had to get a job at the factory in town. We made paper products and I put in a lot of overtime, just to be able to make ends meet.

I didn't mean to be away from home so much, but Danny's daddy didn't send me any money, I had no choice.

When Danny was a teenager he started hanging out with some real bad boys, he also started drinking.

My boy was always getting into trouble. He was arrested for stealing a car, when he was fifteen years old and it just kept getting worse. If I tried to discipline him or ground him, he would call me some real awful names and hit me. I didn't know what to do with my boy. I was at my wits end, by the time he'd turned seventeen.

He had a real nice girlfriend, named Peggy. She put up with a lot from my boy. He actually started to calm down some and he really liked her a lot. So I hoped for the best.

One day, they were both sitting at my kitchen table and Peggy said something to Danny when he went into the fridge for another beer. Whatever it was it angered him, he hauled off and hit her upside the head.

Peggy jumped up from the chair and walked right out of the door. I never saw her again and I didn't blame her either.

A few weeks later, the police came to my door to arrest Danny for murder. I was very confused. Danny told the police that for days he tried to get Peggy to talk to him, but she wouldn't. Apparently a few days before they arrested him, he had killed her. He had been drinking a lot and they had gotten into a fight. He strangled her and then he just left her.

I felt so bad for her family. One of the women at work told me that she was sorry I'd lost Danny after he'd gone to jail. But, I had really lost him years before he went to jail.

JACOB

My grandson Jacob was always a quiet shy boy. He kept to himself pretty much. He came to live with me when he was ten-years-old. My son, Jacob's father was in prison for murdering, Jacob's mother. Unfortunately, Jacob witnessed it. I guess that I should have gotten him some help or counseling. I didn't think about it at the time. I got Jacob when I was sixty-six-years-old and I didn't know what to do with him. I was too old for such a small child to be around, but I couldn't put him up on the county.

When Jacob was twelve, he got into trouble for beating some puppies to death. When he was thirteen, he got caught stabbing one of the neighbors cows. I saw him torture small things like frogs, mice and bugs. But I never thought much of it, he was a boy and as they say, boys will be boys. He sure was a handful!

And school…forget about it. He was always in trouble in school, always getting into fights.

He got worse when he turned fifteen. Jacob, along with some other boys robbed a man and killed him. Jacob went to a detention center for boys, until he was seventeen.

Two weeks after he got out he started dating Sara. She was such a nice, polite girl. They dated for about six months and I saw him hit and slap her, quite a few times. Sara came up to me one afternoon and told me that she was pregnant. 'Oh no.' I thought to myself.

Sara stayed for supper that night and she told Jacob, he got very angry with her. He told her to get rid of it, then he asked her why she would ever want a baby of his. They argued back and forth, I heard her tell him that she was going to keep the baby. Sara thanked me for dinner, then she left and started to walk home. Somewhere between my house and the five blocks to Sara's house, she was stabbed to death.

Later that night, the police came over to my house and arrested Jacob. He swore to me that he didn't do it. I knew that he did it. I wanted to believe him, but I knew that he had killed her.

Jacob went to court and was put into prison this time. The judge found him guilty, even though he continued to deny having killed Sara.

Later, Jacob's attorney told me that he had been convicted because of his DNA. It was under her fingernails and some of his blood was also on her. Apparently he'd been cut with the knife and had dripped blood onto her.

I feel real bad for Sara's parents.

CANDI

Candi was my best friend and she worked in a frozen yogurt shop in the mall. It was during the summer and she was able to get quite a few extra hours. Candi had just turned seventeen a month earlier. I used to go to the mall with my boyfriend to see her at work, well, to see her and to get some free yogurt.

One afternoon, while we were there she told me that an older guy kept bothering her. She said he was a real creep. I told her she should tell her boss and mall security.

"Oh, it was probably just a one time thing." Candi said to me and we let it go.

A few days later, Candi called me from work and asked me if we could pick her up at ten thirty that night. She told me to pick her up at the mall's main entrance. Her mother had to work the late shift and the creep was bugging her again. I told her that we'd be there.

At twenty after ten we parked at the mall and waited until eleven o'clock. I started to get worried. My boyfriend pointed to the security guard in the truck. We flashed our lights, trying to flag him down, as he drove by in the truck. We told him that Candi hadn't come out yet and then we followed him inside the mall. Todd and I looked around the mall and met the security guard back at the main entrance. None of us had seen any sign of Candi.

I tried calling Candi's house and got no answer. Dan, the security guard called the police. While we waited for the police, I told Dan about the creep that had been bothering her.

Once the police showed up, we explained everything. We stood by Todd's car and waited, while they looked around the mall. I heard Dan's walkie talkie come to life with voices and static. I heard 'a body' and more static.

"Oh god." I whispered to Todd as he put his arm around me, having heard the same thing.

Two of the cops came over to us and asked if Todd would be able to identify Candi's body.

"It may not even be her." Todd said to me, before he walked away with the cops.

They were gone for about twenty five minutes and when they came back, I saw that Todd was pale.

"Was it Candi?" I asked him, already knowing it was.

"Yes." Todd said, quietly.

"What happened to her?" I asked him, beginning to cry.

"Someone grabbed her when she brought the garbage out to the trash bin. They pulled her out into the field and beat her up real bad. She's dead." Todd said, starting to shake.

"The creep, he did it." I whispered. "Was she raped?"

"They don't know yet. But they don't think so." Todd said, leaning back against the security guards truck, taking deep breaths.

We talked to the police a while later and then we stopped over at Candi's house. No one was there, so I left a note for her mother telling her that I was very sorry. I miss her so much. I wish that we had gone into the mall to pick up Candi, then she would still be here.

The police never did find 'the creep' and Candi was not raped, but the case still remains open.

JACKIE

Jackie was my older sister, actually she was my step sister. She was always real nice to me, besides she let me go places with her and her friends. I always had fun with her. She was real pretty and she had a couple of boyfriends. Tommy I liked a lot, but Tony was a jerk. They weren't really her boyfriends, but she dated them.

I was ten years old when Jackie was murdered by Tony. He got mad at her, because he found out that she was dating Tommy too. He wanted her to just pick one of them and she told him that she couldn't do that.

Tony picked up a metal pole and hit her over and over with it. He hit her in the face and the head. He didn't stop beating her with that pole, until she didn't move anymore.

Jackie was in a coma for three months and never once opened up her eyes. My mom and her dad decided to disconnect the machines that she was hooked up to. They told me that those machines were the only thing that was keeping her alive. I didn't want them to disconnect her. I had a really hard time understanding why they did it. She was breathing, I saw her. I saw her chest moving up and down.

About an hour after the doctor talked to my parents and the nurse had unplugged everything, Jackie died. She would have been seventeen in two more weeks. We had to have a closed casket for her, because she had been so badly beaten.

Tony went to jail, until he was eighteen. He was actually only in there for a year which made everyone real mad.

That was almost four years ago. I miss Jackie everyday and I wonder if she'd lived, what she would be doing right now.

KARLA

Karla was my only daughter. She had natural blond hair and pretty blue eyes. She was voted Prom Queen, her senior year in high school. All through high school, she was also the head cheerleader.

I always thought that she would go on and do great things. I had such high hopes and dreams for her.

Then she went away to college and that's where she met J.R.. He was studying to become a teacher and she was going to teach the mentally challenged.

I thought that they just dated casually, but after she was murdered I found out that he had been obsessed with Karla.

He had been caught numerous times looking in her dorm windows and following her around the campus. She talked to different people about it, but they all told her that he would get tired of it eventually. No one took anything seriously, not even when he started to threaten her. She never said a word to me, because she didn't want me to worry.

Karla got a part time job in a coffee shop on campus. J.R. would harass her there and after her shift ended, he would follow her home.

She used to write about these things in her journals, which I read a few months after she had been murdered. I also talked to some of her friends. They told me that they watched Kara change from a happy outgoing person to someone who was very nervous and scared.

Apparently one morning while she was at work, J.R. went into the coffee shop. He pulled out a gun and shot twelve people. J.R. killed eight people that day, before turning the gun on himself. That brought the total up to nine people that had been killed, three had been injured. My Karla, was one of those people who died.

I can not bring back that day, but I hope that because of this, parents will stay in touch with their kids more. They need to be more aware of what is going on in their kids lives, especially if they are living away from home.

TANYA

My sister Tanya was a police officer and I always thought that if anything ever happened to her, it would have been job related, not because of her husband. My brother in law murdered my sister, the worst part was he did it with her own gun.

All Tanya wanted to do was help people. I never knew that my brother in law was abusive towards her, she never told me.

No matter what her situation at home had been, I knew that she would never get a divorce. Our parents had a really horrible divorce, I had a bad divorce and our other sister Ayna had an awful divorce. Tanya was bound and determined to make her marriage work.

Donald had a very stressful job, he was an attorney. A pretty high profile attorney and he always had a waiting list of potential clients.

He drank at home, he drank at home quite a bit. We were all aware of that, but he seemed to deal with it okay. No one ever considered him an alcoholic or anything.

Tanya and Donald had been married for four years. We never thought they had the best marriage, but we never suspected that things were as bad as they were.

I did know that they argued about children a lot. Donald wanted kids, but Tanya still wanted to work. She truly liked her job, especially when she got to help out some of the kids.

I worked at the Teen Center and it wasn't unusual for Tanya to drop off one or two kids a night. She had at least a dozen kids that she had taken under her wing, to try to help out. The kids all loved her.

I guess that Donald used to get upset about that. They fought about her involvement with other people's kids. He felt that she was wasted time and energy that she could have been devoting to their own children.

One night from what the detectives can tell, Tanya and Donald argued. He got very violent and pulled out her gun. They struggled and he shot her, she died instantly.

Donald is in prison now. He has never confessed, nor has he ever volunteered any information about what happened that night.

Our family is left to wonder about what really happened that night, which is tearing us all apart.

JANICE

Janice was my daughter and in my opinion, she was murdered by her partner. When she was only nineteen and in college, she dropped what I thought was a big bombshell on me. She told me that she was a lesbian. I think I took it well, I figured as long as she was happy, it was all that mattered to me. I was shocked though.

I met Tara, who was twenty six. It didn't matter to me whether Tara had been a man or a woman. I was concerned about the age difference. Then the two girls moved in together. I didn't like it one bit, I felt my daughter was being talked into things she wasn't quite ready for.

Janice never dated much in high school, so she found herself at a disadvantage, because Tara had been around more. Janice was new to the whole 'relationship thing.'

I also found out that Tara had a drinking problem. She was a very mean and ugly drunk. Unfortunately for Janice, a lot of Tara's anger was directed at her.

They started to fight quite a bit and I saw a lot of it. Janice got really depressed and started to talk about quitting school. I tried talking to her, I wanted her to finish college. But she just seemed to stop caring, about everything.

Tara knocked Janice's self esteem and self worth completely down, to almost nothing. Janice stopped taking showers everyday and she stayed in bed most of the time. She stopped going to her classes and she barely ate.

The last time I saw Janice, she had a black eye and bruises all over both of her arms. I asked her if Tara had done it and she told me yes. I begged her to come back home with me, but she refused.

Two days later, Tara called me and told me that Janice had slit her wrists. My daughter had bled to death in Tara's apartment. I was devastated.

Then I started asking questions, lots and lots of questions. I found out that Tara's fingerprints were on the razor blade that had killed my daughter. I asked why she wasn't a suspect and was told that she had picked up the razor blade. This, the police say, explained that.

They also had found sleeping pills in Janice's system, during the autopsy. Janice hated any medications, she never even took Tylenol.

Janice's right wrist was cut...she's right handed. If she had indeed cut her wrists, she would have cut her left wrist. That is just common sense.

There were also bruises around her mouth like someone had forced the pills down her. No one would listen to me.

The police wrote in their report that it was a suicide. I have never believed that and I never will. I think that Tara killed Janice.

Later that week, I went to Tara's apartment to gather up Janice's things. I was very surprised to meet Tara's new partner, Diane.

No matter what anyone tells me, I will always know in my heart that Tara killed my daughter. And she got away with it.

MARIE

Marie used to live next door to me. She was my best friend, but she was forced to leave. Her husband Tony used to beat on her real bad. We lived in a duplex, so I heard a lot of what went on in the other side of the house. Always after a beating or a yelling match, Marie would seem embarrassed. We had coffee almost every morning. I wanted to help her, but I didn't know what to do. So, I pretended that I didn't hear anything.

As time went on, the beatings became more frequent and more violent. My husband and I weren't sure if we should call for help or stay out of it. He didn't really want to call for help, because he was afraid that Tony would turn his anger towards me and our kids. Obviously, Tony would have known who'd called the cops. So we tried to ignore the screams and cries. I felt bad for not helping her, but I had to agree with my husband.

One day when Marie didn't come over for coffee, I knocked at her door. Then I took out the spare key she had hidden by the front step and I went inside. There was no one there. I looked through her whole apartment and I saw that a lot of her stuff was missing. 'Where was she?' I wondered.

I closed the door and went back over to my side. About an hour later the phone rang and I heard Marie on the other end. She told me that she had left Tony and that she was going to have to hide. I asked her where she was going to go and all she would tell me was the less I knew the better. We talked for a few more minutes and then we hung up. She'd told me she wasn't going to call me again.

I felt really bad after that, I wish I had done something to help her when she had been next door. Marie had been a really good friend and I hadn't been. I'd shut my eyes to what had been happening to her. I felt very guilty and I knew that I had been a lousy person.

Later on that night, Tony came banging at our door demanding to know where Marie was. I told him that I hadn't seen her all day, which was the truth. Tony told me to tell her, he was going to kill her when he found her. I was really afraid for Marie, but I had no way of getting in touch with her. I do miss her and I'd love to be able to tell her how sorry I am. I didn't do anything to help her, I wish I had. If I had the chance to do it all again, I would have gotten involved, no matter what my husband said.

ANDREA

Andrea had been my best friend since grade school. We did everything together. When we got older, we double dated and hung out together all of the time. Freddy started to hang out with us, neither one of us liked him as a boyfriend, but he was okay to hang out with. Although, sometimes he could be pretty annoying. He liked us both and kept trying to get us to go out with him.

One day, Andrea was reading in the student lounge at school and I was in class. Freddy went into the lounge and asked her if she wanted to go have a cigarette with him, by the edge of the woods. She agreed and they left together.

From what the police can put together, Freddy made some advances towards Andrea. When she refused, he strangled her. Then he tried to hide her body in the woods.

Some kids found her about an hour later, when they went to have a cigarette. I was completely and totally devastated.

KEISHA & TANESSA

Keisha and her daughter Tanessa, are my daughter and granddaughter. Keisha married Jeffrey when she was pregnant. I never liked him, but it wasn't my choice. Within weeks of getting married, my daughter came back to my front porch, bag and baggage. Jeffrey had hit her, while they were fighting.

Later that day, Jeffrey came and convinced her to go back home with him. Things continued that way for the entire four years they were married. They would fight and he'd hit her. She'd come to my house and later he'd get her to go back home.

Sometimes she would stay with me a few weeks, before going back with him. I guess it was around the time that Tanessa turned three, when Keisha finally grew tired of the situation.

I babysat for Tanessa, while Keisha went to school during the day. She wanted to be a guidance counselor in a high school. That didn't last too long, because Jeffrey got sick of it and he burned all of her school books. Keisha got very depressed for a while, I really worried about her.

When Tanessa was three and a half, she asked her mother 'Why does daddy hit you?' Keisha's eyes finally opened and from then on she was determined to change things. She left Jeffrey, came back home and got a job. I again, watched Tanessa for her.

Jeffrey was extremely upset by this. He would come to the house and try to convince her to go back home with him. When that didn't work, he would start to threaten her and sometimes he'd hit her.

He even got so that he would go to the mall where she worked and start to threaten and harass her. Needless to say, she was fired because her boss got tired of dealing with Jeffrey. Didn't we all?

It didn't take her long to bounce back and get another job. Again, he would bother her and threaten her.

I took Keisha to talk to some of the women at the shelter and they helped her to leave. Jeffrey would constantly threaten Keisha, Tanessa and me. One time, he pulled Tanessa out of her car seat and did not bring her back for five days. Keisha and I were beside ourselves.

We got together some money and the shelter also gave us some. Keisha and Tanessa left, a few days later. That was probably the hardest thing I ever did. But I knew they had to leave. I wish I could see them, I miss them terribly.

Jeffrey keeps coming to my house and threatening me. At least now I can tell him what I think about him and not have to worry about what he will do to Keisha. I do know the general area they are in, but they don't have a phone.

Maybe someday Jeffrey will get tired of bothering us.

KATIE

Katie and I had lived together since college. We were really good friends. She worked for a lawyer, she was a legal secretary and I am a hostess in a busy restaurant.

Every Friday night Katie and I would go out to dinner. Then we would go out to Charlie's, which always had great bands playing. We would drink, dance and usually have a really good time.

Although the last few weeks that we had gone there, a guy kept bugging Katie. We tried to avoid him, but he would come up to her on the dance floor and move up against her. Or sometimes he would just stare at her. He also kept trying to talk to her, but he was very suggestive and rude.

I walked up to him one night and told him to leave her alone. I also told him we would tell the bouncer, if he kept on bugging her.

That was a mistake, because he got pretty angry. I saw him sitting at the bar and he looked pretty mad. I felt we should be able to enjoy ourselves, without some big oaf bothering us.

When Katie and I left to get into my car in the parking lot, we never saw that guy follow us. The next thing I knew Katie screamed and I turned around to see him standing there. He reached for Katie and I quickly grabbed her by the arm.

The guy hit me hard across the side of my face and he pulled Katie away with him. I got up and ran after them, again I tried to pull Katie away and he hit me. When I fell to the ground, he kicked me in the face, which dislocating my jaw. The whole time this went on, he held tightly onto Katie.

I sort of remember seeing him pull her into an older green truck. The parking lot filled with people from the club and they tried to help me.

I was rushed to the hospital, where they wired my jaw shut for six weeks. Meanwhile, the police searched for Katie and for the green truck.

Two weeks later, they found her body in a rest area, beside the highway. An elderly woman had been walking her dog and discovered Katie's naked body. She had been raped and beaten to death.

To this day, they have never found the guy with the green truck.

CINDY

Cindy was my ex-girlfriend. My name is Amanda. We were together for eight years and I thought we got along pretty good, but I guess I was kind of boring. I work during the day and just like to take it easy and relax at night.

One day, Cindy told me she was moving out. She told me that she wasn't sure what she wanted anymore. We parted as friends and managed to remain close, even after our breakup.

Cindy started to date a woman named Morgan and soon they had moved in together. Morgan was jealous of Cindy's and my relationship. When Morgan and Cindy would argue or fight, Cindy would call me and ask for advice.

Cindy called me one day, crying hysterically. Morgan had hit her a few times. I went over to their apartment and was sickened by what I saw. Cindy had bruises all over her face and arms.

As I was trying to convince Cindy to leave, Morgan came home. She threw the biggest fit I'd ever seen. She told me to get out of her house. I had no choice, I left.

The next day Joanie, a friend of ours, told me that Cindy was dead. Morgan had been arrested for her murder. Morgan apparently stabbed her repeatedly, after I had left. I wish I had stayed that day or had insisted Cindy leave with me. I will always feel extremely guilty about that.

JACKIE

Jackie was my only daughter, in a house full of six boys. Jackie was also the baby of the family. When she got involved with Tom, we were all concerned. Tom was her boss, besides he was a married man. Her father and I were completely against their seeing each other.

She was so sure he was going to leave his wife, we couldn't convince her otherwise, no matter how hard we tried.

Three months later, Jackie was very excited and told me that she was pregnant. Her father and I were very disappointed, but it wasn't our choice. All we could do was support her decision. She was going to keep the baby, end of discussion. I have to admit that I was excited at the thought of having my first grandchild, but I was less than thrilled about the circumstances.

Jackie told us she was going to tell Tom that weekend. They were planning on going boating on Saturday, because his wife was going out of town with his kids. I had no idea there were kids involved.

We talked to Jackie on Friday night, she sounded very excited and upbeat. I couldn't shake a very uncomfortable feeling I had, but she assured me that everything was going to be fine. We hung up the phone, but not before she promised to call us on Sunday night.

By Monday morning I was very upset, because I hadn't heard from Jackie. I called her work and they told me she hadn't shown up. I called her apartment and no one answered the phone. Her father and I thought it was very strange.

Jake, her father and I drove over to her apartment. I let myself in with the key she had given to me. We looked around and saw no signs that she had returned on Sunday, as she'd planned. I went over to her phone and called the police. I told them the last time we had talked to her was on Friday. I also told them, she had planned on going boating at the lake over the weekend.

Within hours the police called us back. They asked us to come to the police station, which we immediately did. We were informed that the body of a young woman had washed up on shore Sunday night. They drove us to the morgue to look at the body. They brought us to see if it was our Jackie and it was. My heart sank, I had never felt such pain in all of my life. Her father took it even harder than I did.

I told the police about Tom. After they investigated him, they told us that they couldn't prove he had been with her that weekend. When the autopsy had been preformed, we found out that she had died due to a blow to the head. Then she had been pushed from a boat into the water, where the fish had bitten her. I was sickened at the thought.

There was nothing anyone could do. This has really ripped our family apart. My husband barely speaks to anyone now and the boys are all acting out in different ways. My husband goes to her grave and just sobs, so do the boys. We were all so close and happy before. Now we are barely civil to each other.

The worst part is Tom is free.

REBECCA

Rebecca was a pizza delivery girl, part time. She went to school during the day. She was a senior in high school and had a very busy schedule. She was also involved in many different clubs at school. She didn't have time for a boyfriend nor did she seem to want one.

Her father and I were very proud of her, she was so responsible for her age. Until the day she met Larry. He was older than her, he was a college student. She was very happy at first, then she became very quiet and withdrawn. She quit all of her clubs at the school and she eventually quit her job.

I knew something was wrong, but I wasn't positive what it was. I watched her and Larry together and found him to be a mean and controlling person. My husband and I discussed how we should handle this situation and we decided that we were going to forbid them from dating.

That did not produce the reaction we had expected. Larry was upset and became extremely violent towards Rebecca and her father. I tried to keep the peace, but to my surprise Rebecca stood up for Larry.

Larry grabbed Rebecca by the throat and he told us he would kill her, if we tried to keep them apart. My husband reluctantly agreed to let them date each other, just to calm Larry down. Eventually, he let my daughter go and after a while he left. When Larry had gone, my daughter appeared to be scared.

I was afraid of Larry and afraid of what he might do to all of us. My husband and I decided to drive Rebecca back and forth to school. We also told her that starting the next day, there would be no more Larry. Rebecca ran from the room and yelled to us, that Larry loved her. My husband and I looked at each other, what had happened to our little girl?

Later that night, Larry came back and my husband told him that he was no longer welcome at our home. Larry left in a huff, screaming obscenities at my husband.

The next morning, my husband drove Rebecca to school and that afternoon I picked her up. While we were in the car waiting in line behind the buses, I saw Larry crossing through the parking lot. He walked right up to my window and peeked in. I was stunned when I saw him reach into his jacket and pull out a gun. Before anything registered in my mind and I realized what he was doing, he shot Rebecca. Then he pointed the gun at me and fired. I heard one more shot, just before everything turned black.

Later when I came to, I saw that I was in the hospital. A police officer and my husband were in the room with me. I knew, by looking at my husband that Rebecca had not made it. They told me that Rebecca had been shot in the head and she'd died immediately. I had also been shot, but I was shot in the neck. I was going to be okay. After Larry shot the both of us, he turned the gun on himself. He shot himself in the head and he died immediately.

My husband and I have tried to make some sense out of all of this. Shortly after I recovered, my husband and I separated. We were each in too much pain. Neither one of us could seem to give any comfort to the other. My entire family unit has been destroyed.

LINDA

My name is Andy and my sister's name was Linda. We were pretty close growing up and even as adults we got along real well. She did tell me a lot of things that went on in her life, but she didn't tell me everything. Like why she let Paul hit her, if she had told me, I would have taken care of him. He would have never hit her again, maybe that's why she never told me. No one in the family knew anything about him hitting her, until we read her journals. At that point Paul was already in jail, so there was nothing we could do.

Anyway, Linda dated Paul for three years. When she died, she had been six months pregnant. According to her journals, Paul didn't want her to get fat and he didn't want any kids.

A week before she was murdered, Paul beat her on the stomach and back with a pair of jumper cables.

The day before he killed her, they argued and he punched her in the stomach, telling her that he wished the kid would just go away.

On the day he killed her, they had argued because she told him she was going to leave him. The next day she had planned to go home, back to our parents house. He struck her a few times and took off for the bar. That was the last entry that she wrote in her journal. I wish she had left him that night, she'd still be alive.

The police said Paul came home drunk and beat her with a hammer, while she lay sleeping in their bed. She never had a chance to fight back or to try to protect herself. She never saw it coming.

They arrested Paul later that day, luckily before I could get a hold of him!

HIS STORY

These stories are the abusers side. They are in no way glamorized. The abuser is never made to look like the victim. These men tell why they feel they abused their girlfriends and wives. Some realize they are to blame and seek help. Others are still blaming everyone else for their abusive behavior.

Some of these men have gone on to have healthy relationships, while others are actively looking for their 'runaway' girlfriends or wives.

Some of these men are sorry for what they have done, while others will more than likely do it again.

KEN

My name is Ken and I don't know why I started hitting my wife. I guess I used to get mad a lot and she was the only one there. She didn't do anything or say anything to get me mad. She would just listen to me complain.

The first time I hit her I felt really bad. I apologized for hitting her, while she cried. I promised her that I would never do it again.

Weeks went by and we both seemed to forget about what had happened. Until one night, when I got home my wife and her sister were sitting at the table, laughing. This really got me mad. The more they laughed and had a good time, the madder I became. By the time her sister finally left, I was a very angry man. I just didn't know why I was so mad.

I guess maybe I thought that they were laughing at me. I went out to the kitchen and slapped my wife. I lost control and kept hitting her. The more I hit her, the better I felt. I just kept hitting her and I didn't realize how long I had been doing it. I seemed to fall into some kind of a trance, I wasn't thinking about anything at all.

Finally, I looked down at my wife. I mean, I really looked at her. She was sitting on the floor with her hands raised above her head. I stopped hitting her and she slowly raised her face up to look at me, tears were running down her cheeks.

"Please," she whispered.

Why did I keep doing these things to her? I loved her and I really didn't want to hurt her. I would just get so mad. I had to hit something and she was there. I wouldn't feel mad anymore after I hit her, but I would feel bad that I had hurt her.

One night she told me she was going to leave me. I couldn't let that happen. No matter what I had done to her, I knew that I loved her. I don't know why, but suddenly I grabbed her and started smashing her head onto the floor. I had her by the hair and just kept pounding her head. When I finally stopped and looked at her, I realized that I was going to end up killing her. I let go of her hair and told her that I was sorry.

I put my head into my hands and I cried. I heard my wife get up and walk out of the door.

She never came back, I guess that I couldn't blame her. I knew that I needed to get some help. At first, I went to counseling to get Kathy back, but after a while I went for me. I wanted to change, I didn't like the person that I'd become.

Kathy and I have been separated for eight months now, but she did agree to go out to dinner with me next week. We are going to take things real slow and see how things go. 'No promises,' she said to me.

I do know that I don't want to hurt her anymore.

STEVE

My name is Steve and I lived with my girlfriend off and on for about seven years. She had two kids when we met. We got along pretty good at first. She didn't work the whole time we were together, but she was on welfare.

Housing paid for her rent, welfare gave her money and all of her medical bills were paid. She got food stamps for food and fuel assistance paid her electric bills. I thought that she had it pretty good, so I started staying with her at the apartment. She paid for everything, I didn't even have to work. I eventually quit my job. Tami had a new car. She let me drive all over and she always put the gas in.

In the beginning it was great. Her kids were okay, they played outside most of the time. I'd go out with my friends or my brothers and after, I'd go home to Tami. Depending on how drunk I was, I would either stay at Tami's or I'd stay at my mom's house.

At first she was okay with it, but then she wanted me to stay at her apartment, no matter how drunk I got. She would get mad at me if I stayed at my mom's, I guess I could see her point.

Tami and I had been together for about a year, before I hit her. Well, I threw the remote for the TV at her. She told me that I couldn't use her car. I felt like I had gotten grounded.

Another time, I was so drunk that I stayed at my dad's house. The next morning Tami showed up and started to yell at me. She told me that she had been up all night, worrying. I finally got up from the couch and went out to her car with her. I climbed in and lay down in the backseat.

I was really hung over, I'd only gotten two hours sleep. Tami kept yelling at me about how inconsiderate I was. I lifted up my leg and kicked out her back window, glass flew everywhere. Tami turned the car around and drove me right back to my dad's.

Things kept getting worse from then on. I didn't have anything to do, so I drank more and more. Tami would get furious with me.

We would split up and then get back together again. Sometimes I'd just leave when she told me to, other times I'd scream and yell at her. Sometimes I'd hit her or slap her. When things would get real bad, she'd call the cops or else a neighbor would. They'd come and tell me to leave, or they'd arrest me, depending on what had happened.

One night when they got called over, they saw my hand prints on her throat. I spent that night in jail. Another time I locked myself in the bedroom, they busted down the door and I was hauled off to jail again.

Sometimes when I'd go out, me and the guys would get some cocaine or do some heroin. I know that when I got home after doing either one of those drugs, I was real miserable to Tami. Those things would make me very violent, but not until I got home.

I don't know why we kept getting back together, we probably should have just stayed split up. But we always got back together. When we had been together for about four years, she told me that she was pregnant. Part of me was really excited and yet another part of me was terrified. How could I be a good father? All that I wanted to do was drink. That was all I knew, I drank with my brothers and my friends. I drank with my dad and uncles. Everyone that I knew drank, it's all we did. My mom even went out drinking every weekend.

I told her that I wanted her to get rid of it. When she told me no, I beat her up pretty bad. A few days later, she ended up having a miscarriage. I don't know if it happened because of me or not.

I went back to the apartment a couple of days later and told her how sorry I was. I wasn't sorry that the baby was gone, but I was sorry I'd messed her up. She had a black eye, a cut up lip and bruises all over. I guess that I had worked her over pretty good. I remembered most of it.

We went back and forth for a few more months, breaking up and then getting back together again. We both knew we should have stayed away from each other, but for some reason we just couldn't seem to stay apart.

My best friend was always depressed around the time all of this was going on. He was always telling me how he was going to kill himself. Whenever he got drunk, which was most of the time, he'd talk about suicide. We ignored him or told him to shut up. One day he finally did it, he hung himself. That really screwed me up, I never knew anyone who had killed themselves before. I got kind of depressed, then all I did was drink and drink some more. Shortly after that, my father died.

I stole a gun from my uncle and I used to really think about killing myself. Tami told me that she was pregnant for the second time, within a few weeks of all of this. I told her to get an abortion and again, she told me no. We argued about it for days, then one night I'd been drinking a lot and we really got into it. She told me that she was going to have the baby, whether I stayed with her or not.

I went into the other room and took out the gun. When I came back out I aimed it at her.

"You will get rid of it." I told her.

"No," she said. "I've already made up my mind."

DOMESTIC ABUSE: ALL SIDES

I pulled the trigger, I saw the blood splatter behind her onto the wall. I stared at the tiny hole in her forehead. When I looked up, I saw gray and red running down the wall. I turned around and vomited.

Now I am in prison for life. I wish we had just stayed away from each other.

ANTHONY

I met Karen at the construction site where I worked. She was so pretty, she had blonde hair and blue eyes. She was applying for a job there. I watched her walk out of the office with an application, sit down and start to fill it out. I managed to get up some courage. I went over to her and sat down beside her. We talked for a few minutes, then I had to get back to work.

A few days later, she was back and working in the office. We started having lunch together every day. She was so sweet and caring. It didn't take long before we started to date.

Karen lived at home with her parents, but that was okay because I lived at home with my dad.

One Saturday I went over to her house to meet her parents. I was pretty surprised when I met her two- year-old daughter, Kelly. Karen was nineteen and I guess I never thought about her being with anyone else. I will admit, that I got very upset about that.

We spent almost all of our time together. Her mother didn't like me, but I didn't care, I was dating Karen! Otherwise, I felt pretty comfortable at their house. I would watch the game with her dad and we'd drink a few beers together. Her mother would get mad at me, when I would tell Karen to get me another beer.

"You have legs," her mother would tell me or else she'd ask me, "Why can't you get it yourself?"

I ignored her, but she sure made me mad. One Sunday, Harry and I were watching the game and the phone rang. Karen's mom called her and told her that 'Bob' was on the phone for her.

I got up and walked out of the house. I went out to sit in my truck. A while later, Karen came running out to me. That's when I slapped her, I had to. She told me she was sorry and that Bob was only a friend. Her mother came out of the house and started screaming at me. I started up my truck to leave and Karen jumped in beside me. She kept telling me that she loved me.

I watched her mom in my rearview mirror as we drove off. I told Karen that I wanted her to move into my dad's house with me. She agreed and we went back to pick up her daughter and her things.

Boy, did her mom beg and plead with her not to leave, but she came with me anyway. My dad liked Karen a lot, so he didn't mind.

Karen called her mom a few times after we had moved in together, but her mom kept giving her a hard time. Eventually, Karen pretty much stopped calling her.

She had to quit her job when she moved in, because she couldn't find a babysitter. One night when I got home from work, I saw a bunch of grocery bags sitting on the counter.

"Where did you go today?" I asked her.

"To the store, we ran out of a few things," she told me, smiling.

I grabbed her by the hair and slapped her hard.

"You are not to go anywhere without me!" I yelled at her.

I hit her again and again, until she picked up Kelly and ran for the door. I grabbed my bat out of the closet and I ran after her.

"Leave me alone." She yelled at me, jumping into her car and locking the doors. "I'm sick of this, I'm going back home."

I was so angry, I started swinging the bat at her car.

"Open the door and come back inside Karen." I yelled at her.

"No," she screamed at me, as she tried to start the car.

I brought the bat down hard against her windshield. I kept hitting her windshield. I could hear her screaming, but it sounded so far away. All that I could think about, was that she was not going to leave me, no matter what.

Kelly was crying. I remember hearing that now, but at the time I wasn't listening. Karen screamed for me to stop and she opened up the door. I brought the bat up high and swung it back down. I heard a horrible crunching sound, I guess that was when the bat crushed her skull. I kept swinging the bat until my arms ached.

Finally things started to come back into focus. I heard Kelly crying, I saw blood splattered all over her. Then I looked down at Karen, I couldn't even recognize her face anymore. I ignored Kelly. I dropped the bat and slowly backed away from the car. I looked down at my hands and saw that they were also covered with Karen's blood.

I walked back into the house, grabbed a beer from the refrigerator and sat down on the couch. Slowly, with shaking hands, I drank my beer.

A while later, I heard sirens and felt myself being roughly pulled up from the couch.

I've been in prison for five years, I've got a lot longer to go. I'm required to receive counseling. My counselor says that I have abandonment issues, stemming from my mother walking out on us when I was a small boy.

This all happened because of my mom. It's her fault, my counselor said so.

RILEY

My name is Riley and I used to beat up my girlfriend. At first I didn't, we got along really good. When I would go to her apartment, she'd have dinner all ready and a cold beer waiting for me. She was great back then, until she started going out at night with one of her girlfriends. At least that's what she told me.

One night after dinner, I saw that she was getting ready to go out. When I pressed her on it, she got mad and yelled at me to leave her alone. I got pissed and slapped her across the face. We were both pretty surprised. Anyway, she still went out and I followed her. I sat in the shadows at the bar and watched, as she and her friends drank and danced.

After a while, she started dancing with a guy. I recognized him. He lived in the apartment building next to ours. So that's what had been going on, I thought to myself.

The longer I sat there and watched her, the madder I got. I ordered another beer and waited. I watched her and I couldn't help but see how comfortable she was with him. He had his arm draped around her, while she talked to her friends.

At twelve thirty, the bar crowd started to thin out. I ordered another beer and went out to my car. I planned on waiting for her to leave.

Finally, at one o'clock she came out with him. They started hugging and kissing next to a car in the parking lot.

I don't know what happened, I just remember being so mad at her. I started the car, put it into drive and pressed my foot down hard onto the gas pedal.

Before I realized what I was doing, I'd ran into them. I pinned them into the car that they had been leaning against, a few minutes before. People were screaming and I saw my girlfriend just staring at me. I couldn't see the guy, because he had his back to me.

Someone pulled me out of my car and backed it up. I watched as they both fell to the ground, screaming out in pain.

Both of their legs were mangled and twisted around, I leaned over and vomited.

Within a few minutes the police and ambulance were there. I was quickly handcuffed and put into the back of the cop car. I watched as the EMT's put them both onto stretchers and drove away. The police questioned everyone, then they drove me to jail.

They let me make a call, but I had no one that I could talk to. I stayed in jail until Monday morning and then they brought me to court. No one told me the whole weekend, how my girlfriend was. I didn't hear anything, until I went to court on Monday.

The judge appointed me a lawyer. That's when I found out, the guy she'd been with had died from massive internal injuries. My girlfriend was paralyzed, from the waist down.

I felt real bad and I was really scared. The judge wouldn't let me get out of jail. When court was finally over, eight months later, I was found guilty of attempted murder and vehicular manslaughter.

I am still in jail and I will be here for quite a while. No one comes to see me in here. My family has disowned me and none of my friends come here.

The time goes by so slowly in here.

I am so sorry Mary Ann. I don't know why I did it.

TODD

My name is Todd and I am a senior in high school. I used to be on the football team. I also had a girlfriend, her name was Annie and she was a cheerleader.

We used to fight all of the time. We'd break up and then go back out again a day or two later. That is, until I found out that all the times that we had been broken up, it was so that she could go out with other guys. That really pissed me off.

She made me look like a fool. Everyone was laughing at me and talking about me behind my back. She played me so bad and I was so stupid not to see it.

Finally, my sister told me what was going on. That's when I figured out what I was going to do about it.

One Friday night we went over to the tower. All the guys took their girls there. I pretended that everything was fine, for a while.

After we'd had sex, I put my hands around her throat and squeezed as hard as I could. She kicked me, she scratched at my face and hands, but I didn't let her go. I held onto her throat, until she stopped fighting me. When I let her go of her, she didn't move. Then I tried to think about what I was going to do with her.

I remember yelling at her, telling her I knew what she had done and that she was never going to hurt me or embarrass me again.

I started my car and drove down the dirt road, until I saw a bunch of brush by the side of the road. I pulled over and picked her up, then I put her down behind the pile of brush. I looked around, saw no one and I quickly drove off.

When I got home I tried to act as normal as possible. My sister could tell that something was wrong and she kept asking me if I was okay. I lied to her and said that everything was fine.

A couple of days went by and they still hadn't found Annie. I was afraid to go back there. I wanted to see if her body was still there. I knew that it had to be, because no one had said anything yet.

On Monday, kids in school were asking where she was. I told them I didn't know, I told them that we had broken up after school, on Friday. Everyone believed me, because we had been broken up so many times before.

It wasn't until Monday night on the news, they said they had found a body up on Tower Road. I was really afraid for the next couple of days.

On Wednesday afternoon, the police came to the school to arrest me.

They said they believed I had been the one to kill her. They put a thing, like a big q-tip in my mouth. A while later they said that my DNA matched the DNA that I'd left inside her on Friday night. They also told me she had skin under her nails and I just happened to have scratches on my face.

My parents got me a really good lawyer and I denied that I'd done anything, for a while. Then, one day during the trial, I just couldn't take it anymore and I broke down. I told them what I had done and why I'd done it.

I'm in prison now. I turned eighteen a month before I had killed her. They tried me as an adult. I'm taking high school classes here in the prison, at least I will be able to get my diploma while I'm here.

I feel bad about what I've done. I just couldn't handle the fact that she'd made a fool out of me. I will be in here for a really long time.

ANDREW

My name is Andrew and I was married to the most beautiful woman in town. All the guys had a crush on her and when she was with me, she ignored all of their stares and whistles.

I was a truck driver and would haul long loads, sometimes I'd be gone for a week at a time. The money was real good and I wanted to be able to give Patty all the nice things that she wanted.

We had been married for five years and I desperately wanted kids, but Patty kept telling me that she just wasn't ready yet, so I waited and waited.

One day my boss offered me a local job. I would be able to haul my load locally, except for one weekend a month. Then I'd have to haul a longer load. To me that sounded great, I'd be able to spend lots more time with my Patty. I thought that maybe I could convince her to have a baby, since I'd be around a lot more to help out. Patty wanted me to keep the other job. She said that it would be harder to make it without the extra income.

I talked with my boss and we came up with an idea. I'd make one long haul a month, a weekend haul every other month and short hauls the rest of the time.

The money wouldn't be that much different. He told me that if I really needed more money, he could use me in the warehouse.

I didn't tell Patty right away, I wanted to surprise her. Surprise her I did!

One night when she thought I was on my regular route, I came home early. When I pulled into the driveway, I saw a car that I didn't recognize. I sat in my rig for a few minutes, then I grabbed a metal pole, that I check my tires with. Slowly I climbed down from the truck and walked to my house, holding the pole.

Quietly I let myself in and I noticed how quiet it was. I was drawn down the hallway to our bedroom.

Slowly I opened the door and saw my wife in bed with another man. She was sitting on top of him, as he lay on my side of the bed! I went crazy. I clutched the pole and walked up behind her. I swung the pole as hard as I could. My wife fell to her side of the bed, with a loud cry.

The man looked up at me and begged for me to let him go. He kept saying he was sorry and that he didn't know.

I lifted the pole and brought it down on him, striking him over and over again. I couldn't believe he had been in bed with my Patty. When I was done with him, I turned to her and I beat her with the pole.

When I stopped, I realized there was blood everywhere, I had blood covering me. I walked into the bathroom and took a shower, then I put on some clean clothes.

I went back into the bedroom and looked down at my wife. Why had she cheated on me? I gave her everything that she'd ever asked for.

I went out into the kitchen and picked up the phone to call the police. Then I sat down and waited for them to come. Once they got there, I told them what I had done and why.

I heard one of the cops talking to another one. He was saying that he wondered when I'd find out about my cheating wife.

Now I'm in prison on two counts of murder.

I know now that I should have just walked away and divorced her, but I wasn't thinking clearly at the time.

BEN

My name is Ben and my girlfriends name was Carla. She was a waitress in this really dumpy diner when I first met her. We started dating and things were pretty good, at first.

We were together for about four months and I was sure that I loved her. She told me that she was in love with me, too.

I worked for the cable company, so I spent a better part of my day on the road. I guess that Carla and I started to fight a lot the last month we were together. We fought all of the time.

One day, I hauled off and slapped her in the head, so that she'd shut up. She told me she wanted to break up with me and she called me stupid for hitting her. Carla walked out of my apartment that day and she avoided me for weeks.

I called her everyday. I left messages for her all over the place, but she never called me back or got in touch with me. I didn't know what to do. I couldn't eat, I couldn't sleep. I missed her so much. Then I started to get really mad. Did she think that she was too good for me? I made a mistake, I loved her and I knew that she loved me.

I decided to wait for her outside of her apartment the next day. While I waited in my cable van, I played with a flat head screwdriver that I used for work. You know, tapping it on the steering wheel, while I listened to the radio.

To my horror she came out of her apartment with her arms around a big blonde guy. I watched as they kissed, then he got into his car and drove away. I thought that she loved me! How could she be with someone else, already?

Carla walked to the corner, to wait for the bus. I got out of the van and walked over to her. I didn't even realize that I was still holding the screwdriver.

"You bitch!" I yelled at her. As she turned to face me, I plunged the screwdriver deep into her chest. I heard a sucking sound as I pulled it out, then I stabbed her again and again.

The next thing I knew I was being roughly pulled away from her. I saw that a crowd had gathered around us and two cops were pushing me to the ground.

I was taken to jail and then to court. I found out, she had died before an ambulance had been able to get there.

Now I am in prison, probably for the rest of my life.

STEVE

I was married to Jenna for three years and during that time we would get into fights all of the time. She'd say things to purposely piss me off, she'd make me hit her. I never hit any girl before, but she'd just keep running her mouth.

When she was pregnant I only hit her a couple of times, but after my son came, man! We fought about money, mostly about the lack of it.

If her friends came over she'd say, "Steve makes minimum wage." So I didn't make lots of money, at least I worked and I was making an honest living.

On my son's first birthday, Jenna bought him all of these expensive things, to impress her family and friends. I knew that we couldn't afford them. When I confronted her about it later, we got into a huge fight. I hit her a few times, it was no big deal.

She turned around and threw a glass ashtray at me. It hit me in the shoulder, that's when I lost it. I choked her until she passed out. When she came to she seemed okay, but she didn't say a word to me for the rest of the night.

The next day I went to work as usual. When I got home Jenna and my son weren't there.

I've been looking for them for three years now. My wife has left no trail leading to her. I don't know if my son is dead or alive. I won't stop looking for them, ever.

JAKE

My name is Jake, my girlfriend Kelly and I met in a bar. I went out with my buddies every weekend. Kelly showed up on a Friday night with a couple of her friends. I watched her as she danced with her friends and when she came to the bar to refill their drinks.

By her fourth trip to the bar, I got up the courage to talk to her. I was pretty surprised when she sat down at the bar next to me. We talked for a while and by the time the bartender called out for last call, we were getting along really good.

Within a few weeks we'd moved in together, well, actually I moved out of my mothers house and into Kelly's apartment. We kept going out to the bar on weekends. She worked during the week, she was a waitress. I painted houses, so my job wasn't a guaranteed every day deal. But we got along pretty good, for a few months.

After we'd been living together for about three months, we started to fight. She'd get mad at me, it was winter and I couldn't work. She was upset because we were living off of just her money. We'd still go out, but she'd leave me with the guys and she'd go over with her friends.

One night while I was sitting at the bar, I watched a guy walk over to her. They danced a few dances together, then the guy went downstairs to use the restroom. I followed him and beat him up pretty bad in there. I went back up to the bar and sat down, like nothing had happened.

After a while it got pretty quiet in the bar, that's when I noticed a couple of guys were bringing up the guy I had beaten up earlier.

"He did it," the guy said, pointing at me.

"Call the cops," someone told the bartender.

"No, forget about it." The guy said, as his friends helped him out to his car.

Kelly came over to the bar and stood next to me. "You sick bastard, stay away from me!" she yelled at me.

I got up and grabbed her by the arm. "It's your fault, you were the one dancing with him."

"We were only dancing!" she said to me, pulling her arm away.

She walked away from me and I heard a couple of people laugh. I quickly ran up behind her and punched her in the back of the head. She had embarrassed me in front of my friends and the whole bar. Kelly fell forward onto a table and knocked over all of the drinks. She was helped up by a couple of her friends.

"Don't you ever come near me again," she said to me. She took a napkin that someone handed her and put it on top of the big gash that was on her hand.

"I will do whatever I want to." I said, slapping her hard.

Two guys came up behind me and dragged me out of the bar. In the parking lot they beat me up pretty bad, then they left me there. Before they left, they told me to stay away from Kelly.

I guess that I must have passed out, because when I woke up, I was alone in the parking lot. I was covered in my own blood.

I tried to call Kelly, but for the first few days all that I got was a busy signal. The next time I tried to call, I got a recording saying that the number had been changed.

I drove by her apartment and saw her standing outside talking to a couple of guys. I didn't know who they were, but they sure looked big.

About a week later, all of my things were sitting on my mothers front yard. I guess that Kelly had been serious.

I don't go out to the bars anymore. Mostly I just sit in my mothers livingroom, drink my beers and watch the TV.

BILL

My name is Bill and I used to be a police officer. I met Maggie when I pulled her over for running a red light, well, actually it was a yellow light. I saw her go through the intersection and I thought she was pretty, so I pulled her over.

We started dating and things went really well, for a while. I worked the four to midnight shift, so we only got to see each other two days a week. Although, I would drive by her apartment a few times each night, during my shift. Sometimes I'd stop by, but I was afraid the Sergeant would see me there, when I should have been working.

I thought we were getting pretty serious, but in August when the college opened back up, she started taking classes again. I soon began to see a strange car parked in her driveway, usually once a week.

Then it was parked there a few nights a week. I asked her who was visiting her and she told me that it was her cousin. Maggie told me she'd promised her aunt that she would watch out for him.

I didn't believe her, she was twenty years younger than I was and he was young too. Maybe she wanted to be with him instead of me, I thought.

One day, I drove by around five o'clock and I saw his car. I kept driving by and each time I did, I saw his car was still parked there. I drove by right before my shift ended and he was still parked there, in her driveway.

I did my paperwork at the station, got into my car and drove to Maggie's. I saw that his car was still there at her house and I pulled into the driveway across the street. I waited and waited. Finally at two o'clock, they came out.

I saw Maggie hug him, before he got into his car. I was furious. I knew that she had lied to me. I picked up my gun, which had been sitting on the front seat beside me. I aimed it at her and squeezed the trigger. Maggie fell against the car and I fired again. I thought that I'd hit him, but I found out later that he had crawled onto the floor of his car.

A neighbor called the police, within minutes there were cops everywhere. One of my fellow officers handcuffed me and put me in his backseat. From there I watched them help the guy out of his car, I saw the ambulance slowly take Maggie away.

Maggie was dead and now I'm in jail. I don't know why I did it, I can only say that I wasn't thinking clearly. I was a cop, I knew what was going to happen.

And guess what…that guy was her cousin.

TODD

My name is Todd and my wife's name is Karen. We were married for three years. During that time I hit her, actually I hit her a lot. I'd hit her over stupid things, like if the dishes weren't done or dinner wasn't ready. I sometimes felt like she would deliberately do things to get me mad at her, maybe she did.

When our son was six months old, he died. I guess it was my fault that he'd died.

Karen was holding onto Jimmy when she told me that she was going to leave me. I got so mad at her. When she was walking away, I punched her hard in the back. She fell forward and accidently let go of Jimmy. I watched as his little body flew through the air and slammed against the kitchen counter.

He just lay there on the floor, he didn't move. I could see nothing wrong with him, but a tiny cut above his right ear.

When he didn't move, Karen jumped up and ran over to him. She started screaming at me. I tried to take him from her, but she wouldn't let me. I went over to the phone and I called 911.

My son Jimmy is dead and my wife has left me.

In court, my lawyer got me off on all of the charges, except for the anger management classes that I am required to take.

I went to the funeral and was shocked to see the tiny coffin that held my son's little body. Once Karen saw me there, she started screaming and yelling at me. She called me a murderer.

A few men, I think from the funeral home, asked me to leave or they would have to call the police.

I don't think that my son's death was completely my fault, Karen was the one who let go of him.

JASON

My wife's name is Brenda and she has been missing for over a year. I have looked everywhere for her. I've asked her family where she is, over and over again. All they tell me, is that they don't know where she is.

She took off with my two kids, she even told everyone that I used to beat her. I never beat her, but I would slap her occasionally. What man doesn't slap his wife? I mean lets face it, we have to keep them in line.

Someday I will find her and she'll be sorry that she messed with me!

BOB

I met Aimee in the grocery store, we were both doing our shopping. We started talking, while we waited in line. She was really pretty and seemed so nice. I found out that she had two kids and no husband.

Aimee lived in the same apartments that I lived in. She lived with her kids and I lived with two other guys.

I waited for her by the exit door and we walked together to her car. I helped her unload her cart and then we talked for a while longer. By the time I watched her drive away, I'd been invited to dinner.

She was a few years older than I was, but I didn't care. I took classes at the university in town and she worked there in the admissions office. We started seeing a lot of each other, after that day. Her kids were great, Sally was five and Diane was three.

Aimee used to get a teenager from her building to babysit. Then we could go places together. We went out to eat dinner a lot, she loved to eat out.

One night while we were at a nice Italian restaurant, our waiter kept smiling at her. At first Aimee just laughed it off, then I noticed that he slipped her a piece of paper. I asked her what was on the piece of paper he had given to her and she told me that it was his phone number. What got me mad was when she put the paper into her purse.

We fought about it that night. I wanted her to throw it away, but she wouldn't. We were still fighting about it a few days later. Aimee told me that when she went home she had thrown it away, I didn't believe her.

About a week later the phone rang while I was at Aimee's apartment, she answered it and then told the person to call her back later. I was sure it was the waiter who had called her. Aimee laughed at me and said I was crazy, then she told me that maybe it would be better if we saw other people. I told her, I didn't think so.

On Wednesday nights I usually have a class, so we don't see each other. One time I cut class and went over to her apartment instead. I saw that her car was in the parking lot and her lights were on, but she wouldn't answer the door when I knocked.

I started to bang on the door and she still wouldn't open it. I gave up after a while and went back to my apartment, then I called her. The phone was busy, that's when I knew she had the waiter over, I just knew it.

I went back over to her apartment and waited by the bushes, it seemed like I waited forever. I could hear voices inside her apartment, I also heard the TV.

By the time it started getting real cold outside, I had grown tired of sitting out there. I knocked at the door and no one answered. Then I remembered that she hid an extra key in a little metal box, under the statue next to the door.

I took out the key and slowly slid it into the keyhole. Then I quietly turned the key and the doorknob at the same time. I stopped short at what I saw, Aimee was sitting on the couch with the waiter from the restaurant. He was sitting there and he had Diane sitting on his lap.

"What the hell is this?" I yelled.

Aimee and the waiter both looked at me, surprised. I walked over to her before either one of them could react. I punched Aimee in the face as hard as I could.

Before the waiter could stand up, I'd hit him too. Then I turned my attention back to Aimee and kicked her a few times, before I walked out the door.

Both of Aimee's kids were screaming and crying as I closed the door. I felt pretty good. Well, at least until I got back to my apartment, then I was mad again.

I decided to go back over to Aimee's. When I got there I saw two cop cars in the parking lot. I couldn't believe it, she had called the cops on me. I wasn't sure what to do, so I decided to go back home. I was laying in bed when I heard a banging at my door. Slowly I got up knowing that it was the cops. As I made my way to the front door, I promised myself that Aimee was going to be sorry for causing all of this.

TODD

My name is Todd and I was married to Carrie for four years. We met at a restaurant, we both had been fixed up on blind dates that never showed up. In the lounge we started to talk to each other and found out that we had a lot in common.

We decided to have a late dinner ourselves, despite having been stood up. Carrie and I really seemed to hit it off. We had a good time that night, so I asked her if she'd like to go out with me again.

We went out to dinner a few nights later and again had a great time. We continued to see each other for the next two years, then we decided to get married. The whole two years that we dated, we'd gotten along great. We never fought about anything.

After we were married things continued to go well for us. Carrie designed her own clothing line and I was an advertising executive. We were so happy, we had our careers and each other. We lived in a nice house, in a nice neighborhood and we drove nice cars.

Our lives consisted of dinner parties for both of our potential clients or quiet dinners at home. Carrie and I both loved our lives, at least until she found out that she was pregnant.

At first she agreed with me to get an abortion, the baby would have been a mistake, I told her. Our lives were so perfect, a baby would just ruin everything. For some reason Carrie kept stalling. Two months had passed, that made her three months pregnant.

"I'm thinking about maybe keeping the baby." Carrie told me one night.

"What?" I couldn't believe what she had just said to me. "Baby, you can't keep it, it will just complicate everything."

"Todd, I feel different about things, this baby is growing inside of me. It is our baby," she said, smiling at me.

"Have you lost your mind? What about your career? I don't want a baby and you told me that you didn't want one either." I said, trying to make sense of it all.

"I do now. I went to the doctors today and saw the baby, our baby, on an ultrasound." she said, trying to make me understand.

"What is an ultrasound?" I asked her.

"It's a really cool machine, it let's you see the baby. I saw our baby inside my stomach. I can't get rid of it now, it's too real," she said, reaching for my hand.

I pulled my hand away from her. "You can't keep it, we agreed that you'd get rid of it." I said. "Before we got married, we said 'no kids.' You agreed."

"Todd, I've decided, I'm going to keep it. I'm going to raise this baby with or without you. I want to be a family, but I will do it alone if I have to," she told me.

"I won't allow it." I said to her.

"Todd, I'm having this baby and that's it. I've decided, actually, I decided today." Carrie said, standing up.

I had to think about it, there was no way that I wanted to be a father. No way was I going to get stuck paying child support for a kid, that I didn't even want. I had to make Carrie realize she was about to make a very big mistake.

"If you want to keep it, then I am going to file for a divorce. We both agreed that we didn't want kids, you are going back on that agreement. I love you very much, but I do not want a kid, ever. You make a decision, either the baby or me." I told her, feeling pretty confident that with this ultimatum she would decide to get rid of the baby.

"Todd, I love you too, but I am keeping this baby. If that means I lose you, then I'm sorry. But I want this baby," she said, firmly.

At that point I saw red, I couldn't believe that she was going to throw our lives away over a mistake. A mistake that should have never happened. I should have put my foot down and made her get an abortion right away. I was furious with her, our lives were crumbling apart. She just calmly ruined everything, four years of a perfect marriage were being thrown away.

I asked her again. "Carrie, please reconsider. How can you throw everything away? You are making a very selfish decision."

"I'm sorry Todd, but I want this baby. I'm going to keep this baby," she said to me.

I don't know what happened, but I suddenly swung my fist at her. I hit her pretty hard in the head and I just couldn't seem to stop myself. I hit her again and again. Slowly I stopped feeling so frustrated, then I realized what I had done.

Carrie was on the floor crying, I mean really crying.

"I'm sorry Carrie." I told her, reaching for her.

She cowered away from me, I saw confusion and hatred in her glare.

"Stay away from me!" she yelled.

"I'm sorry, I didn't mean to." I said to her.

She was already starting to bruise. I saw blood in her mouth and her nose was starting to bleed.

"Carrie..." I said.

"I'm leaving," was all that she said.

I watched helplessly as she pulled herself up. She packed a few bags and walked out the door.

I didn't see Carrie again, until we were in court for our divorce. She had filed for a divorce the very next day. I signed a paper at the court, relinquishing all of my parental rights.

I will never have to pay child support, but I will also never be able to see Carrie's baby. She moved out of the area after we went to court, she also got half of everything that we owned.

I do miss her and the life that we had together. But I am happy to not be tied down with a kid.

DONALD

My name is Donald, I never meant for things to turn out the way they did. I am sitting in jail right now, because of my wife.

You see, we were married for twelve years when my wife decided that she wanted a divorce. Out of nowhere, one day she told me that she wanted a divorce.

"Oh, there is no one else," she had told me.

I didn't believe her and I was determined to find out for sure one way or the other.

We had been separated for a few weeks when I decided that it was time to find out. I drove back to my house one night and saw a red jeep in my driveway. I felt my temper begin to rise, we had only been separated for a few days, we weren't even divorced yet!

I parked my car and walked up to the back door. I listened for a few minutes, yes I heard two voices, my wife's voice and a man's voice. I pushed against the door, splitting the door casing.

My wife was sitting on the couch, she had a surprised look on her face and the man quickly jumped up off the couch. I lunged for my wife, knocking her to the floor. As she fell, she smashed her head on the corner of the coffee table.

I jumped up ready to hit the man. I saw a woman run into the room, she was holding a bowl full of something in her hands.

"Who are you?" I asked her.

"Samantha Barrows, this is my husband Tom. Who are you?" she asked, nervously looking down at my wife.

My wife didn't move, she lay on the floor as a puddle of blood began to form around her head. I slowly sat down on the couch and put my hands up to my head. What had I done?

"We need to call for help," Tom said.

"Are you having an affair with my wife?" I asked him.

"No, my wife and I came over to visit. We just moved in down the street, a week ago." Tom told me.

Samantha went over to the telephone and called for an ambulance. I just sat there on the couch, I knew that my wife was dead. This was all her fault, if she hadn't wanted to get a divorce this would never have happened.

Now I am in jail and I will be for a long time.

BEN

My name is Ben and my wife filed for a divorce, after we'd only been married for four months. Okay, so I hit her a few times, but it was no big deal. I didn't break any bones or anything.

One day I came home from work and Tamie told me that she felt like she'd made a big mistake.

"What did you do?" I asked her.

"I am really unhappy. I don't think that we should have gotten married. I made a mistake, we weren't meant to be married. It was a mistake," she told me.

"We love each other, what better reason to stay married?" I asked her, really confused.

"But I don't love you. I thought that I did, but I guess that I was wrong." Tamie said.

"I'm not going to let you leave me, not without really trying to make this work." I told her.

"Ben, I'm leaving you today," she said, firmly. "I wanted to tell you before I left, I felt that I at least owed you that much."

"What did I do wrong?" I asked her.

"Nothing. It's me, it's my fault," she said, as she stood up.

I suddenly got very angry and swung at her, slapping her across the face. Then I pushed her against the wall and I kept hitting her.

I felt like I wasn't really there for a few minutes, I guess that my anger just took over.

I realized what I was doing, when I finally heard Tamie screaming for me to stop. I apologized to her and I still really felt like things were okay between us.

She went into the bedroom and I sat down on the couch. After a while I lay down on the couch. I guess I fell asleep, because when I woke up it was light outside.

I went into the bedroom looking for Tamie and that's when I saw that she'd left me. She walked out on me…on us. Almost all of her things were gone from our bedroom.

A couple of weeks later, I got served with divorce papers. She had filed for a divorce, I couldn't believe it. Anyway, we are divorced now and I haven't seen Tamie in a long time.

I can't figure out why she left me. My new girlfriend, Emily hasn't left me and I've hit her a few times.

MARK

My name is Mark and I married my girlfriend Sara, when I found out that she was pregnant. I still think that she tricked me into marrying her.

I didn't love her, but I felt like I had to give my baby a last name. So we got married when she was seven months pregnant.

We never really got along, but after we got married, I really started to resent her. I felt like I had lost my freedom. I didn't want to be married, especially not to her. We started fighting a lot, by that, I mean that we fought all of the time.

I hated everything that she did and I was disgusted by how fat she seemed to be getting. Just having to look at her every day, would get me mad.

She loved to spend my money, too. No matter how much money I gave her, she always seemed to need more.

Finally, she had the baby. I'll admit I was disappointed, it was a girl. But I was even more disappointed later on.

When little Amanda was four I began to wonder if she really was my kid. She didn't look like Sara and she certainly didn't look like me. I told Sara that I wanted a blood test, she got really mad at me and started screaming and yelling.

I let it go for a few days and then I called a lawyer. I don't know how and I didn't ask, but somehow he arranged for blood tests with the pediatrician. Sara didn't know what was going on, when the pediatrician ordered some blood work for Amanda.

That night, after Sara had gotten home from the doctor's, I couldn't help but mention that I wanted some blood tests done. She got really mad at me, because I kept bringing it up. I told her that if she wasn't lying, then she wouldn't get so upset and she had nothing to worry about.

We got into a really big fight and I slapped her a few times. She kept mouthing off to me, so I started to choke her, just to get her to be quiet. Sara started to hit me, that's when I realized that she couldn't breath. I let her go and she crawled over to one of the kitchen chairs.

"I'm sorry, Sara." I told her. I went over to the refrigerator and grabbed a coke, then I went to the couch and sat down.

Sara didn't talk to me for the rest of the night. The next morning, while I got ready for work, she ignored me. I tried to concentrate on work, but my mind kept going back to the fight we'd had the night before. Why would she get that upset when I asked her for blood tests?

When I got home that night, I found that Sara and Amanda were gone. I reported them missing and then I waited. I didn't know what else to do.

After a month had gone by, I got the results back from the blood tests in the mail. My hands started to shake, as I read the lab report. I was 99% excluded from being the father of Amanda.

I talked to my lawyer and found out there was nothing that I could do. I had loved that little girl for the first four years of her life.

I have never heard from Sara or Amanda. The police dropped the missing persons search. Apparently, they'd found her and she told them that I wasn't Amanda's father, maybe she told them that she feared for their safety. I was told not to pursue them in any way.

JOEY

My wife Carla was a wonderful woman, she didn't deserve to be treated the way that I treated her.

I had a hard time controlling my temper, I used to get mad so easy. Carla and I got married when we were just nineteen years old. I got a job and we lived in a dingy trailer for two years, while I saved to buy us a house.

Finally, we had enough money for a down payment. We found a small two bedroom house, with a small yard. But it didn't matter what it looked like, because it was ours.

After we moved in, Carla fixed it up and made it look real nice. She sewed curtains and went to lots of yard sales to get any extras she felt we needed.

Carla wanted to start a family shortly after we had moved in. We tried and tried, but she just never got pregnant. That started to create a lot of friction in our marriage.

That and the fact that I was having a hard time keeping up with the bills. At work they had cut back on everyone's hours. My pay each week was quite a bit less, than what I had been making.

By the end of the month, I really dreaded sitting down at our kitchen table to try to pay all of the bills. Carla was great about it and she cut back wherever she could. She tried to help out as much as possible.

I started to have a hard time coping with just about everything. Carla wasn't getting pregnant and our financial situation was weighing heavily on me. Then there was talk at work about how some people were going to be laid off. The bills kept coming in, with 'Past Due' stamped across them.

I don't remember what Carla said that day to set me off, but I slapped her. Then I jumped up and I punched her. I just lost control and she was the closest one there.

I remember being just so damn angry, it was almost like I was watching someone else hurt Carla. It was like I had become someone else.

I heard Carla in the distance crying and screaming, but I wasn't focusing on that. I was only focusing on my own anger and frustration.

Finally I stopped, I don't even remember why I stopped. I looked down at Carla and saw that she was sitting in a heap on the floor, crying.

I reached down to help her up and she whispered for me to leave her alone. I watched her as she slowly got up and walked into the bathroom. I didn't know what to do, I felt so bad about what I had done.

Carla came out of the bathroom and then she went into the bedroom. I tried to apologize to her, but she told me that she didn't want to hear it. I watched helplessly as she packed up some of her things and walked out of our house.

I didn't hear from her again. Then I got served with divorce papers. We went into court and I tried to talk to her, but her lawyer told me to stay away from her.

Today we are divorced. I lost my wife and I even lost our house. I am living in another tiny trailer. I can't believe that in a matter of minutes I lost my wife. I wish I could take back that day, but I know that I can't.

I also wish, I could tell Carla how sorry I am.

ANDY

I dated Sandy for six years. We lived together for five and a half of those years. I didn't like it when she tried to tell me what to do and for the most part she didn't. Occasionally she would try to tell me to do this or to do that, but I wouldn't listen to her. Sometimes she would get pretty upset with me. I didn't care, I'd just go out with my buddies. I figured that she'd get over it, eventually.

She got pregnant and I was pretty upset about it. I didn't want to be a father, ever. So we argued for a while and then we really fought. I punched her a few times and I walked out.

Later that night, when I came back home she was gone. She never called me and I never saw her again.

PAUL

My name is Paul and I am in prison for murder. I killed my girlfriend a few years ago. I don't remember doing it or how it really happened.

I don't remember what happened that night at all, I actually thought that what happened was a dream. I do remember having a dream where I strangled Tanessa, but I don't remember actually doing it.

We used to fight a lot and it almost always turned physical. I admit that I hit her, quite a bit.

Apparently, I was too strung out on heroin to remember anything, well, heroin and alcohol. We had some friends over that night and that's how the cops found out what happened.

I hate being here in prison, besides I don't think I should be in here. I don't remember anything about that night, so why am I in here?

JAKE

My name is Jake and my wife took off with our kids. I hit her a few times, but only when she deserved it. Our sons were five and eight, when she left. Now they would be fourteen and seventeen.

I looked for her everywhere, but it was like she had disappeared right off the face of the earth.

The night before she left I did hit her a few times. Probably more times than I had ever hit her before. She used to tell me all the time that she was going to leave me, but I never took her seriously. She always said it when she was mad at me.

I went to work as usual and when I got home that night she was gone. So were my boys.

I don't think that she needed to leave like that, a lot of my friends hit their wives. It's really no big deal.

UNKNOWN

It was Amanda's fault that I used to hit her. If she didn't do stupid things and make me mad at her, I would never have hit her.

I know that someone helped her to leave me, because she was afraid to do it on her own.

If I find out who helped her, I'll beat her and whoever helped her.

BILL

Kari and I met at a bar. I thought she was the most beautiful woman I'd ever seen. She was a flirt though, she was a waitress at the bar and she used to flirt with everyone. She told me that when she flirted with people, they would give her bigger tips.

I asked her out a lot of times and finally one night she told me that she would go out to breakfast with me, but only as friends.

She got into my car and I drove down the road to an all night diner. We ate some really bad food, but I didn't care, because I was sitting with Kari. I felt real good, because the diner was filled with people and a lot of guys were watching us.

I could tell that she really liked me and after we ate, I drove her back to the bar. She said good night, then got into her car and left. It was okay, because I knew I would see her the next night. I hardly slept that night, because I was so excited about seeing her again.

The next day seemed to drag on forever. Finally, when I knew she was working, I drove over to the bar.

I kept trying to talk to her while she worked. I knew that it was pretty hard for her to talk, because the bar was so crowded. I watched her move from table to table. She seemed to be avoiding me, which really started to make me mad.

When the bar was closing, I walked over to Kari again.

"Are we going out for breakfast again?" I asked her.

"Bill, I can't. I'm going to go out with Todd for breakfast." Kari told me.

"I thought that we were going out, I don't want you to go out with anyone else." I said to her.

"We are not going out and never will be. You are not my type. We had breakfast and that's all." She said, turning away from me.

"Don't walk away from me." I told her, as I grabbed her by the arm.

"Tom!" Kari called out to the bartender.

Tom rushed over to us and I let go of her arm.

"What's the problem?" Tom asked.

"He thinks that I'd go out with him." Kari told him, as she started to laugh.

I watched as Tom began to laugh. I felt embarrassed and very angry at them.

"Bitch!" I said to Kari, as I walked out of the bar.

I sat in my car and waited for Kari to leave the bar. I watched her as she got into her car. I followed her to the diner and waited outside, watching her.

When she finally left the diner, I followed her. She drove for a while, then pulled into a parking lot. I also pulled in and parked my car. I got out and I ran over to her, just as she was getting out of her car.

"Bill!" she said, as I surprised her.

"No one makes a fool out of me." I told her, grabbing her by the throat and squeezing. She struggled for a few minutes, then I felt her body go limp. I let go of her and she fell to the ground.

I ran back to my car and sped out of the parking lot.

About a week later, I was arrested for Kari's murder and now I'm in jail. It was her fault, everything was her fault.

TOM

I used to get very angry at everyone. I'd especially get mad when things didn't go right at work. By the time that I would get home, I'd be very mad. Some of the guys at work used to pick on me and I felt like I had no control, except for when I was at home.

My wife was a lot smaller than I was, so I had no problem overpowering her. I used to slap her a lot, even when she did nothing wrong.

Sandy begged me to go to counseling with her, but I told her no.

One day I gave her a bloody lip and a black eye. I felt so bad about it, I felt so guilty. When I got home the next day, Sandy told me that she was going to leave me unless I went to counseling with her. She had an appointment set up for the next day.

At first I was really mad at her and then I thought about it for a while. I loved Sandy so much and I really felt bad about the way I'd been treating her lately. I agreed to go with her.

We have been going to counseling for three years now and although I still have to catch myself, we are getting along pretty good. I haven't hit her in months and I don't want to ever hit her again.

UNKNOWN

My wife Connie took off on me. I have been trying to find her for months and when I do, she'll wish that she'd never left me.

UNKNOWN

My wife Sally divorced me after we'd been married for eight months. We started to fight quite a bit. I guess that when I felt like she was right, I'd lash out against her. I hated to be wrong about anything, it made me feel weak.

Mostly I'd just slap her around and always with an open hand. I never hit her with my fist.

One day she told me that she was tired of being my punching bag. Then she walked out on me.

Sally, I made a mistake and I am truly sorry.

FRANKIE

Karen was my girlfriend and we were both seniors in high school. I was on the wrestling team and she was a cheerleader. We went out for five months and I thought that she loved me.

I heard that at one of the football games she cheated on me, but instead of asking her about it, I just blew up and I hit her a few times.

The next day in school, one of her friends told me that she wanted to break up with me. I was so angry at her and at everyone that day. I found out who the football player was and I beat him up.

Then I watched her. I watched her and I waited. Within a week she had a new boyfriend, his name was Mark. I watched the both of them together for a few days. On the outside I seemed fine, but on the inside I was very angry.

I followed them to McDonald's, I took out the hunting knife that I carry in my car and I stabbed Mark.

When Karen realized what I had done, she started to back away holding her mouth. I grabbed her and I swung her around. Then I slammed her head down onto the pavement.

I stood up and looked at the both of them, then I realized what I had done. I went into McDonald's and asked them to call the cops.

Now I am in prison. I guess that I won't be using my scholarship to go to college.

HECTOR

Tanya was the mother of my two children and I did the most horrible thing that anyone could do. I killed her in front of my two kids. I heard them screaming and crying, but I didn't care. I was so angry at her. I heard the kids in the background, they seemed so far away.

Tanya and I argued a lot and one day she just kept nagging at me. I was hung over, I felt like crap and she just wouldn't shut up. I yelled at her, telling her that I would mow the lawn later on. But she wouldn't close her mouth, so I got up and put one of my hands around her throat. The other hand I used to cover her mouth, anything to just shut her up. I had her backed up against the wall and I guess I didn't realize how hard I was pushing against her throat.

Finally she stopped nagging at me, she stopped doing everything. I let go of her and she fell to the floor.

When I realized that she was dead, I looked over at my kids who were screaming. I knelt down and pushed on her chest and I tried to give her mouth to mouth, but it didn't help. I ran over to the phone and called for help. I was arrested and my kids were sent to live with their grandparents.

I'm in prison now. This wouldn't have happened if she hadn't been nagging at me. If she had just shut her mouth...

JACOB

My name is Jacob and I'd actually see my mom beat up on my dad. For no reason at all she would just land into him. She would start hitting him.

I eventually got married and slowly I started to do things to my wife and kids. It was a very gradual thing, so I wasn't even aware that it was happening.

It started out as yelling, I would yell at my wife and at my kids. Then I started to slap them and from there, I gradually moved on to punching and kicking them.

I never realized how bad I made it for my family, until they left me. Then I had time to think about things. I felt real bad about the way I treated my entire family. I don't know where they are now. My wife left one day with the kids and I have no idea how to find them or where to begin looking.

I know that I caused them to leave because of my behavior. I only wish that I had treated them better.

TOMMY

My name is Tommy and my wife's name is Mary Ellen. I have been looking for her for three years now and I will never give up.

I hit her a few times and she left me. She has left me before, but she would always come back to me, eventually. This time is different because she hasn't come back yet.

When I had hit her a few times before, she'd leave. I would tell her that I was sorry and everything would be okay for a while.

We never had any kids and I guess that was a good thing. Mary Ellen was a nurse in a pediatricians office in town. I still can't believe that she would just walk away from her job and from me. She left everything behind.

Someday I will find her and she had better not be with any other guy.

BUTCH

Carrie was my first crush in school, I asked her out over and over again. Finally she agreed to go out with me. Once a month at our school, they held a dance and it was always on a Friday night.

After we had been going together for a few weeks I asked her if she wanted to go to the dance with me. Our parents were going to drop each of us off and we were going to meet out in front of the school.

I got there first and waited for Carrie near the stone wall. I sat and smoked a cigarette, while I watched everyone and waited for her. A while later, I saw Carrie get out of a car, along with her friend Annie.

I watched as Carrie looked around and walked over to Carl, he was a friend of mine. They looked around again and then they kissed. I'm not talking a little kiss, I mean a real kiss.

I got very mad and I walked over to them. I punched him and slapped her a few times. I couldn't believe it, he was my friend and she was my girlfriend.

I walked away from the both of them and I kept walking, until I got home.

When I went to school on Monday, Annie told me that Carrie wanted to break up with me. Later on that same day, I saw Carrie and Carl walking together down the hall holding hands. It bothered me some, but not as much as I thought that it would.

TOM

My name is Tom and I am in jail for beating up my wife. I beat her up so bad that she ended up in the hospital. I didn't realize how badly I had beaten her, but I put her in a coma.

The doctor's don't know if she will ever wake up and if she does she may never be able to function normally again.

I did love her, I do love her.

All of this happened, because she spent too much money on groceries. What a stupid reason to hurt someone.

UNKNOWN

My wife and I were married for three years and during the entire time, I maybe hit her a total of ten times. But I know that she remembered each and every one of those times. I made sure that she would remember them.

I wanted things done a certain way in my home. I figured because I paid the bills, that whatever way I wanted things to be, that's the way that they were going to be.

For some reason she didn't or couldn't understand that and occasionally she would try to test me. And on those occasions I would again lay down the law for her.

I don't know where she is right now, she left me. But we are still married and she is still my wife. One day I will find her and she will be sorry that she walked out on me.

MARVIN

My name is Marvin and I was dating a girl named Jessica. We only actually went out a few times, the first time we got along pretty well. I thought that things were going good between us, but apparently I was wrong.

By our third date she told me that things just weren't working out between us. I admit that I got upset and I slapped her, I know that it was wrong. I quickly apologized to her, but she walked away from me and wouldn't listen to me.

I felt bad and the more I thought about it, the worse I felt. I tried to call her, but she wouldn't accept any of my calls. I sent her some flowers with a note and then I stopped bothering her. I never did hear back from her, I didn't want her to think I was stalking her.

I had never hit a woman before that or since then.

STEVE

My name is Steve and my girlfriend and I went out together for a few years. Usually we got along pretty well, but when I wasn't working we fought. We fought verbally and physically, sometimes I would slap her, choke her or punch her.

I guess that I took out my frustrations on her. The police were always coming over to our apartment. Sometimes, they would arrest me and other times, they would just make me leave.

Eventually I'd go back, but only after promising her that I would never hit her again. She always took me back.

Then one day I'd blow up and I'd hurt her again. I can't explain why I did it and I know that I always felt bad after I hurt her.

I wasn't really mad at her, she just happened to be there. My brother and I used to argue a lot about our painting business. Each one of us wanted to be the boss and we would get pretty frustrated with each other.

My girlfriend walked out of our apartment one day and she never came back. If we could start all over again, I know that I would be able to treat her better.

TOM

Sylvia and I worked together and dated once in a while. We joked around at work and everyone got along great. She was a secretary and I was one of the ad executives.

I thought that Sylvia and I had a relationship outside of work, but I found out later that she went out with a lot of other guys from work.

I started to follow her, so I could see for myself. I followed her home from work, then I sat in my car outside of her apartment, waiting and watching.

I didn't have long to wait, because within forty five minutes she came out. She was all dressed up and I watched her get into her car.

I followed her again, this time she drove to a restaurant and parked her car in the parking lot. I saw her walk up to the front door and wait outside.

Within a few minutes a man walked up to her and they kissed. When he turned around, I saw that it was Eddie from work. They went into the restaurant together, holding hands.

A few hours later they came out, they kissed again and then Sylvia walked over to her car. While they were inside the restaurant, I had moved my car over next to hers.

She unlocked her car door and then I jumped out in front of her.

"What?" she asked, surprised.

"What were you doing with Eddie?" I asked her.

"Tom, you and I are just friends." She told me, as she pushed past me to get into her car.

I felt like she had dismissed me and that made me mad. I reached into her car and pushed her back against the seat. Then I put my hands on her throat and squeezed as hard as I could.

She fought me a little, but when she realized that she was going to die, she stopped struggling. She seemed to be in shock. It was over pretty quickly and when I saw that she was dead, I backed out of her car. I got back inside my car and I left.

When I went into work the next day, everyone was talking about how Sylvia's body had been found. I tried to act natural, but eventually everyone started to become suspicious.

It didn't take the police long to find out that I had done it. I probably shouldn't have told anyone, but I did. I told a co-worker that I had done it, but they promised me that they wouldn't say anything to anyone.

Obviously they did, so now I am in prison.

WILLIAM

My name is William and I have been sentenced to life in prison. I killed Amanda, actually I killed seven people. They were all my co-workers, even Amanda.

Amanda and I dated for a while. When she told me that she wanted to date other people, I got pretty mad. I kept asking her to change her mind, but she would just laugh at me and tell me 'no way.'

So, one day I went to work with a gun. I opened fire on everyone I saw on my way to Amanda's cubicle.

CLARK

Janie was a girl who lived in the apartment next to me. She was so beautiful and popular. There were always lots of people at her apartment.

I was always a little slower than the other kids in school. They used to pick on me.

I'd get real shy when I was around Janie and I just couldn't seem to talk to her. When I tried, I would stutter and Janie and her friends would laugh at me.

One day, I got up the courage to ask her out and she started laughing at me. She kept on laughing. I got really upset and all I wanted was for her to stop laughing at me, I stopped her.

I strangled her and now she is dead. She won't ever laugh at me again. Now I live in the state hospital.

BRUCE

Crystal and I were married for eleven years. We had two daughters, Pam and Ashley. We never got along very well and I'm actually surprised that we stayed together, for as long as we did.

I used to hit all of my girls, but I used to really hurt Crystal. I sent her to the hospital more than once, to put in some stitches or to fix broken bones. I broke her arm, her ribs and I even knocked out a few of her teeth. I wish that it hadn't happened, but it did. I can't take any of it back.

Crystal took my two girls and left me one day while I was at work. I looked everywhere for them, I even grilled Crystal's family. No one knew where she'd gone. I eventually went to a shelter and I found them there.

I threatened everyone that was staying in the shelter and the next day they took off again. I have no idea where they are, but I don't think that they are anywhere near here anymore.

I do miss all of them, but I know if they were here, I'd still be hurting them.

ALAN

Cissy and I were married for fourteen years, then she filed for a divorce and moved out with my boys. Everything changed for us, once she started taking classes at the community college. She changed, it seemed like she would stand up to me a lot more.

She told me that she was tired of the violence inside our home. She said that she was going to make a better life for herself and for my boys.

We went to court and she got custody of the boys. I only got visitation every other weekend. The judge said that I also needed to go to counseling, for anger management.

Cissy rented a small house in town and I was so angry about everything. I remember thinking if I couldn't have us all together, that she wasn't going to have my boys with her. I just couldn't allow for that to happen.

One night, I took a full can of gas with me and I poured it all around that rented house of hers. Then I lit a cigarette and took a few puffs from it. I looked around and saw no one, it was two thirty in the morning. I threw the cigarette onto the gas and watched it catch on fire.

Man, it caught fire with a big whooshing sound. I watched as the flames swallowed up the entire house. I was pretty sure that I heard screaming coming from inside the house, but I ignored it.

When I was sure that no one was going to come out, I ran to my car and I left.

Three days later, I was arrested for the murder of my wife and kids. Stupid me, in my hurry to get away from there, I left the gas can with my fingerprints all over it.

STEPHEN

When my wife Alex left me, I was devastated. I felt like my whole world had fallen apart. She left me, because I had hit her a few times.

After she left I tried to talk her into coming home, but she wouldn't do it. I begged her and pleaded with her, but I still couldn't convince her.

One day I decided that I was going to kill us both, so that we could always be together. I went over to her mothers house and pushed open the door.

I grabbed Alex and sliced her throat with the knife, I was holding. Then I took the same knife and plunged it deep into my stomach.

I felt the blood draining out of my body and I passed out, I actually thought that I had died. But, I woke up in a hospital bed with my hand cuffed to the bed rail.

I had somehow managed to miss every major organ and artery, I was going to make it. Alex had died within minutes, of my cutting her throat.

As soon as I am able to leave the hospital, I'm going to prison.

TODD

Toni was separated when we started dating and I guess I thought she would file for a divorce soon. I moved in to her apartment with her and her two kids.

Things went okay for a while and then I heard from our neighbors, that Toni's husband had been coming around during the day, while I was at work.

I confronted Toni and she told me that they were going to give their marriage another try. She said they owed it to the kids, to try to make things work. She told me she was waiting for the right time to tell me.

I was so pissed off at her and I told her so. I even hit her a few times. I felt like she had made a total fool out of me.

I left the apartment that day, but I went back that night. Oh yeah, I went back. I took my shotgun with me and I busted down their door. I saw Toni and her husband sitting on the couch together. I raised my gun, I aimed and fired it, twice. I watched as they both slumped down on to the couch.

That's when I saw Toni's two kids, sitting on the floor. I pointed the gun at them and came very close to pulling the trigger. But I couldn't shoot those two little kids.

I guess that a neighbor must have called the cops, because before I could leave, they were there. I was roughly shoved down onto the floor and handcuffed.

Now I am in prison. I am glad that I didn't hurt the kids.

JACOB

My name is Jacob and I lived with my girlfriend Delilah for eight months. We argued a lot and sometimes I would slap her. I never punched her and I always hit her with an open hand, never a closed fist. I know that I shouldn't have ever hit her at all, but I did.

On a Wednesday, she told me that she wanted me to move out. She wanted to be able to date other people. She said that things just weren't working out between us. I moved out that day, but I went back on Thursday night.

I took a gun with me and I had planned on shooting her, for hurting me so bad. I went inside the apartment and walked into the bedroom, where she was sleeping. I stood next to the bed and I pointed the gun at her.

I stood there for what seemed like a very long time, with the gun pointed at her head. But for some reason, I couldn't pull the trigger.

I put the gun down and quietly left the room. I walked out of the apartment and I never went back.

Delilah never knew how close she came to dying that night. I am so glad that something stopped me from shooting her.

When I think back about that night, my hands still shake and I feel sick to my stomach.

BRICE

Sharon and I dated for a long time, but we never got married. She used to nag me constantly about getting married and I used to tell her not yet.

One afternoon, Sharon told me that she was pregnant. Man, did I get mad. I remember yelling something about her trying to trap me and then I slapped her.

She left me later that day and I haven't seen or heard from her since. I don't know if I have a kid out there or not.

ARNOLD

I remember when I was younger I used to hear my dad pounding on my mom. Usually he would punch her on the head, sometimes I'd see him kick her or throw food at her.

I don't remember how I felt when it was happening. I don't think that I felt anything. I guess, I thought it was normal. I thought that's what it was like in everyone's house.

I met Karen in college and we started going out. After we graduated we got married and moved into a small apartment.

I don't know why, but I started to hit her. Karen told me that I was going to go to counseling with her or else. I really did love Karen very much and I was afraid of what the 'or else' would be.

I had only slapped her about three times, but I guess that was enough for her. She used to get pretty disgusted when we would go over to my parents house and my dad would slap my mother in front of us.

Karen would tell my mother that she should leave before it got worse, but my mother didn't want to hear it.

Anyway I loved Karen and I wanted to be with her. I wanted to raise a family together. So I agreed to go to counseling with her.

That was five years ago and we still go to counseling. I haven't slapped her and we have three beautiful kids now.

I thank god every day that I had enough sense to go to counseling. Karen is the best thing that has ever happened to me and I will never again do anything to jeopardize that.

KEN

Jamie and I used to argue a lot, we still do, although I am much better about it now. Now I like to call it disagreeing, we disagree.

I punched Jamie once and she walked out on me for a few weeks. During that time, I came to realize how much she really meant to me. I missed her terribly and I knew that I didn't want to spend another day without her.

I went over to her sister's and told Jamie that I wanted to be with her, no matter what it took. We hugged and I apologized to her. I really did mean it this time.

We started going to therapy and we still go today. We probably will for quite a while, but I know how empty my life felt without her in it. I am willing to do whatever it takes to stay together.

SAMUEL

Andrea and I used to argue a lot, but I never hit her or punched her. Although, I once threw a hard boiled egg at her. We eventually broke up, but not because of that.

CHESTER

I was with Janet for two years and in the beginning, we got along great. She is an accountant and I am a mechanic. I always felt beneath her, because she was college educated and I wasn't. All of her friends were smart professional people and I felt inferior when I was around them.

I quit high school and got a job as a mechanic. I had worked there for fifteen years and I was now the manager. I met Janet when she brought her car in to be repaired. We flirted with each other and got along good.

We dated for almost two years, then we got married. I did want kids, but Janet said that she wasn't ready to start a family yet. So we started to fight over that and then we started to fight about money.

Eventually, we started to fight about anything and everything. I always felt like her friends were saying things behind my back. If I walked into the room, they would suddenly get very quiet. I automatically thought that they had been talking about me. If I would hear them laughing, I knew that they had to be laughing at me.

Janet would tell me that her friends liked me and that they would never say anything bad about me. I knew better, I could feel it. They all thought that because they were college graduates, they were better than me.

Janet told me that I was a good provider and that she loved me, but I wasn't so sure about that. Janet got a promotion at work and her friends threw a party for her. I went out onto the balcony for some fresh air and heard a few of her friends talking.

"And he's a mechanic." I heard one of them say. I heard it and then I heard them all start to laugh.

"She needs the promotion to be able to buy the extras." I heard another voice say.

I knew it, I knew that they had all felt that way. I was furious. I went back inside and I walked over to Janet.

"You are such a bitch!" I said to her, before I punched her in the face.

A group of guys tackled me and I was pushed to the floor. The rest is kind of blurry, I know that they dragged me out of the house and that they told me to leave.

I slowly walked home, because we had driven to the party in Janet's car. When I finally made it home. A few of the guys from the party were already there, waiting for me. They told me I had better just leave and not bother Janet again.

One of her friends brought me out a bag with some of my clothes in it. A few days later, a friend of Janet's called me and told me to come pick up the rest of my stuff. When I drove up to our apartment, I saw my things sitting out front in the grass.

Mark, an accountant friend of hers, was sitting in a lawn chair next to my stuff. I started to load up my things and he helped me. I never even saw Janet. Mark told me that Janet had filed for a divorce.

The next time I saw Janet, we were both standing in front of a judge.

DEVON

Tracey and I have been married for eighteen years. I never once raised a hand to her. At least not until our sixteenth year together. I guess I started hitting her because I was frustrated.

At work they had begun downsizing and no one seemed to know who was going to be let go next. It seemed like they let someone go each week, it was all very frustrating.

Tracey and I had started to argue more than ever. I even hit her a few times, which surprised us both. She told me that she wasn't going to throw our marriage away, not without a fight.

I loved Tracey, I really did, but I had so much on my mind at that time. I was worried about losing my job. Where would I get another job? Especially one that offered me all of the benefits, that this one did.

One night Tracey and I sat down and I told her all about what was going on at work. I told her how worried I was and how sorry I was that I had hit her. I cried, I sat there in front of my wife and I cried. For the first time in my adult life, I actually cried.

Tracey came over to me and hugged me. She told me that together we would get through all of this.

That was two years ago, I got laid off, but I found another job. It doesn't offer as much as the other one, but I also don't have the deductions taken out of my paycheck each week. I'm even making more money now.

Tracey has started working part time and she loves it. We get along so much better now. She said that she was becoming bored sitting home all the time. We both feel that having a job has been a good thing for her.

We also go to counseling with our pastor once a week. We couldn't be happier and I hope to spend our seventy-fifth anniversary together.

HOMER

Sami was a woman who I was very attracted to. For some reason, she seemed to like to hang around real loud guys. I was a pretty quiet guy. I kept to myself and never bothered anyone.

We lived in the same building, sometimes we even rode up in the same elevator. I liked those times in the elevator, because we would talk. Even if it was just a few words, that was okay with me.

I had such a crush on her. I used to write her notes and poems, then I would slide them under her door. I never signed them though, because I didn't want her to know that they were from me.

One day when I was in the elevator, the doors started to close. I noticed Sami running towards the elevator. Quickly I put my arm out, to keep the doors open.

"Thanks." Sami said, smiling and winking at me.

Okay, I thought to myself. I finally felt like I had the courage to ask her out. All that I had needed was a little encouragement.

"Do you want to go out sometime?" I asked her, quietly.

"Are you joking?" Sami asked me, starting to laugh.

"No. Do you want to go out to dinner with me?" I asked her again, confused as to why she thought that what I had asked her was so funny.

"Do you really think that I would go out with you?" she asked me, still laughing.

"What about the poems, did you like them?" I asked her, trying to think of something to say.

"You wrote those pathetic things? Oh god, this is too funny." she was laughing hysterically now.

"You didn't like them?" I asked her, starting to get mad.

She was holding onto her stomach when she said, "Oh please, stop. This is just too funny."

I was furious. How dare she laugh at me, I thought as I pushed the stop button on the elevator. She looked very surprised when I roughly pushed her back against the wall of the elevator. Then I pushed the plastic dry cleaners bag I was holding, against her face.

"Who's laughing now?" I yelled at her.

She tried clawing at me and at the bag I was holding against her face. I heard her whimpering, but I didn't care. I just wanted to erase the sound of her laughter.

I never would have written those notes and poems for her, if I'd known that she was going to act like this. Slowly she slipped down to the floor and I pulled my bag away from her face.

She was so ugly now, her eyes were bulging and her tongue was sticking out of the side of her mouth. I stared down at her and then I gave her a good hard kick.

"You shouldn't have laughed at me, you bitch." I said to her, even though I knew she was dead and that she couldn't hear me.

I pushed the number three button. When the doors opened up I saw Mr. and Mrs. Sanford, standing there. They looked at me and then they looked down at Sami.

"Oh my god!" Mrs. Sanford whispered.

Mr. Sanford grabbed his wife by the arm and they quickly ran down the hall, back to their apartment.

I stepped out of the elevator and looked back at Sami before the doors closed. I walked down the hall to my apartment and waited for the police to show up. I didn't have to wait for very long. I was arrested a short while later. I had a trial and now I am in a psychiatric hospital.

HANK

Jasmine and I had a very strange relationship. Most of the time we fought. Although sometimes, we actually got along. I would get so angry at her, sometimes I would hit her and once in a while I would choke her. A few times I punched her or I would kick her. Once I sat on top of her and beat her bad.

She would leave me for a while and then I would find her and convince her to come back home. She almost always came home.

One time she didn't come back and I couldn't find her anywhere. I looked in all of the places that I had always found her before, but it was like she had just disappeared. I still haven't found her.

TONY

Britney and I went out together when we were seniors in high school. She was much smarter than I was, but that didn't bother me at first. I was a big guy and whenever anyone gave me or Brit a hard time, I'd just pound them.

One afternoon in January, Brit told me she wanted to break up with me. She told me that she had gotten a scholarship to go away to college. She wanted to start all over, she wanted no ties at all to the past.

"No way." I told her. "You are not going to leave me, you are never going to leave me."

"Tony, I am leaving here. You can't make me stay here." she said, as she started to get out of my car.

I punched her on the side of the head and she fell back against the seat, dazed. I drove out of the parking lot and pulled on an old dirt road, which led into the woods. I looked over at Brit and saw that she was crying, quietly. I grabbed her by the wrist and pulled her closer to me.

"You are not going to leave me. I love you." I told her.

"We've only been going out for three months! How can you possibly be in love with me?" she yelled at me.

"We are going to stay together, always. We will be together, dead or alive." I told her, squeezing her harder.

"You are crazy! I am going to go away to college. We are now officially broken up," she said, pulling her arm from me.

"You are not going to leave me." I yelled at her. She opened the car door and got out.

I jumped out of the car and opened up the trunk. I grabbed out the tire iron and ran up behind her.

"You bitch!" I yelled at her, swinging the tire iron as hard as I could. I hit her in the back of the head and she fell to the ground. There was blood running down the side of her face and she didn't move. She didn't move at all, she just lay there very still. I could see that she wasn't breathing.

I panicked and rolled her body down the embankment, then I wiped the blood from the tire iron on some leaves. There was still a little blood on it, but I figured that it would dry. I put the tire iron back inside my trunk and I drove home.

Later that night, the police came to my door and asked me some questions. Her parents reported her as missing, when she hadn't come home for dinner. I guess some of the kids at school saw us leave together, earlier that day. The cops asked if they could search my car and my dad told them okay. I was a minor, so my dad could give them permission, even if I didn't want them to.

One of them found the tire iron, with the blood from Brit still on it. They took me to the police station and they also impounded my car. When they searched my trunk they found more of her blood on the carpet.

They tested the blood and found out that it was hers. I admitted what I had done to her and I told them where they could find her body. I was arrested for her murder.

Today as the rest of my class graduates, I am sitting alone in a jail cell.

I wasn't allowed to go to her funeral, even though I told them I had really loved her.

RYAN

Farah was my wife, well actually she still is. I just don't know where she is at the moment.

We were married for six years, before she left me. Today is our anniversary and we would be celebrating our tenth year together. Our daughter Katie, was four at the time and now she would be eight-years-old.

I was a lousy husband and a terrible father. I was really a miserable person. I have made a lot of changes since then and now I really feel that I am a better person.

I wish I knew where they were, so I could tell them I am sorry and ask them for another chance.

I have been going to counseling for the last three years. I really didn't like the person that I had become. I wanted to change and I am pretty sure I've changed for the better.

I'd love to have my family back again.

BRYAN

My girlfriends name is Kate and we lived together for two years. Then she walked out on me. We have a baby named Caleb, she took him with her.

We got along pretty good, well, at least until she started to work. Then my dinner wouldn't be ready, when I got home. Most of the time, she was pretty lousy about keeping up with cleaning the house and doing the laundry. That used to get me mad.

Caleb used to go to work with her, because she worked in a day care center. They told her that she could take him with her. She told me how much he used to enjoy watching the other kids play.

Anyway the longer she worked, the more independent she became. I hated it, I felt like she didn't need me anymore. I would get mad at her and yell or slap her. She really didn't do anything wrong. I just wanted to feel needed and I didn't feel like she needed me anymore.

One day she came home and I was already on my way to getting pretty drunk. She said something, I can't even remember what it was. But I remember getting real mad at her and I know that I hurt her bad.

She took Caleb and spent the night in the guest room, with the door locked. I guess that I passed out, because when I woke up it was light outside and I was still sitting in my recliner.

I didn't see her at all that morning, but I'll bet that she came right out after I left. I made myself some breakfast and ate it alone that morning. All that day, I tried calling her from work. I called the day care center and they told me that she had called in sick. Then I called our house and no one answered.

When I got home at 6:30 that night, the house was totally dark. I opened the front door and called out her name. I went from room to room looking for Kate and Caleb. I found no one.

That was six years ago, but I can remember it like it just happened yesterday. I knew that I shouldn't have let her go to work. That ruined everything for us.

RICK

Sasha worked in the ice cream shop in the mall. She looked so cute, in the uniform that they made her wear. I worked in the book store and I used to watch her all day long, I never got tired of watching her. I was a little older than she was, but I was okay with that. She was seventeen and I was thirty eight. They say that age doesn't matter, right?

A lot of times I'd watch guys walk over to her and try to talk with her, but I could tell that she didn't like any of them. She was always so busy working, she didn't have the time to talk much, even to me. Besides, why would she waste her time with any of them? They were all high school kids who probably still lived at home with their parents. I had my own apartment and a full time job.

She had come into the book store a few times, when she was on a break. We said hello to each other and I would try to think of things to say to her. I found her to be very polite and very friendly. I liked her very much.

Sasha didn't act like a seventeen-year-old and I never saw her hanging out at the mall on her days off, like other kids did.

One day I took a break right before Sasha was due to come into work. I waited in the parking lot for her to show up. I finally saw her pull up in an older looking Chevy. I waited in my car and I watched her walk into the mall. I got out of my car, walked over to her car and I pulled out two of her plug wires. I put them inside my trunk and then I quickly walked back inside the mall.

Later, when I took my dinner break I went over to the ice cream shop. Sasha and I talked for a few minutes and I told her that if she ever needed anything, all she had to do was ask.

That night as the last few shoppers left the mall, I quickly did everything I had to do, so I could close and get out of there. I had noticed about ten minutes before closing, a large group of people had gone inside the ice cream shop. I couldn't believe my luck.

I walked by the ice cream shop as I was leaving. I saw that she was almost ready to lock up. I quickly went out to the parking lot and got into my car. I started my car and waited for Sasha to come out. I noticed that there were only a few cars left in the parking lot.

About ten minutes later, I saw Sasha come out of the main mall entrance and head towards her car. She walked quickly, the temperature had dropped quite a bit and it was pretty cold out.

I watched Sasha get into her car and try to start it. I saw her get out and open up the hood. For a few minutes I panicked, thinking that she might notice the missing plug wires. Then I could tell that she knew absolutely nothing about cars, she looked totally lost as she looked around.

She looked like she was trying to decide whether or not to go back inside the mall. I didn't want to blow my chance, so I drove over to her and opened up my car window.

"Are you having problems?" I asked her, trying to sound concerned.

"My car won't start, I don't know what's wrong with it. I guess it's just too cold out here." She said, shivering and pulling her jacket tightly around herself.

I got out of my car and told her to try to start her car up, of course it didn't start. I knew that it wouldn't.

"Why don't I hook up my jumper cables and you can wait in my car, while your battery charges up." I suggested to her.

"No, I'll be fine out here," she protested.

"Nonsense, I insist. My car is warm and it should only take a few minutes to get yours going." I pressured her.

"Okay," she said quietly, walking over to the passenger door of my car. "Thanks."

I watched her get inside my car, then I walked over to my trunk. I got out my jumper cables and hooked them up to my car. Then I went over to her car and pretended to hook them up. I shut both of the hoods down a little and I walked back over to my car. I smiled at Sasha as I climbed into the driver's side.

"It shouldn't take too long." I told her, with a smile. "I've got a new battery."

We made small talk for about ten minutes, then I suggested she try to start her car. I followed her over to her car and watched as she tried to start it, again it didn't start.

"Well, I can give you a ride somewhere if you want, because that about covers all of my knowledge about cars." I offered.

"No. Thanks for trying, but I'll just go back into the mall and call my mom. She'll come get me and then her boyfriend can look at it in the morning," she said, climbing out of her car.

I didn't want her to leave, that would have ruined everything. I took the flashlight I was holding and I hit her over the head with it. I dragged her over to my car and shoved her into the front seat. Then I went back to her car and shut her car door. I took my jumper cables out and threw them back into my trunk. I shut down both of the hoods and then I climbed back into my car.

I drove for a while, until I found a quiet place to pull over. I wanted to get off of the main road. It was a good thing that I pulled over when I did, because Sasha was starting to moan and move around. It looked like it had been an old road at one time, but parts of it were now grown over with tall grass and weeds.

"What happened?" Sasha asked me, rubbing her head.

"I think that it's time for us to begin our lives together." I told her.

"What are you talking about?" she asked me, her eyes widened in surprise.

"I know that you like me and I like you. I can tell by the way you talk to me. You are so friendly to me." I said to her.

"We have only talked together a few times. I don't even know your name," she told me. "I don't know anything about you. Besides, I have to be friendly to everyone. It's part of the job."

"I have been watching you, since the first day that you started to work at the mall. I want to be your boyfriend." I told her with a smile, not listening to her.

"But you are way older than me. I already have a boyfriend and his name is Danny." She said, as she tried to back away from me. "You are so old, that's just too creepy!"

"No!" I said, slamming my fist onto the dashboard. "I am your boyfriend now. I care about you and I am the only one who can really love you."

"Please, let me go." Sasha pleaded, as she started to cry.

"Why are you afraid of me?" I asked her. "I love you and we are going to be together forever."

"No!" she yelled. She opened up the door and tried to get out.

I pulled her back by the hair. "You are not going to leave me, ever. I'll kill you first." I told her. She grabbed at me, trying to get me to loosen my grip on her.

Suddenly she punched me in the face, I was completely caught off guard. I didn't expect it at all and I let go of her hair. Seeing an opportunity, she jumped out of the car. I saw her start to run off, but she wasn't running very fast. I think that it was a combination of not knowing exactly where she was and the fact that I had knocked her unconscious earlier. She seemed a little dazed.

I started the car and quickly caught up to her. She kept running and looking back at me. I chased her for a while, kind of enjoying it. But, I soon got bored and gunned the engine.

I watched her fly up onto the hood of my car. I slammed on the brakes, she rolled off the hood and then fell onto the ground. I drove over her and I slammed the car into reverse, then back into drive again. I kept going back and forth over her body. Each time that I ran her over, I felt the car rise slightly.

I stopped and backed up, so that my headlights were shining on her still body. I could see that her blond hair was now mostly red, matted together from her blood. I felt sick to my stomach. I opened the car door, I leaned out and threw up.

I got out of the car and walked over to Sasha's body. I suddenly realized how still it was outside, alone on that dirt road. No one else was around and I kind of got spooked out there, with Sasha's dead body. I ran back over to my car and jumped inside. I threw the car into gear and sped out of there, sending gravel flying as I left. I went home and then I went straight to bed. I tried not to think about what had happened.

The next day, I went to work as usual. I noticed that someone else was working in the ice cream shop. I took my lunch break at around noon. When I went back into the book store, I was surprised to see my manager talking to a couple of cops. Betsy, my manager, pointed over at me. The officers walked up to me, they roughly handcuffed me and told me that I was under arrest for Sasha's murder.

The mall security guard had seen me talking to Sasha in the parking lot the night before. I also found out that when I leaned out of my car to throw up, I dropped my name tag onto the ground. Apparently, Sasha had ripped it off me when we'd been struggling in the car.

HUSBAND ABUSE

These are stories that are rarely ever told or heard about and yet this is becoming more and more common. These men bravely open up and tell their stories. Stories about being hit and even beaten by their wives or girlfriends. Some of the abusive relationships lasted for just weeks, while others stay in their relationships, where the abuse lasts for years.

These men have no one they can turn to. No one they can talk with about these things, without the fear of being ridiculed.

JACK

My wife Hilda has a terrible temper. I was raised to never hit a woman…no matter what she did to me. Hilda will slap me and punch me, when she is angry. There is no one that I can turn to. Do I want to admit that my wife beats me up? Of course not.

MARK

My name is Mark and my wife Denise is a mean and awful drunk. When she starts to drink, I try to stay out of her way, because she gets very, very angry.

I have gone into work more than once with a black eye. I hope that everyone at work thinks I get into fights at the bar, but that couldn't be farther from the truth. Denise fights like a man and I have never hit her back.

PHIL

My wife Sheila is a very hot tempered woman. Actually it would be pretty comical, if I wasn't the one getting hurt. I'm six foot two and she stands at five foot two, she maybe weighs a hundred pounds, soaking wet. It doesn't take much to get her mad and then watch out!

I have gone to work with cuts and bruises all over my face and neck. I have never raised a hand to her, although I do try to protect myself. When I can tell 'a mood' is coming on I try to avoid her, but that isn't always possible.

I have mentioned to her that we should get some counseling, but she gets upset about that. She has hit me with objects like glass, silverware and especially her fists.

I don't know what to do. Who can I talk to about it? I feel alone. I love my wife, but I am tired of being her punching bag.

CARMINE

My name is Carmine and I once dated a woman who I thought was perfect. Well, at least until she began to get abusive towards me. Trudie would hit me, punch me, kick me and ridicule me.

One day she hauled off and slammed me on the head with a beer bottle. I had it, that was when I split up with her. I told her that I was done.

The next night I woke up to the sound of glass breaking. I looked out of my window and saw Joan and one of her friends, hitting my car windows with a baseball bat. I called the cops on her and both of them were arrested.

When Joan got out of jail, she came back to my apartment and pounded on my door, screaming that she was going to kill me. For about two weeks she came back almost every night, drunk and sometimes sober. She'd bang on my door.

Then I started to get phone calls, breathing at first and then threats were whispered into the phone.

I got so sick and tired of it, but there was no one I could tell. What kind of a guy would I look like?...a big wimp!

I did what I had to do, I moved. I left my apartment and moved in with a friend of mine. I hired movers to get my stuff and put it into storage for me. It cost me a lot of money, but it was worth it. She never bothered me again after that.

RON

My name is Ron and I dated Kevin for six months. During that time, he was very dominating and controlling. At first I must admit, I was kind of flattered. But soon, I grew tired of being questioned about what I did, as well as being told what I could and could not do.

I stood up to Kevin and told him that I wasn't going to continue to live like this. To my surprise, Kevin slapped me! Tears welled up in my eyes, I had never been hit before. Kevin grabbed me by my wrist and twisted it.

"Leave me alone." I begged him.

Kevin laughed at me and called me a whiny little bitch. I felt the tears slide down my cheeks. Kevin looked at me with disgust and pushed me away from him. I fell back onto the coffee table where I hit my wrist. I heard a loud snap and then I felt a very sharp pain, followed by a throbbing.

"I'm going out." Kevin said to me, as he slammed the door shut behind him.

I picked up the phone and called my friend Donald. Half an hour later, with the help of Donald, I was packed and I left the apartment.

Donald brought me to the emergency room, where my wrist was x rayed. I discovered I had broken a bone in my wrist. The doctor put on a temporary cast and I was told to make an appointment with an orthopedic surgeon, for the next day.

I slept at Donald's apartment for two weeks and then I moved in with my friend Tom, who had an extra bedroom. I never went back to that apartment and I never saw Kevin again.

My wrist healed up after six weeks and it's as good as new. I have a new man in my life now, who treats me great. Charles and I are very happy together.

ANDY

Valerie was my girlfriend for two months. The first time that she hit me, I kind of laughed it off. Then she steadily became more and more violent.

I was afraid of her. She could be so nice and then all of a sudden, she could turn on you.

She used to tell me if I ever left her, she would kill me. I did believe her, because she seemed pretty unstable to me.

I got tired of walking on egg shells around her. Even my friends were concerned about her frequent and violent outbursts.

I split up with her and got some real annoying phone calls for a while, but they eventually stopped.

BILL

My name is Bill and I met Ann Marie five years ago. We are still together and I can't explain why. I know that I should leave her, but I love her. Besides, she isn't always abusive and violent towards me.

Sometimes we will go for months, without any outbursts from her. Other times, she stays grumpy and bitchy for days at a time.

I never know what to expect from her when I walk through the door. It is kind of like living with Jekyll and Hyde.

I guess that we will always be together anyway, I don't really want to leave her. She is the most beautiful woman I have ever been with. She loves me and she sure knows how to keep life exciting.

Don't get me wrong, I don't like to get beat on. I get embarrassed when she cuts me down in front of my friends or when she hits me in front of them.

But I also know that I'm not the best looking guy and I know that she could do much better than me.

AL

My name is Al and I dated Martha for over a year. That was the longest year of my life. Martha wasn't physically abusive, but she sure was verbally abusive. She cut me down all of the time, she would tell me that I was ugly or fat or even stupid.

Martha used to make me feel like dirt. She would flirt with other guys all of the time and she made me feel pretty bad about it. She never thought about how I felt or if her words and actions hurt me.

I kept hoping that she would change, but I also found myself wondering if she might be right. Was I fat? Was I ugly or stupid? Was I really ignorant?

I admit that I probably had little or no self esteem when I was with her. My work started suffering and my friends stopped coming around. They told me that it was too painful to watch her degrade me.

Finally, I walked out on her and I never went back. Today I am doing great and dating a really wonderful woman, who treats me with respect.

RODNEY

My name is Rodney, I am plain looking and kind of short. I manage a grocery store. People look up to me and listen to me there. I am respected at work. I am confidant and in charge.

But at home things are very different. My wife Penny wears the pants in our house. She runs me and all four of our kids. When Penny talks, we listen and if Penny yells, we run! I would be so embarrassed if anyone from work knew what it was like inside my house.

I can't leave her, because I would be too worried about the kids. They are the only reason that I stay with her. If we didn't have any kids or if they were grown and gone, I would leave her.

Through the years she has gotten worse. But I am here for now, at least until the kids leave home. Then maybe I will too.

TOM

Tara and I have been dating for a little over a month, but that is about to end. She is constantly belittling me in front of my family and friends. They all laugh, uncomfortably. I can see they are embarrassed for me.

She has even punched me in the face a few times. Okay, maybe it was wrong to look at another woman, but that is all I did. I just looked, I didn't say anything or even flirt…nothing.

Those punches were totally unprovoked and I didn't deserve them. I am splitting up with her this weekend…over the phone!

JIM

Phyllis was a little older than me, but the age difference never seemed to be an issue, until we started to hang out with her friends.

She started to treat me like a waiter, 'get me this or get me that.' I did at first, but then she started to talk down to me in front of her friends. She made me feel inferior, because I was not only younger than they were, but I wasn't a college graduate either.

Phyllis started to be real rude to me. Then one day I told her that I didn't feel like making her a coffee. She looked at me with fire in her eyes. I noticed that her friends were waiting to see what she would do next. She stood up, walked right over to me and punched me in the face.

"Don't ever talk to me in that tone." Phyllis said, staring at me.

I didn't. I turned around and walked out. I never went back there.

BEN

My name is Ben and I met a girl named Alex at a club. We both went to the same college, which made things real convenient.

I lived in a fraternity and she lived off campus, in an apartment. I spent a lot of time in her apartment. Her roommate Carla was nice, but kind of a flirt. I tried to ignore her for the most part, because Alex would get mad.

We dated for about four months and things were okay. But the longer we were together, the more possessive she got. She didn't want me to talk to anyone else. She didn't want me to hang out with my friends and she wanted me to spend all of my time with her. I was just dating her, I wasn't married to her.

One night there was a party at my fraternity and I went to it. A while later, Alex came storming inside and walked right up to me.

"What do you think you're doing?" she asked me.

"Having a good time." I told her.

She made a fist and I felt it land across my cheek. Boy, was that a surprise! People that were standing near us, turned to see what was going on.

"Let's go." Alex said to me, grabbing me by the arm.

"No." I told her. "I'm not going anywhere with you."

She slapped me again. "I said, let's leave now!" She yelled at me, causing more people to turn towards us.

"What are you? Psycho?" I asked her, quietly.

Alex totally lost it and she went after me. Her fists started flying and she made contact with me.

"Let's go!" she yelled at me, even louder than before.

"We are through." I told her, as I turned to walk away.

Suddenly, she was clinging to me and hitting me in the back and on the head with her fists. Some of the guys managed to pull her off of me. They led her outside and told her not to come back or they were going to call the cops on her.

I was really embarrassed, as I looked around the room. But everyone was real cool about what had happened.

Some girls even came over to me and talked for a while. I did manage to somehow enjoy myself after that embarrassing scene.

Alex followed me around campus for weeks. She was always standing across the street, outside of my frat house.

Eventually she got tired and she gave up. I haven't seen or heard from her in months.

JACK

My name is Jack and I was married to Jessica for fifteen years. During that time she was very abusive; emotionally, mentally and physically. But I stayed with her, because I was too ashamed to explain to people what was happening.

Most of the time the abuse was just verbal, but sometimes she would hit me, punch me, bite me or kick me. I had no one to talk to. Who do you talk to about these things?

When Jessica would start to beat on me, I could see the disgust on my kids faces. Why didn't I do something? Why didn't I stop her? How could I let her do these things to me?

I sure couldn't talk to my father about it. He would have called me a big sissy and I would have never lived it down. I would never have even thought about telling my friends or co-workers. There is no place to go or no one for a man to talk to about these things. This is a taboo topic.

When I felt that our kids were old enough, I left Jessica. Since moving out, I found that more men are coming forward, but still not that many. How many men want to admit that their wives are beating them up?

ANDY

I'm Andy and my wife, Carol was physically abusive towards me. The first time she hit me, I let it go.

The second time I called the police. When they finally showed up, they laughed at me. One of them asked me, "Can't you control your wife?" I felt like a real loser. I was ashamed and embarrassed. After the cops left, she really showed me how angry she was!

After living with the abuse for a few months, I walked out. I moved in with a male friend of mine.

A week later Carol was banging at his door and threatening me. Phil let her in and he asked her what her problem was. Carol completely ignored him. She came after me, clawing me, kicking me and spitting at me. All I did was hold up my hands, trying to protect myself.

Phil came up behind her and he grabbed her.

"What is your problem?" he asked me. "How can you let this psycho bitch, do these things to you?"

"I left her to stop this." I told him quietly, avoiding his eyes.

He led Carol to the door and pushed her outside, then he quickly closed the door and locked it. Carol continued to pound on the door, creating quite a disturbance.

"Call the cops." Phil told me.

I went to the phone and placed the call. Within minutes, a police car pulled up and they took Carol away.

A few hours later the cops came back and arrested me and Phil for assault. Carol had pressed charges against us, saying that we had hit her, repeatedly.

We went to court and everything. Carol stuck to her story about the abuse that we had inflected on her. The judge believed her, even after Phil and I told our side of it.

"You mean to tell me, that this tiny little woman was beating up on you?" The judge asked me, as he chuckled.

"Yes she did." I responded, embarrassed.

"I'm sorry, but I don't believe your side of the story. I can't see how this woman could have possibly done all of those things to you." The judge said to me.

Phil and I looked at each other.

"Furthermore, I am very disturbed that you two grown men, would try to blame this quiet defenseless woman. I am ready to pass judgement now. Both of you two gentlemen will spend ninety days in jail, attend an anger management course and you Mr. Barrows, are to stay at least fifty feet away from your wife. I can't believe that you both would stand in my courtroom, before me and lie about a thing like this. Perhaps you'll learn your lesson." The judge said, as he started shuffling through some of the papers on his desk.

I looked over at Carol and she was smiling sweetly at me. I went to jail for three months and was labeled as a wife abuser. I lost my job and all of my things. I couldn't understand what had happened. All I do know, is that we had a real ignorant judge. The only good thing to come from this, is that I got rid of Carol.

ERIC

My name is Eric. Bonny and I were married for sixteen years. During that time I was physically abused, there, I said it and the walls didn't come crashing down.

Bonny used to bite me, slap me, punch me, kick me and put me down constantly. The worst part is, I just took it. I never once laid a hand on her, I was raised to never hit a woman.

Things got so bad that even my daughters used to abuse me. I didn't know what to do or who to turn to.

My whole family treated me like dirt, all that I was good for was to bring home the money. No one respected me or even listened to me.

When my daughters were thirteen and fifteen, I left. I had put up with the abuse for way too long. My self worth was so low. Honestly, the only reason that I left when I did, was because I met a woman at work.

Nikki listened to me, she respected me and she was the only person who I told . She encouraged me to leave, she had also been in an abusive marriage. Together we bonded and started a wonderful friendship, which in time grew. We eventually fell in love.

Today Nikki and I are both divorced. I am feeling really good about myself. Nikki and I are very happy together.

I hardly ever see my ex wife. My daughters don't have too much to do with me, but I am okay with that. I have tried to have a relationship with the girls, but they treat me so badly. I feel I'm better off, just seeing them occasionally.

GEORGE

My name is George and I was married to Sarah for two years. I thought that I was a good husband and a good provider. I took care of Sarah, I gave her a nice place to live and nice things. But no matter what I seemed to do, it just never seemed good enough for her.

Sarah used to hit me quite a bit and she didn't care who saw. I was embarrassed by her outbursts, but they didn't seem to phase her at all.

If I brought her the wrong item back from the grocery store, she would hit me in the head or slap me across the face. People would always turn around and stare at us, when she had an outburst. I couldn't wait to get out of wherever we were, because people would laugh, whisper or point at me.

We went to my nephew's graduation party and Sarah went nuts. She had been drinking and got very loud. I was talking with my sisters friend, Ann. We had grown up together, but there had never been anything more than a very strong friendship between us.

Sarah saw us talking, came over and started pounding on my chest and face. Everyone just stared, not sure what to do and trying to figure out what was happening.

I tried to walk away from her, but she wouldn't let me. She jumped up onto my back, she pulled my hair and scratched at my face. Without thinking I twisted around, trying to push her off of me.

Sarah fell to the floor, hitting her head on the edge of a table. I turned and looked down in horror as she just lay there. She didn't move and it didn't look like she was breathing.

Someone finally reacted and ran over to her, someone else called for help. It was so quiet in the room, all I heard was the pounding of my heart in my ears. Slowly people began to talk and whisper, but I didn't pay any attention to what they were saying.

I knew that I had killed my wife. I was sad and yet in some strange way, relieved.

The ambulance and the police came. The ambulance took Sarah away and the police began questioning everyone. I wasn't arrested, because they considered it an accident. I was trying to walk away from the situation. I was trying to remove myself. I was the one being attacked and all that I did was try to get her off my back. I didn't expect her to hit her head. There were enough witnesses there to confirm it.

I feel bad that she died, but now I don't have to deal with anymore abuse.

SAM

Lucy and I dated for several months and during that time she hit me twice. The second time, I left her. There was no way that I was going to let any woman use me as a punching bag. She could find another way to take out her frustrations.

Today, I am very happy. My wife and I recently had a beautiful baby girl. We have a wonderful life together, filled with love and a mutual respect.

MARK

Donna and I dated for a while. My name is Mark and I have a band, which plays out in clubs quite a bit. I actually met Donna at a club. She seemed real sweet at first, but then I realized how insecure and jealous she really was.

Of course, being in a band, girls tend to flock to you. I didn't encourage it, but some of the other guys did.

One night a real pretty blond girl walked up to the edge of the stage to request a song. Seeing this, Donna ran up onto the stage and shoved me away from the girl. Then she started to pound on my chest with her fists. I grabbed her by the wrists, so she would stop. All that did was get her even angrier.

One of the bouncers saw what was going on. He ran over and grabbed Donna around the waist. He pulled her back, away from me.

I walked over to my guitar and picked it up from the stage floor, then we started to play again. The bouncer talked to Donna, trying to calm her down.

He walked away, I guess he figured that everything was okay. Donna grabbed a pitcher of beer from off one of the tables and she threw it at me. It hit me right on the head and it felt like my head split open. The beer ran down the side of my face and I remember thinking that it felt extremely warm. The pitcher had smashed and I had quite a gash on the side of my head from it. Everyone started yelling and screaming.

The bouncer jumped up and grabbed Donna, he held her while a few of my band members tried to stop the bleeding. I blacked out and when I came to, I was in a recovery room. I received over one hundred stitches on my head and I also had a concussion.

I had to take some time off from playing for a while. Donna kept calling me and coming over to my apartment. I stopped answering my phone and the door.

Eventually, she seemed to get tired of bothering me. But as soon as I started playing out again, she was right back at the clubs. I told her I didn't want anything to do with her and I wanted her to leave me alone. She was furious and she started screaming at me right there in the club. The bouncer came over to us and he told her that she had to leave the club.

After our gig was over, I went out to my car. I discovered that she had gone to the bathroom on the hood of my car and smeared it all over my windshield. I was so disgusted. What was wrong with her?

Five months later, Donna sent me a letter telling me that she was six months pregnant. She said that I was the father. It was impossible. I hadn't seen her for five months and I had been laid up for two months before that. There was no way that the kid was mine, if she was even pregnant. I didn't respond to her letter and I never heard from her again.

TODD

My name is Todd and I dated Lynn in high school. She was kind of loud, where I was kind of quiet. We got along pretty good, well, at least until she started to accuse me of cheating on her.

I never did cheat on her, but I had lots of friends, both male and female. Anyway, I guess that she was just insecure. Whenever I talked to a girl or just looked at a girl, she would go crazy.

At first she used to get mad and yell, but then she started to hit me. That totally threw me, because I never knew anyone that got violent. My parents never even fought!

One day we had a fight in the lunch room, because a good friend of mine sat down next to me. Lynn threw the food from her tray at me and then she beat me in the head with the tray.

Finally someone came over and pulled her away from me. I must have looked funny with spaghetti hanging from my head and face, but after I wiped it off I saw that I was bleeding. She had cut me in the head with the tray. I went to the hospital and got eleven stitches. Three days later I broke up with her.

TIM

Rachel started out being real nice to me. She cooked for me, washed my clothes and was even good to my friends. Eventually I moved in with her, which turned out to be a real big mistake.

After I moved in she changed, she started demanding money from me. I didn't mind paying her money, you know, for rent and for food. But then she wanted me to hand over my whole paycheck. No way!

We would argue about money a lot. Then she started complaining about my friends. She told me that she didn't want my friends to come around anymore. I couldn't all of a sudden tell them that they weren't welcome. Besides, I had moved in, I paid rent and it was my place too. I told her that I wasn't going to tell my buddies they couldn't come over. She slapped me and told me that it was her apartment.

"Okay." I told her and I walked out. I never went back there either. The way I figure it, I can always buy new clothes.

RANDY

My partners name was Tico and my name is Randy. We were together for a little over two years. During that time, he would constantly tell me that I was stupid or ugly. Then he started to slap me and get more and more violent towards me.

Most of the time I never provoked him at all. I do admit that I would sometimes get upset and say things to him. I wanted to hurt him like he hurt me. It didn't always work, he would hit me.

But most of the time he would just come home in an ugly mood and slap me or choke me. If he had a bad day at work or if someone made a comment to him about being gay, he'd vent his anger on me.

I put up with verbal abuse from him too. Tico would call me a little queen or a fag. Duh! But it was the way that he said it. He spit the words out with such venom.

Sometimes after we would be intimate he would hit me, punch me or call me a fag. Maybe he was upset because he enjoyed it, I don't know.

The last time that he hit me, I ended up with a split lip and a black eye. I waited until the next day when he went to work, then I gathered up my things and I left. I walked out on him and I never went back.

Now I am in a loving, respectful relationship with a wonderful man and I am extremely happy.

JOSH

Bobbie was a small woman, but she was like a tiger. She could certainly take care of herself in a brawl. I saw her get into fights with women twice the size of her and walk away banged up. But she was still in better shape than them.

That was okay, until she started to vent her anger out on me. She would have to jump up to punch me in the face or on the head. I didn't ever do anything to warrant being hit by her.

At first I thought that it was funny, but I quickly grew tired of it. Maybe without even realizing it, I had encouraged her. I don't know, but when I'd tell her to knock it off, she wouldn't. So I'd grab her by the wrists, until she calmed down.

Soon she got to the point where she wouldn't calm down, while I was restraining her. She became more angry and more violent.

I decided that I'd had enough and I split up with her.

MARV

Tanya and I fought from the beginning, but she was stubborn and bullheaded. She was a spoiled little rich girl and she was used to getting what she wanted.

At first, if I didn't give in to her she would throw potatoes across the room at me. Those are hard to dodge and boy, do they hurt when they hit.

When she started throwing dishes and silverware, I got out of there quick.

Now I am married to a wonderful woman and we are expecting our first child this year.

MARK

My wife's name is Allison and she has done lots of really mean things to me. We got married when we were seniors in high school, because she got pregnant. We have a great kid named Mark, he'll be six this year.

Allison said it's my fault that she never went to college and it's my fault she got pregnant. Everything is always my fault. I basically ruined her life. It's funny, I remember there being two people.

She blames me for everything, 'If I had kept my grubby little paws off of her,' she wouldn't have gotten pregnant. Allison is also terribly mean to our boy, I think because he looks just like me. She blames him for ruining her figure and her life. My son and I just can't seem to win.

Allison get's so mean and spiteful. I also had planned on going to college, but I don't blame her or Mark for my not going. Besides, he's a great kid. Mark and I do a lot of things together. Mark loves sports and so do I.

Sometimes insults aren't enough, Allison will throws things at us. Occasionally she will even hit us. She started out just using her mouth as a weapon, which hurt, but when she throws something and actually makes contact, it really does hurt. She is also constantly calling Mark, a little bastard.

Allison really isn't much of a wife, she's even less of a mother. I can't take Mark and leave, because Allison told me that she would get custody. She doesn't want him, but she doesn't want me to have him either. I am not going to leave my son alone with her. So I guess that I will be staying here with her, for a while.

TAD

My name is Tad and my wife's name is Maria. We have been married for four years. During that time, I have been hit quite a bit. The worst is when she does it in front of people.

Maria has a very demanding job and lots of pressure, which she doesn't handle well. One time she got passed up for a promotion, which she felt she deserved. She came home and she was so miserable, she punched me a couple of times. It wasn't my fault.

They also have a big Christmas party at work, her boss throws it every year. This year, Maria drank a little too much and acted really stupid. Plus, she slapped me when I tried to convince her that it was time to leave. I got embarrassed, but she didn't care. I turned away from her and I left to go home. I refused to go to another one of her office parties. When Maria got home that night, she was livid. She abused me more that night, than she ever had before.

Maria has punched me, slapped me, kicked me, thrown things at me and she's even bitten me.

CARLOS

My name is Carlos and I guess I'm what you'd call a house husband. My wife and I have five kids. I stay home with them, while Constance works. She makes way more money than I did. Besides, day care would have hurt us pretty badly. So we decided that it made more sense for me to stay home, with the kids.

Sometimes after a long day at work, Constance will come home in an ugly mood. She expects me to have dinner ready for her and have the kids fed, bathed and ready for bed, by the time she get's home. She treats me terribly. If things aren't perfect she will throw things at me or hit me.

I have never hit a woman in my life and I refuse to start now. My parents would have been so disappointed in me, plus I don't want my kids to see any more violence. They've seen enough.

I am so afraid that she will hurt one of our kids, but for now all of her anger is directed at me. I can't leave her, because I have no place to go and no money to get there.

She controls all of our money, because as she says, it's hers. She is the only one who is working. Constance has told me that if I ever try to leave her, she'd make sure that I never got to see our kids again. Maybe someday when the kids get older, I'll leave.

JACK

My girlfriends name was Abby and she was so beautiful. Everyone always turned to look at her when we walked into a room, she would just light up the whole room. I was so proud to be seen with her.

No one realized the verbal abuse she inflicted on me, when we were all alone. She would point out that I hadn't attended college, she had. She would point out that she made more money than I did, she did. Abby would say that her job was more important than mine was, it was.

I felt pretty low on the totem pole when she would start rambling off all of the things that she had accomplished. Then she would point out that I had done nothing.

She had traveled to England, France and Germany. I'd barely made it out of our state. I felt pretty inferior around her. I admit that I did kind of enjoy the looks of envy on the other guys faces when she and I were together.

Eventually I grew tired of the constant put downs, no matter how perfect and beautiful she was, it was time to walk away, which I did.

DON

My name is Don and I married Margaret right out of high school. We never got along really great, but we did okay. At least until we had our baby. Troy was a big baby and she had a lot of problems while she carried him. She was sick a lot and she gained a lot of weight. He even came out bottom first. Then he had colic for the first six months.

Margaret started to resent Troy and me. She blamed me for everything. I helped out, I honestly did, but it was never enough.

I worked sixty hours a week. When I got home she wanted me to take care of Troy, clean up, do the dishes or the laundry and make dinner. What did she do all day long?

I was exhausted by the time I finally went to bed. If Troy cried during the night, Margaret would wake me up to take care of him.

I guess that I finally got tired of it and I told her that she needed to do more around the house, I couldn't do everything.

She got pretty upset with me and she hit me over the head with a ceramic pot. The pot smashed and cut my head. I drove to the hospital and they put in twenty five stitches.

When I got back home she started to punch me on the head and face, because we didn't have insurance to cover a hospital visit. By punching me, she tore eight of my stitches. They ripped open and I had to go back to the hospital.

She was furious when I got back home. She started to punch and slap me, again. There was no way I was going to have them put any more stitches in. I picked up Troy, left the apartment and drove over to my sister's house.

I stayed with her for three months, until Troy and I had enough money to move into our own apartment. I have custody of Troy. Margaret never comes around. We are divorced now, too.

SCOTT

My wife's name is Amber and I'm Scott. We had been married for two years, when the abuse started. Amber's parents died in a car crash and she got very depressed, which is understandable. Then, two months later, her sister was diagnosed with a brain tumor.

Amber didn't know how to deal with everything that was going on and she started to verbally abuse me. She got very cruel and mean.

Then she started hitting me. Sometimes she would punch me and she almost always threw things at me. I wasn't sure how to react, I never hit her though. No matter what she did to me, I never fought back.

Finally after about four months of this abuse, I talked her into going with me to see a counselor. At first she was completely against the idea. Then her sister slipped into a coma and she died shortly after that. This left Amber extremely depressed and she agreed to go with me.

We have been going to counseling for three years now and it has helped. Amber doesn't strike out at me anymore. She hasn't hit me in months. Although occasionally she still gets snippy and verbally abuses me, but she is trying very hard.

I plan on going to counseling with her for as long as it helps her and the both of us. I love Amber very much and I wish that she didn't have all the heartache that she's had. We are both trying hard to be very happy together and maybe we will even have some kids someday.

SETH

Chris and I were married for a little over a year.

One day I came home from work early and I caught her with another guy. She started hitting me and punching me. She was the one who had been caught doing something wrong!

Anyway we stayed together for a while after that, but the abuse never stopped. Then came the day when my eyes finally opened up and I walked out. She had cheated on me and was abusing me. I knew that I deserved to be treated better than that.

I have been dating a wonderful girl recently. Will I ever be able to totally trust another woman again? I hope so.

TREVOR

Rebecca started slapping me the second week we were dating, but I stupidly laughed it off, I thought it was funny.

Then it progressed to her punching and kicking me. Eventually, she started throwing things at me. For a five foot woman, she had a lot of anger in her tiny body. I am six feet tall and I tower over her quite a bit. But she knew that I would never hit her back.

Things steadily got worse and her violent outbursts became more frequent. She used to act out when we were alone. But then she started doing it when we were at friends houses, in the mall or anywhere else she'd get upset about something.

One night when she was beating on me, she tripped and fell, hitting her head. I rushed her to the hospital and after the doctor had stitched her forehead, he said he needed to talk to me.

He had noticed the cuts and bruises on my face and arms. The doctor asked me if I abused my wife. I laughed and told him that I had never raised a hand to her. Then he quietly asked me if I was the one being abused by her. I stopped laughing and admitted that was what happened and that it happened frequently.

The doctor asked me a lot of questions about our situation. He asked me about what would trigger the abuse and her outbursts. We talked for quite a while and he asked me if he could admit her for observation, I agreed. I felt that maybe there was some kind of a cure, at least I hoped there was.

I explained to Rebecca that they wanted to keep her in the hospital, because she had suffered a head injury. She reluctantly agreed and I went home to a peaceful, quiet house.

The next night, I went back to talk with the doctor. He told me they had talked with her quite a bit and he felt she was bipolar. BIPOLAR? I had never heard of that before. He asked me if I would sign papers to admit her for two weeks. Then during that time they could get her on medication. I reluctantly agreed and signed the papers.

The doctors suggested that I not see her and that I just go back home. He said he would handle it. He gave me some pamphlets to read about bipolar illness. He told me to call him at the end of the two weeks or before if I had any questions.

I had lots of questions and I called him pretty regular during those two weeks, plus I was curious about how she was doing. He told me that she was responding well to the medications, they'd had a problem with the first one.

At the end of two weeks I went to see her. Rebecca smiled at me, she stood up and hugged me. At first I thought that she was going to hit me, so I unconsciously stepped back.

"Thank you. I'm feeling much better now," she whispered in my ear.

Was it true? Did she feel better or was she just trying to get out of the hospital?

The doctor, Rebecca and I decided that she would stay for an extra week. Then she could come home for four hour increments during the fourth week, to see how things went.

During her 'home time' things went great. She seemed so different. Then came the time for her to leave the hospital. I was unsure and she seemed pretty nervous.

I picked her up from the hospital and we went home. Things went good the first day, the first week and then the first month. I was hopeful, but cautious.

We went to counseling as a couple once a week and she went once a week on her own. The medication only had to be adjusted once, but she is doing great now.

We are very fortunate that we found out what the problem was. Rebecca and I are very happy and we get along great. We love each other and respect one another.

The doctor told us that Rebecca will probably always be on medication, but at least we know what we are dealing with.

We will be getting married in three weeks.

DONNY

Roseanne was the love of my life. We never had any problems and we got along really great, until she was diagnosed with a brain tumor. Slowly, over time the tumor spread and grew. The doctors said that it was possible to operate and try to remove it, but Roseanne told them 'no.'

I was afraid that if she had surgery, she wouldn't make it. Especially when the doctors gave us only a seventy percent chance she'd survive for more than six months. I didn't like those odds. Although, we knew she didn't stand a chance at all without the surgery. She just wanted to spend whatever time she had left with her family.

When she started to get worse, she stopped going to the doctor. She said that she didn't want to waste any more of my money on something the doctors couldn't fix.

She started to get terrible headaches, around the same time she started to hit me. I knew that I should have said something to her. I didn't want to fight with her, I didn't know how much time she had left. She had enough going on without my picking on everything.

When I would bring a tray of food in to her, she'd throw the food at me. She would either say it was too hot or too cold. Roseanne would punch me or hit me with different things. I used to pray to God asking him to take my Roseanne. I wanted to end the horrible pain that she was in. She suffered so much from those awful headaches.

One day Roseanne came after me with a knife, she cut my shirt and sliced my arm a little. Then she started slapping and punching me. I assumed it was because of the tumor, so I just tried to put up with it. At night she would cry while I held her in my arms, her pain was so intense.

Then one night she went to sleep and in the morning she didn't wake up. I miss her, but I'm glad that she isn't in any more pain. I'm also happy that the abuse has stopped.

MARVIN

My name is Marvin and I was married to Sylvia for three years. We both drank quite a bit on weekends, but nothing we couldn't handle. Well, we were also on a bowling team, so we drank a few extras on Wednesday nights.

We got along pretty good, except when we went bowling. If we were losing the game or she drank a few too many, we would argue. Sylvia was not a happy drunk, she could get quite mean and violent.

I enjoyed going out for a few drinks, but I seemed to handle it much better. Maybe because I had been drinking for a longer period of time. I used to drink quite a bit when I was younger.

Six out of the last eight games that we bowled, we lost. This really got Sylvia mad and she would start complaining about how lousy I had bowled. Then she would go on to say that I couldn't do anything right. She would tell me in front of other people, that she was embarrassed to be seen with me.

I would get so frustrated with her, I did try to bowl better. I kept thinking, 'If we could just win, then maybe she would stop nagging me.' But she didn't stop, she kept going on and on. After the game and on the entire drive home, she would keep yelling at me.

Every time we lost a game, she would hit me in front of the others. I was embarrassed and so were our friends who had witnessed it. Most of them tried to pretend they hadn't seen it happen. I was grateful for that, because I didn't really want to make eye contact with anyone. The last time that she did this to me, one of my buddies asked me why I put up with it? I thought about it for a minute and I couldn't come up with one good reason. So, the next day I packed some of my things and I left.

TONY

Rhonda was an executive in a mortgage company. My name is Tony and I got hurt on the job, I couldn't work for eight weeks, which was driving me crazy. I had hurt my hip, so on some days I was in so much pain that I had to stay in bed or sit down. I was collecting Workman's Comp, so I was at least contributing some income.

Sometimes Rhonda would come home and complain that I hadn't cleaned the house or done the laundry. On those days I could barely make it into the bathroom! She'd storm through the house, having a major fit and throwing things around.

A few times she even hit me on the head with her fist and walked away. I didn't know what to do. We had only been married for eight months and I knew no one that I could turn to. I didn't even have any money, because I gave it all to her.

This continued for a while and didn't get any better, but it did get steadily worse. I called an abuse hotline and was told that they only dealt with women. When I asked them who I could call, they told me they had no idea and hung up on me.

I called the police, the dispatcher thought I was joking and laughed at me. I didn't know what to do, so I went to my friend Kevin's house. When I told him why I had left, he just stared at me in disbelief.

The first night that I was gone, she came over to Kevin's and screamed at me from outside the window. She told me that I made a big mistake by leaving her. Rhonda screamed out that she was going to kill me.

When I went out the next morning, all four tires on my car were flat. I got a ride from Kevin and went to the courthouse. I filed charges against her and I asked for a restraining order. The judge actually laughed at me, he said something about having a tighter rein on my woman. I left the courthouse embarrassed, frustrated and completely humiliated.

Kevin told me that he had a cousin in the next town, who was looking for someone to help him out on his farm. I readily agreed and I haven't seen Rhonda in over three years. What was supposed to be a temporary thing, turned out to be indefinite. I love working here and my hip has completely recovered.

FRANK

Allison and I dated for a little under a year. Things went okay for a while, well, for about the first six months. All that she did was pick on me. She would say that everything I did was wrong, that I didn't take care of myself or that I was stupid.

I wasn't the smartest guy around, but I was far from stupid. I may have been big, but I wasn't fat. I used to work out back in the day, but I wasn't so good about doing it anymore. I did notice that just above my pants, I was starting to get a patch of extra skin on each side. Allison would grab those and pinch me pretty hard. 'Fatty,' she'd say to me, grabbing onto it.

Then she would pick on my appearance when we would go out. 'Your hair is all messy' or 'Can't you do anything about that gut?' She would also make comments about my clothes like, 'Those pants are getting really tight' or 'I'll bet you barely squeezed into that!' I know that these sound like little things, but it was the way that she said them, the tone of her voice.

If we went to a store or the mall, she'd tell me to walk ahead of her or behind her. She told me that she didn't want anyone to know we were together, I just couldn't figure her out.

She always cut me down and acted like she was ashamed of me. It took me a while, but I did finally break it off. I figured that I owed myself at least a little dignity.

TOM

My name is Tom and I dated a girl who used to go nuts on me. She would get so violent sometimes. When I finally split up with her, she bothered me quite a bit. She would threaten me on the phone or she'd follow me around. Sometimes she would punch or hit me.

I went into court and I talked to the clerk, but all he did was tell me that restraining or stay away orders were intended for women, not for men.

She eventually grew tired of bothering me, but I had no legal recourse. Things really need to change for men.

MARC

My wife Lottie and I got divorced after eight years. I was awarded custody of the kids, it is pretty unusual for a man to get custody. But enough people had testified on my behalf about the abuse my children and I had suffered. Although the judge did give her unsupervised visitation, which I didn't agree with.

One Saturday afternoon she picked up the kids as usual. Sunday afternoon came and I still didn't have the kids back. Where were they? Why hadn't they come back? What was she doing with them?

I waited a while longer, then I drove over to Lottie's apartment. I didn't see her car in the parking lot, so I walked up to her door. No one answered when I knocked, which I had already figured that no one would.

I filed a missing person report and a judge issued a warrant, but we never found any of them. My kids have been gone for six years now and I don't know if they are alive or dead. I worry about them everyday, because I know that Lottie is not the most stable person.

I hope my kids are okay and I hope they know that I love them. I haven't given up hope that they will all come home, someday.

GARRETT

Janet and I went to high school together and then on to college. We always figured that we would get married someday. We both wanted a family, a house and a career.

Unfortunately, somewhere along the line Janet changed her mind. She decided she wanted someone to pay the bills and she wanted a career. We used to argue about having kids, but she wanted a career. Sometimes in her anger she would lash out at me, she would hit me or punch me.

Eventually I realized that she and I didn't want the same things anymore and I left.

BRIAN

My name is Brian. Marcie and I dated for about four months. At first she was so great, but then I discovered she had a dark side. Marcie would and could get extremely violent. She was depressed a lot of the time. She would say really mean and hurtful things to me. I figured because she was depressed and hurting maybe she wanted to hurt me too.

It didn't take long for her words to change to her throwing things at me. I'd been hit with a coffee pot, pans and dishes. She had a heck of an arm on her! Plus, it was always so sudden, she would just have these outbursts for no apparent reason.

At about our four month marker, I ditched her. I told her that things just weren't working out and that was the last time she ever swung at me!

CURT

Joanna was an emergency room nurse and she had two kids. I am a police officer, actually that's how we met. I was quite taken with her when I saw her at the hospital. She was so beautiful and smart.

We started dating and eventually I moved in with her and her kids. The kids were great, although they seemed very quiet and sometimes they appeared withdrawn.

Joanna worked the three to eleven shift and I worked four to midnight. We really didn't see a whole lot of each other and she didn't see much of her kids. I didn't either, because they were in school from eight to three.

But we tried to make up for it on the weekends, we tried to plan fun things to do. We would go to an amusement park or just go to the park. I began to notice that when we were all together, it didn't take much for Joanna to blow a fuse.

If she got mad at one of the kids, she would suddenly backhand them. I was quite surprised by her anger. One day she completely shocked me and she backhanded me. I almost slapped her back because it was my first reaction, but I somehow managed to stop myself.

The abuse continued with her, she began to hit me quite a bit. I found it harder and harder to stop myself from hitting her back. That's when I walked away. I didn't want to hit her and I knew that if I stayed, that's exactly what would happen. I feel bad for her kids, but there really wasn't anything I could do for them.

JACQUE

Jamie and I had what I thought was a good marriage, but I found out I was wrong. We would argue like most couples and it was almost always about money.

I worked in a paper mill with a woman named Karen, who was just a friend. No matter how hard I tried to explain that we were just friends to Jamie, she wouldn't believe me. She started to accuse me of cheating on her, which I never had.

Jamie made the mistake of going to a psychic, which confirmed her suspicions that I was cheating on her. The psychic seemed to encourage her. Although the more often she saw the psychic, the more money she paid her. So of course the psychic would feed her a bunch of garbage.

The accusations grew stronger and more frequent. It got to the point where I couldn't handle them anymore and I screamed for her to shut up. She made a fist and punched me in the nose, she actually broke my nose. I was furious with her, as I drove myself to the emergency room. They had to pack my nose with gauze to stop the bleeding.

When I got back home I still had the gauze in my nose. I told Jamie that I was going to leave her if she ever raised a hand to me again. To my surprise she asked me if Karen had met me at the hospital. I told her no and she called me a lair. She punched me in my already aching nose, which literally brought tears to my eyes.

I must have blacked out, but when I came to I grabbed some of my things and I left. I never went back.

JACK

My name is Jack. Sharon was my girlfriend for a while. We used to go to bars, listen to the music and dance. For the most part we usually had a good time.

One day one of her girlfriends went over to Sharon's apartment. She was upset because she had caught her boyfriend cheating on her. She asked us if we wanted to go out for a while, she said that she needed to be around lots of people.

That night her friends boyfriend also showed up at the bar and her friend got extremely upset. Sharon went with her to the restroom, because she had started to cry.

Another friend of ours came over to me and she asked me to dance. We had danced before, so I really saw no harm in it. We walked over to the dance floor and started to dance. It wasn't even a slow dance and we weren't even touching.

Well, Sharon came up from downstairs and she saw me dancing. I don't know why, but she grabbed a pitcher of beer from one of the tables. She walked right up to me and hit me in the head with the glass pitcher. I know I screamed out really loud, because the band stopped playing.

The girl that I was dancing with quickly took off. Sharon started punching me, as the blood poured down my face. I walked maybe five steps and collapsed onto the dance floor.

When I came to, I was in the back of an ambulance. At the hospital they wheeled me into the emergency room, where they stitched up my head. I don't remember how many stitches I got, but I know there was a lot of them.

They kept me in the hospital overnight, I had also suffered a mild concussion. I went back to my apartment the next day and I didn't return any of Sharon's phone calls.

RAY

My name is Ray and my partner George, became abusive towards me. After we had been together for almost a year. George was always extremely jealous, I know now that he was a very insecure person. He started to call me names and humiliate me in front of our circle of friends and family.

I decided to leave when George started to throw things at me. He hit me a few times with a clock, a pan and cans of vegetables. I finally had enough and I left him. I know that I deserve to be treated better than that.

PHIL

I'm Phil and my girlfriend, Melissa was abusive towards me. She used to hit me, punch me, slap me and kick me when she got upset, which was a lot of the time. Melissa sold real estate, but sales weren't going well for her. She was a very forceful woman and a lot of people didn't like that about her. That was actually part of the reason why I fell in love with her. At first our relationship was pretty good, but then it changed to bad very fast.

Her being forceful and demanding was an embarrassment to me. She began to talk down to me when we were out in public. She would call me an uneducated hick, because I had only graduated from high school. Melissa would also punch me and kick me in front of our friends.

After a few months of this, I decided that whatever attraction had been there at first, was gone now. I split up with her.

TYRONE

My name is Tyrone and I dated Chenise for all of about eight months. It was the worst eight months of my life. She didn't hit me. I never thought of it as abuse, but now I realize that it was abuse. Chenise would threaten me and call me names. No matter where I went she would accuse me of cheating on her. She verbally, emotionally and psychologically abused me.

It took every ounce of my inner strength for me not to pop her a good one and I am happy to say, I never did. Instead, I left. I walked away from that situation and from Chenise.

Today I am happily married and we are expecting our third child.

WALTER

Walter was my partner for many years and for the most part we got along good. In all fairness, Walter treated me well, except for when he would drink. He didn't drank that often, but when he did, he was miserable to be around. He would call me horrible names, slap me and force me to have sex with him. Walter was very rough and pretty crude when he had been drinking.

I tolerated it for quite a while because it didn't happen that often. At least not until the last six months that we were together. Walter had lost his job and he began to drink quite frequently. I put up with it for as long as I could and then I left him.

RAY

My name is Ray and my wife's name is Marie. We got divorced three months ago and I was awarded custody of our kids. I had enough witnesses to prove that Marie had been neglectful and abusive towards me and our kids.

After the divorce Marie constantly called me and threatened me, as well as the kids. She told me that if she couldn't have the kids, I sure as hell wasn't going to get them. I listened to these threats for almost three months, then I packed up the kids and we left. We are in a whole new area now and doing just fine.

KURT

My girlfriend got pregnant after we had been dating for two months. She got real mad about it and she blamed me. I told her that she could get an abortion, but she said no. I almost wish she had, maybe she wouldn't have become so mean.

She started hitting me, kicking me, slapping me and just being plain horrible to me. A few weeks later she had a miscarraige. It was almost a blessing when she had the miscarriage. I feel bad that the baby didn't make it, but I took the miscarriage as a sign to get the hell out of that relationship!

BERNIE

Kylie and I dated for about four months and during that time she hit me twice. The second time was the last time, then I split up with her. But things didn't stop there, she kept calling and following me. I got a stay away order, but that didn't stop her at all, if anything it got her more upset. Things intensified; the calls, the threats and the banging on my door during the night.

I've had my tires slashed, my headlights smashed and my windshield busted out of my car. I couldn't have her arrested, because I couldn't prove it was her. I knew that it was Kylie, but I hadn't actually seen her do it.

This continued for a month. Then I guess she got tired of bothering me or she found a new victim. I don't know, all that I do know is that she was leaving me alone and that was just fine with me.

JACK

My name is Jack and I was married to Valerie for a little over two years. During that time she was verbally abusive towards me. I know that I should have left her, but I truly believed in my marriage vows. I didn't want to be considered a failure for getting a divorce, I didn't know anyone who had ever gotten a divorce.

I did love Val, but her words really were hurtful and mean. I met a woman named Janet at my church, Val never went to church with me. The woman told me that her husband had been verbally abusive towards her. She left her husband eight months before and was told that verbal abuse was the same as domestic abuse.

A few months later I left Valerie and I filed for a divorce. I go to a counselor now and I hope to someday be in another relationship, a much better, loving relationship.

TONY

My name is Tony and my wife Casandra is in prison for attempted murder. She had always been abusive towards me, it originally started with verbal abuse. Then it steadily progressed into a very violent situation. Casandra would kick me, hit me and punch me.

Then suddenly she'd stop and start acting really nice towards me, I was completely confused by her. At times, she almost became loving towards me. She certainly tolerated many more things. At that time, I had really high hopes that things were changing and I even hoped things were getting better between us.

Within the month I started to get very sick. I went to the doctor numerous times, but after running many tests they couldn't find anything wrong. Each day I became more and more ill. I had no strength and I noticed that my heartbeat wasn't regular. I also began to vomit quite a bit. It got so bad that I couldn't even get up off the couch by myself.

My sister Katie came over to visit and she rushed me right to the emergency room. What they found out that day shocked me, my body was full of arsenic. Apparently Casandra was trying to poison and kill me.

When she was arrested, she told one of the cops that she had taken out a rather large insurance policy on me.

While I was in the hospital, I started to slowly get better. I don't know how close I came to dying, but in my opinion it was way too close.

BEN

My wife Janie and I were married for less than six months when I left her. Once we got married she changed. She went from being quiet to bossy and sweet to mean. It was like I was living with two different people. I liked the sweet, quiet one much better than the bossy, mean one.

During the time that we were together Janie hit me, threw things at me and punched me. But that isn't why I left her. I left because one time Janie stabbed me with a kitchen knife. She stabbed me in the arm. It really didn't cause too much damage, but she had still stabbed me. I didn't know what she would try next. I should have pressed charges, but I didn't. I just left. Seven months later we were divorced.

RON

My name is Ron and I dated a woman who was verbally abusive towards me. At first it didn't bother me. I would just laugh it off, but then it became rather annoying. She was constantly belittling me when we were alone and even when we were with our friends. I finally had enough and I dumped her.

TONY

Tony was a happy go lucky kind of a guy. He was always smiling and cheerful. Tony seemed to get along with everyone and he was a very likeable guy. He met Sarah and they seemed to hit it off right from the beginning. Tony treated Sarah very good, but Sarah seemed to lash out at him as time went on. Tony was in love with her and tried to ignore her mood swings, at least for a while. When Sarah started to become violent towards Tony, he couldn't ignore it.

One time when they were out in a restaurant, Sarah had gone to the ladies room. When she returned, she saw Tony talking to a female co-worker of his. She flew into a rage accusing them of fooling around, embarrassing them both. When Tony tried to explain to her that they worked together, Sarah punched him in the face. Tony's co-worker wasn't sure how to react, when Sarah suddenly slapped her. People in the restaurant watched them, wondering what was going to happen next. Sarah was the only one who wasn't embarrassed.

The next day at work, Tony's co-worker told another employee what had happened the night before. Sarah stopped by Tony's work and she felt as though all of his fellow employees were staring her, she again flew into a rage. She started yelling at everyone, throwing things and then she attacked Tony. When she finally left, Tony was extremely embarrassed and ashamed. He quietly apologized for what had happened.

A few of the women at work got together and talked to him later that day. They told him that this kind of situation would only get worse. They also told him that he should split up with her.

Tony took their advice and told Sarah that he was through. Sarah suspected that some of his co-workers had planted that idea in his head and she was even more furious. She hit Tony a few times, before he left her apartment.

The next day at work Tony told his co-workers that he had taken their advice. He thanked them and admitted that he felt a lot better about things.

After lunch the same day, Sarah showed up at Tony's job. She walked right over to Tony and started yelling at him in front of everyone.

"Please Sarah, don't do this. Let's just try to not make this any worse." Tony pleaded with her, but Sarah wasn't listening to him.

"No one splits up with me, especially because some stupid bitches have to stick their noses into our business!" Sarah yelled at Tony. She looked around the room at his co-workers. Everyone was staring at her, unsure of what to do. Sarah reached into her purse and pulled out a gun.

"Stay right where you are!" Sarah yelled at a women who had started to move towards the door. "You first," she said, pointing the gun at the woman from the restaurant. "This is all your fault."

"Sarah, put the gun down. Let's talk about this." Tony begged her.

"It's too late for talk, Tony. She split us up, I know she did. You left because of her and now I am going to kill her." Sarah said, still pointing the gun at the woman who's face had turned pale, she was also shaking uncontrollably.

"Please," the woman whispered.

"You are not going to take Tony away from me!" Sarah screamed at the frightened woman.

Suddenly the gun went off and the woman fell to the floor.

"Don't anybody move!" Sarah screamed, when she saw a women move towards the woman she'd shot. "Just stay where you are."

"What did you do? Sarah, please. This is between the two of us. Let these people go." Tony said to her.

Sarah turned the gun towards Tony. "You're right baby, it is between us," she said as she squeezed the trigger, shooting Tony in the chest. "You see ladies, no one is going to have my Tony. Not you…or you…or even you."

One by one the other women in the room fell to the floor, as they were shot. Then Sarah pointed the gun at herself and she pulled the trigger. But before she did she said, "Now we will always be together, Tony."

Four people died that day and two were critically wounded, thankfully they did survive.

BIFF

Jenny and I were both juniors in high school when we started to date. We got along pretty good for a while, at least until Joanie started coming to our school. Joanie transferred from another school and all of the guys liked her. I admit that I found her attractive, but I never thought about doing anything. I was with Jenny. Occasionally, Jenny would hit me when I'd look over at Joanie.

One day Jenny broke up with me, so that she could go out with Brad. I was okay with it, because I sort of wanted to go out with Joanie. When Jenny found out I was going to go to the movies with Joanie, she told me we were still going out together. I explained to her that she was the one who had broken up with me.

Jenny really got mad, she started punching and kicking me. I tried to shield myself, but she just kept coming after me. I pushed her and I walked away. What I didn't realize, was that she had hit her head on one of the lockers.

Later that day, I was called into the principal's office. A cop stood in the middle of the room, waiting to talk with me. He told me he was going to arrest me for beating up on Jenny.

What? I didn't beat her up. What was he talking about? I didn't know what to do as he led me away in handcuffs. I was later released into the custody of my parents.

The next day we went to court and I saw a big bandage on Jenny's forehead. Jenny told this unbelievable story about how she had split up with me to date someone else and how I had just gone crazy. She went on to say that I had slapped her, punched her and finally pushed her into the lockers. That was how she suffered a cut to her head, which required several stitches. She was lying!

When it was my turn to tell my side of what had happened, I told the truth. The judge didn't believe me, he believed Jenny. He told me that I was lucky I hadn't killed her. I was found guilty and sentenced to six months in a group home, community service and I was to attend an anger management course. I didn't do anything. I was just trying to get her away from me.

My parents believed me, but no one else did. I had no proof to back up what I had said. She was the one with the injury, I had nothing.

ERNIE

Carla was my first love, she was beautiful and smart. She was also very mean. She threw things at me and usually her aim was pretty good. She made contact more times than she didn't. I loved her and I put up with the abuse for much longer than I should have. I can't think of any other reason why I stayed with her for so long, before getting help.

Carla and I talked about lots of things. We talked about how we could make things better between us. She wasn't even aware that she had a problem. Carla went on to tell me that her mom had been very abusive towards her and to her dad. To my surprise, Carla suggested that we go to a counselor. It has helped us tremendously.

Today Carla is so sweet and loving. She can control her temper much better now. We get along so good, it's like living with a different woman.

PAUL

My name is Paul and I was forced to leave my job, my home and my whole life, because of Paula. Paula and I dated for over a year. Then she started to go crazy with jealousy, which I never gave her a reason to be jealous. She started to hit me, slap me, break my things and then she started to follow me around.

It just kept getting worse, finally I told her that I didn't want to see her anymore. I was actually becoming afraid of her. Paula told me that she would kill me before any other woman could have me. She became very unstable and emotionally unbalanced.

After I broke it off with her I found the tires of my car slashed and all the windows of my car were smashed out. I got threatening phone calls at all hours of the day and night. When I called for help, everyone told me that there really wasn't much they could do. I was told to file for a restraining order and at the same time, I was also told that it was generally just given to women.

The next day I went to court and filed for a restraining order and after a bit of a fight, the judge gave me one. But all that proved to do was make Paula get more upset with me. The phone calls increased, as did the threats.

I decided that I had enough, I made arrangements for a realtor to rent my house and I left. I took just what I needed and I moved away. It's been three years and I haven't gone back yet. I'd like to, but I don't want her to start bothering me again. The realtor tells me that she is having a hard time keeping any tenant in my house, because Paula keeps bothering them. Maybe in time she'll stop.

I miss my mother and brother very much. We have gotten together a few times since I left, but never back there. They have come to visit me. We've spent Christmas and Easter together so far this year, which was pretty nice.

JONAH

I almost died because of my girlfriend Darlene. I was talking to another girl one afternoon, outside of our apartment building. She had just moved in and had locked herself out of her car. I was trying to help her, that's all. Darlene came home and started yelling at me in front of her. I was pretty embarrassed, I apologized and slowly followed Darlene into our apartment.

Another time, the same girl had her arms loaded with groceries and I offered to help her carry them. Darlene saw this and started to scream at me. I was only trying to help her out. I would have helped anyone out, no matter who they were.

I didn't see the woman for a while and I forgot all about her. Then came our annual block party. We block off our street and all of the neighbors get together and have a huge cookout. It's really fun and everyone has a great time.

Unfortunately, the new girl came over to me and we started talking together. I introduced her to some of our neighbors, Darlene saw this and she was furious. When we got back to our apartment later that night, Darlene proceeded to ruin a perfect day by arguing with me. We must have been arguing for hours before she hit me. I was pretty upset with her, but I somehow managed to walk away and I went into the other room. Darlene followed me and continued to yell at me.

I turned around and faced her, "Look, please, just leave me alone." I yelled back at her.

"You want her don't you?" Darlene screamed at me, then she started to beat her fists against my chest.

I grabbed her by both of her arms and held her firmly.

"Darlene, things just aren't working out between us and I am not going to continue to live like this. I think that you need to go back to your apartment, right now." I told her, as firmly as I could.

"I'll leave, but we are not even close to being finished." Darlene yelled at me, then she spit in my face.

I watched as she grabbed her purse and left. I wiped away the spit with my sleeve as it dripped down my face. 'What the hell was wrong with her?' I asked myself.

I went into the livingroom, sat down on the couch and turned on the tv. I sat there until around midnight, then I went up to go to bed.

The next morning, I went to work as usual. When I got home, I found that my apartment had been trashed. At first I thought that I had been robbed, but then I saw that nothing had been taken. I slowly went through each room, shocked by all the damage I saw.

In the kitchen, the food that had been in my refrigerator and freezer was dumped out all over the floor. Everything from the cupboards was thrown onto the floor. All of the canned items had been opened and were also dumped out onto the floor.

In the livingroom, my tv was on the floor, my couch was ripped and the stuffing had been thrown all over.

The bathroom mirror was smashed and everything from the medicine cabinet was dumped out into the sink.

My bedroom was the worst, my clothes were all cut up and thrown around. The bed was tore apart and my sheets were all ripped up. All of my family pictures had been ripped in half.

I was so upset, when I called the police my eyes began to well up with tears. The police came over and wrote up a report. They looked around and surprised me by telling me that there hadn't been a forced entry. I knew right away that it had been Darlene, although I couldn't prove it.

She actually had the nerve to call me later that night. She laughed when she told me what a lousy house keeper I was.

Two days later Darlene called me. She was furious because the police had questioned her about my 'break in.'

When I got home, I was surprised to see her waiting in the parking lot. 'Should I go over to her or pretend that I don't see her?' I wondered, for about a second. That's when I decided it was best to ignore her.

I started to walk towards my apartment, in the distance I heard a car start. I didn't think too much of it, until I heard the car accelerate. When I heard it get closer I turned, that's when I saw Darlene's car. Before I could register what I saw and react, I was hit. I felt such excruciating pain! When the car hit me, I felt myself roll up onto the hood, slam into the windshield and then I fell to the ground. I watched as Darlene drove off with her hand sticking out of the window, her middle finger raised.

I thought that I must have lay there for a long time, but really it was only a few minutes. A few of my neighbors came running over to me. I couldn't move my legs, I couldn't feel anything from the waist down. I looked down at my legs and saw that my hips seemed to be crooked, they leaned to the side.

I must have passed in and out of consciousness, because I only remember bits and pieces after that. I remember that a crowd had gathered around me. I remember the paramedics and I remember the drive to the hospital, well, actually I remember parts of all of those things.

I don't remember much about my time in the hospital. I know that I was on a lot of pain medications. I had a few surgeries, lots of physical therapy and more than enough doctors.

Darlene did go to jail, but she didn't do enough time in my opinion. I am now in a wheelchair, but the doctors are very positive and upbeat. They feel that I will be able to walk again, someday. I hope they are right.

TOM

My name is Tom and my partners name was Biff. We were together for two years, but Biff had a lot of problems. He was extremely jealous and he could become extremely violent.

He was a cook in the same restaurant where I was a waiter. By being a waiter I had to be friendly to the customers, which used to get Biff very angry. He didn't have to be a 'people person', he was tucked away in the kitchen.

I have been hit, punched, kicked and choked. I have also been spit on, had things thrown at me and I have even been cut with a knife. I didn't know what to do and I didn't know who to turn to. I felt so alone.

I can imagine that reporting domestic abuse for a man is hard, but it is twice as hard for a gay man, trust me on this one. I couldn't go to anyone.

I just kept putting up with it and praying that it would all stop, but it didn't. It steadily got worse. I hinted around to people at work, but no one there really knew that Biff and I were gay. Well, they knew I was gay, but Biff didn't want anyone to know that he was. People thought we were friends, as well as roommates. I think that Biff was ashamed of me and embarrassed by his own sexual preferences.

I put up with the abuse for as long as I could and then I left. I just took off, going as far away from Biff as I could. I left my job, all my friends and my apartment. To this day, I am still afraid that Biff will find me.

J.R.

I met Kim at work, it wasn't until later that I found out she was a very abusive person. We were both teachers, well, actually I was a teacher and she was an aide. We got along pretty good at first, but I guess most people say that. She worked in my classroom with me, which in the beginning was pretty convenient, but then it became a real burden. She started to insult me in front of my students after we had been dating for a few months. I didn't know how to handle that and when I tried to talk to her about it, she'd get worse and make it a big deal.

I taught eighth grade science, so we did a lot of hands on type activities, experiments and things. One day she got mad at me because I was trying to help one of my students, who had a pretty well known reputation. I didn't care about her reputation, I was there to teach. From across the room a glass beaker flew at me and almost hit me. I looked quickly and saw that it was Kim who had thrown it. Glass shattered everywhere and luckily none of my students were cut, although I did get a small cut on my forehead.

After class that day, I went to talk to the principal of our school. I explained what had happened. He agreed with me that Kim had to be let go. We were very lucky that nothing had happened to anyone.

That night, I told Kim that I was going to stop seeing her and she got very angry with me. Before I could herd her out of the door, she hit me a couple of times.

The next day, I had quite a few students of mine come up to me and tell me that my car had flat tires, all four were flat. I knew who had done it, but I couldn't prove it.

I kept getting phone calls where they just hung up on me and the school got numerous bomb threats during that time. Again, I knew who had done those things, but I couldn't prove it.

Eventually, Kim got tired of bothering me or she found a new victim, because I was soon free of her. All of the weird things that had been happening, suddenly stopped. I am much more careful about who I date now.

CHRIS

My wife Jen was a terribly mean person and she sure seemed to enjoy tormenting me. When we got a divorce, I got custody of the kids. Jen got visitation every other weekend, which I didn't agree with. I begged for supervised visits, but the judge told me that a mother would never harm her own children. I wonder what that judge is thinking now!

Jen took our three sons, Tommy who was five, Robby who was three and Junior who had just turned one-year-old, for her visit. I received a phone call from the hospital about five hours later, telling me that I had better get there as quickly as I could.

I immediately thought that there had been a car accident, so I rushed down. When I got there I saw my three little boys all hooked up to machines. None of them were moving as I stood there watching them. I was told to wait for the doctor and that was when I saw Jen being led away in handcuffs. I ran over to her and the policeman. I started yelling at them to tell me what was going on. Jen just smiled at me and told me that now I could have our boys.

The doctor came over to me at that point and he told me that my boys had been given Drain-o. He said that there wasn't much more they could do now, other than to try to make them comfortable. DRAIN-O? What the hell was going on? The doctor went on to say that Kim kept telling everyone, if she couldn't have the boys, I wasn't going to have them either. I admit, I tried to attack Kim, the cops pulled me away before I could get to her.

I couldn't believe what had happened. I sat by my boys for three days and I watched each one of them as they convulsed and died before my eyes. None of them ever opened their eyes again. I felt as though my heart had been ripped out of my chest. Kim couldn't have hurt me any worse than she did that night. I was devastated and felt like my life had ended.

Then I got angry and I went to all of her trial dates. I even made enough noise so that the state investigated the judge, who had allowed the unsupervised visitations. I know that this will never get any easier and I will never feel like justice has been served.

Kim was sentenced to a hospital for the mentally disturbed, which I was very unhappy about. I had no doubt that she knew what she was doing.

I miss my boys everyday and no, it does not get any easier, no matter what they say.

REX

I dated Donna for about eight months and never realized that she was an abusive person. She never beat on me or hit me, but she would talk down to me all of the time. Donna would call me stupid, but I never knew it was a form of abuse.

A few times when we would have a fight, she would tear up some of my clothes, which actually kind of sucked. I can't figure out why some days she would be so nice and other days she was mean and miserable.

At around our eighth month together, she started to bug me all the time about getting married. I didn't want to get married. We argued a lot and she always made me feel like a little kid. When I told her no, she'd begin to throw everything around. She even told me to get out of our apartment and never come back. So, that's just what I did. I grabbed what I could and I left.

For the last two years Rebecca and I have been together and she is really great to me. It's funny, Rebecca works at a domestic abuse shelter.

SAM

Debbie and I were dating exclusively for about six months. I really thought that she was the woman who I was going to marry.

I thought we got along good, at least most of the time. Then I was introduced to her parents. We drove to Maine to spend a week with her parents. What a big mistake, actually it was quite an eye opener for me.

Her mother treated her father like a dog or she totally ignored him. She constantly downed him, even in front of us. Debbie's father would just sit in his chair and watch the tv. It seemed like he ignored her, which I couldn't blame him at all. It was sad to watch, because he just sat there and took it. On the rare occasion that he would open his mouth, she would get even louder and drown him out.

In other words the entire week was terrible. I noticed that Debbie treated her father the same way that her mother treated him. She had no respect for her father at all. I wasn't really sure how to react or what to think.

When we got back to her apartment in New York, I realized she was treating me the same way. Had she been doing it all along and I just hadn't noticed?

I stayed with her for two weeks after we got back and then I left.

TODD

My name is Todd and my girlfriends name was Carla, we had been dating for about six months. The reason it didn't last very long was because Carla had this awful habit of insulting me. No matter what I did, it was wrong and I was stupid. I knew I wasn't stupid, but she made me feel that way. Sometimes I just wanted to shut her up, she just had such a way of goading me.

For months I listened to her and I took it. I tried to ignore her, but sometimes she would just get right in my face and nag at me. One day after trying to walk away from her, she slapped me hard across the face. Unfortunately, on instinct I hit her back. I honestly didn't even think about it, I just lashed out. I was hit and I hit back.

I regret doing it, I'd never hit a woman before, not ever. That same day, I left. I didn't want to ever do that again. I was afraid too. I was afraid that if I ever hit her again, I'd hurt her.

TOM

My name is Tom and my wife's name is Cassie. We have been married for six years. Cassie is a very dominating woman, she controls the house. I don't have a problem with it, because she is much better at handling money and paying the bills than I am.

The problem is that she started to become abusive towards me. She actually started out by calling me names, then hitting me and finally punching me. It got really bad and I found myself with no place to go, no one to turn to and no money to leave. All the money that I was given, was accounted for each day. I had no chance to save and put any extra money away.

I hinted around to a few of the guys at work, about what was happening at my house and they told me that I should just slap her back. One of the guys called me a wimp for letting her treat me that way. I felt alone and stuck in a situation that just wasn't going to get any better.

When I tried to talk to my mother about it, she laughed at me. "Yeah, I raised myself a real man," she said to me.

I called the police and got nowhere with them, I even tried calling a domestic abuse shelter. They told me that they had no facilities for men. That is when I realized there was nothing I could do…

Today I am still with Cassie and the beatings have gotten much worse.

PEDRO

My wife's name is Patricia and we have been together for three years. We fight quite a bit and have since the beginning. She is, what my dad would have called 'hot headed.'

Patricia thought nothing of throwing a plate, a potato or whatever else was handy, across the room at me. Together we have a two-year-old son and she has a daughter who is eleven years old. When she is mad or upset with the kids, she also throws things at them. We have all gotten pretty good at ducking! When Patricia starts to yell, my son usually just sits down by the couch and seems to wait for her to stop.

I love her, but if things don't calm down soon, I'm going to leave her.

CARLOS

Emily was my girlfriend for two years. I had to leave her and today my name is different. I had the help of an abuse shelter, although they did tell me it was unusual for them to help a man. Emily was very abusive towards me and I made more than one visit to the emergency room.

My life with Emily was miserable, each day I hated to come home from work. I was afraid of her. Some days she would be fine and others she just seemed to lose it.

One of the times that I was in the emergency room, a nurse asked me what had really happened and I told her. To my surprise she didn't laugh, instead she called a woman in, who worked in an abuse shelter. She told me that because I was a man they couldn't bring me to the shelter, but they did put me up in a motel.

Two days later, Emily found me and beat me with a baseball bat. The motel manager called for help, the police and the ambulance came. I was admitted to the hospital for two weeks and by the end of that time I had a new name, all my papers and a new place to live.

The shelter helped me out so much. I don't know what would have happened to me if I had stayed with her. I am so grateful to the women at the shelter, I know 'men' are not their normal clients.

Today I have a good job and a nice girlfriend. I still worry about Emily finding me, but not as much as I once did.

JAKE

I once dated a woman who was verbally abusive to me. She cut me down all of the time and she made me feel like I was worth nothing. If I tried to do something nice for her, I was criticized. If I tried to help her out, like make a nice dinner, there was always something wrong with it. It was never good enough for her.

Eventually, I grew tired of it and I split up with her.

ELLIOTT

I dated Roger for six months and the first time that he slapped me, I left. I knew that I didn't deserve to be treated that way. I am a nice person and not bad looking. I am fun to be with and I enjoy being around people.

Today Pierre and I are very happy together.

SAM

When I was in college I dated a couple of different girls. One of them, I eventually ended up marrying. The other one I swear was a psycho. She used to follow me around campus, she threatened my wife to be. She threatened to kill herself and me if I didn't date her, exclusively.

I was in college, I wasn't ready to get serious with anyone at that point. I finally got tired of her threats and whining. When I split up with her, that's when she really went crazy on me. First she told me that she was pregnant, then she told me that she was going to have the baby and torture it if I didn't marry her. I couldn't figure out what was wrong with her.

When I went to the clinic with her, I found out that she'd been lying to me. She wasn't pregnant and had never been pregnant. I was so upset with her.

A few days later, she went over to my wife to be's dorm and she beat her up for no reason. She ended up with a black eye and a couple of bruises, but she still didn't deserve it.

I went to the campus police with my wife to be and we told them what was going on. They suggested that we call the police, which we did. The police didn't do anything, they said there wasn't much they could do, unless things happened off campus.

During Christmas break, I went with my wife to be to visit her parents and then we went to my parents house for a few days. While we were at my parents house, we kept getting hang up calls. Again, we went to the police, but without proof they said they couldn't do anything. It felt as though we were at a dead end.

I finally confronted her and she acted kind of crazy. I was afraid of her and what she was capable of doing. I wished I had never started dating her. What a terrible mistake that was.

Luckily for us she got kicked off campus for 'unknown reasons.' I heard rumors that she had been caught with drugs, which would have explained a lot of her behavior. I also heard rumors that she had propositioned the dean, but whatever happened, she was told to never go back on campus grounds.

Three years later my wife and I got married. One of our wedding presents just happened to be a box of black roses with a dead bird tied to the stems. I figured they came from her, but I will never know for sure.

Today we are still happily married and expecting our third child.

JUSTIN

I have been married to Reba for three years and I thought that we were basically a happy couple. Apparently, I'd been wrong for all of this time. I found her in our bed with a guy from down the street. I started screaming and yelling at her. She turned around and slugged me in the head. It wasn't the first time that she had hit me, but this time it certainly was the most painful.

I knew we had some problems, but I chocked it up to just part of being married. She could get violent at times, but I pretty much ignored it. This time I didn't and I couldn't any longer. I walked out and I never came back.

ROB

My girlfriends name was Nora and I thought I was in love with her. We dated for about eight months and I was even thinking of asking her to marry me, at least until the day she seemed to go mad.

Nora found my old 'black book' one day at my apartment. She went crazy and she started throwing things around. I yelled at her to stop, because she was destroying my stuff.

Nora ignored me and she continued to ruin my things, she even hit me. I tried to tell her that the book was old, very old. I told her that I hadn't used it in years, but I guess she didn't believe me. She punched me and kicked me a couple of times.

Finally she seemed to calm down enough, so I could talk to her. I thought I was getting through to her, but as soon as I stopped talking she attacked me again. I guess my neighbors heard the noise and called the cops.

The cops banged on my door and then pushed it open. Nora didn't stop hitting me, she kept throwing punches at me, even as the cops were pulling her away from me.

It took about an hour for the cops to calm her down. They asked us what had started all of this. In the end, they made her leave. As she left, I told her it was over.

PARKER

My life was miserable for about all of nine months, which happens to be how long I dated Joy. From the first day I saw her, she was a pain in the neck. She started out being demanding, then she would tell me where I could go and with who. She didn't like my friends or family and none of them liked her either. She was rude to all of them. She told me that she didn't want me with them.

There was no way I was going to let her tell me who I could or couldn't see. I did what I wanted to and it sure used to get her mad. I didn't do it on purpose, but I wasn't going to stop seeing my friends and family for anyone.

It started to get so bad that every time I left the house she'd accuse me of seeing them or else she accused me of cheating on her. It seemed like I couldn't win, no matter what I did.

So, I finally broke it off with her. Now I happen to be with the most wonderful woman.

GARY

I dated Jackie in high school and I thought that she treated me good, but then after a while she started hitting me. She would usually hit me when we were alone together. One day she hit me in front of my parents.

Later that night, after I had dropped Jackie off at home, I went back to my house. My parents sat me down and wanted to talk to me. They told me that what she was doing to me was just going to get worse. My dad told me that Jackie obviously didn't respect me. If she did, she wouldn't treat me that way. My mother told me that I must not respect myself, because I allowed her to do it.

The next day I broke up with Jackie, my parents were right about her not respecting me. But they were wrong about me not respecting myself. I did respect myself and I deserved to be treated better than Jackie was going to treat me.

MARCUS

My name is Marcus and my partner Raoul was verbally abusive to me. Raoul and I had a relationship for about seven months. Raoul was a carpenter and none of the guys that he worked with knew he was gay. He was embarrassed by our affair, embarrassed and ashamed. I didn't know it at the time, though.

I loved Raoul, I treated him like a king. Every night when he came home from work, I had dinner on the table waiting for him. I always had a clean house and he always went to work with a gourmet lunch. All the guys at work were jealous of Raoul.

I was so proud of him, I knew I kept a neat house and I took very good care of him. Everything was fine, until the day Raoul forgot his lunch and I decided to bring it to him. I guess I embarrassed him when I showed up.

Raoul grabbed me tightly by the arm and led me away from the construction site. When we stopped by my car he started to yell at me. He called me "Queenie" and many other awful things. As I got into my car, I felt the hot tears streaming down my cheeks.

That night when Raoul got home he and I started to argue terribly. Mean and hurtful words flowed so easily out of Raoul's mouth. I was surprised and heartbroken.

Raoul told me that no one at work knew about me and no one was ever going to, ever. I was proud of Raoul and happy in our relationship. I didn't realize until that day, how ashamed and embarrassed Raoul was about our relationship. How could we stay together if he felt that way? Why would we want to?

I brought that up to Raoul and he got very upset with me. To my surprise he slammed me against the wall. Then he slapped me across the face as he continued to yell at me. I wasn't sure what to do at that point, so I just stood there.

After a few minutes of hearing those insulting words he flung at me, he turned and walked out of the room. I stood there for a few minutes longer, still trying to understand what had just happened.

Okay, that was all I could take, I thought to myself. I walked into our room and grabbed a small suitcase, then I proceeded to pack some of my things. When I was done I walked right past Raoul and out the front door. I must admit, I was a little upset that Raoul didn't try to stop me as I walked out of the door.

I did go back to the house the next day, when I knew he was at work, to get the rest of my things. It was so hard to leave Raoul, but I am happier now and my partner is not ashamed of our relationship.

TOD

My wife and I were married for fourteen years and in the beginning we got along great. After the boys were born, she seemed to be very frustrated and unhappy.

We started to fight a lot and she even struck me a few times. We had triplets and the pressure was a lot for her. She was home all day long with our three boys and they were a handful. When I got home from work at night, I tried to help her out.

Slowly our marriage felt as though it were fading away. We didn't talk anymore, we yelled. We didn't discuss things, we ignored each other. I knew things were getting worse between us, but I didn't know what to do, or how to approach her with this issue. I just didn't know how to make things right again.

As the boys got older, they seemed to be harder for Alice to control. I tried to help her out as much as I could, but she was verbally abusive towards me, which made it hard for me to deal with.

The boys started to lose respect for me too, they started to talk to me like my wife did. I began to feel like less of a man, almost like I was nothing in my own home.

I tried to talk to my wife about it, but felt as though I was getting nowhere. I didn't want to live like this any longer. I wanted to be respected, especially in my own home.

After figuring out that I wasn't going to be able to talk with Alice about how I felt, I decided to leave. I needed to get away for a while. To be able to think.

I told Alice I felt I had to leave. She told me to go if I wanted to, but I had better plan on still paying the bills, because she couldn't leave our unruly boys with a sitter. She was right, our boys would have driven anyone to drink!

I moved out and stayed in a motel for three weeks. During that time, I stopped in at the house almost every day. I sometimes stayed for dinner and other times I actually stayed until eleven o'clock.

A funny thing happened during the three weeks that I was at the motel...Alice and I started to talk. We started to talk together and really listen to each other, it was wonderful. We were beginning to have actual conversations again.

By the end of three weeks, we were back together. We also started to see a counselor once a week. Now we get along much better and find ourselves talking about everything. It is wonderful and we have the kind of marriage I always wanted us to have. Our boys are still somewhat unruly, but we are working on that, together.

HARLAN

I was married to Tricia for over forty years, until she died of cancer. My dear wife was sick and in much agony for the last year of her life. We went through so much together. I loved her dearly and it was almost a blessing when she finally did pass away.

We had two daughters and they stood by Alice and me, through all the doctors appointments and the chemotherapy. Towards the end, when we realized that we were just grasping at straws, Alice begged me to let her come home. She had been in the hospital for three months, prior to that day. The doctors told us that the cancer had spread, there was no hope left.

I agreed to sign Alice out of the hospital, to bring her home so she could spend the rest of her days with our daughters and our grandchildren. We all knew Alice was dying and we tried to make the rest of her days as happy and worry free as we could. Alice spent every day basking in the love of her grandchildren, daughters and her husband.

On the day that Alice died we were all there with her. It was a very sad time for our entire family. Right before Alice died, she held onto my hand and whispered in my ear for me to get married again. She told me with a smile that I needed someone to take care of me.

Six months after Alice had died, I met a woman named Jane at the hardware store. She was younger than I was, much younger. She was actually closer to my daughter's ages. I guess looking back on it now, my daughters were upset. They had reason to be.

Jane was a very beautiful girl and she was fun to be with. We did a lot of things together. We went on cruises, many other trips and attended lots of dinner parties. I am a retired lawyer and I still own and oversee my law firm. I just wasn't as active as I had once been, but I still had my dinner parties, colleagues and clients that I kept in touch with.

I slowly began to back away from the firm and I found myself spending much more time with Jane. This began to concern my daughters very much, they didn't like Jane and they didn't hide it well at all.

Jane didn't like my daughters or my grandchildren, either. I didn't realize it at the time, I found out later that she was very rude to my girls. She told them that if they gave her a hard time, she would make it so that they would never see me again. Jane threatened to turn me against the girls, by telling me the things they said to her.

Unfortunately my daughters didn't come to me with these things at the time, which is probably just as well. I was pretty caught up in Jane. I would like to think that I would have listened to them, but I honestly probably wouldn't have.

Jane and I dated for about a year and during that time my daughters seemed to distance themselves from me. I can see it so clearly now looking back on it, but at the time I guess I was so flattered that someone as beautiful as Jane was interested in me, I didn't pay attention. She was young, fun and I truly enjoyed being with her.

Jane and I were vacationing in Cancun when my oldest daughter called. There had been an accident involving my son in law, I was needed back at home. I told Jane that I had to cancel the rest of our vacation. She told me that she had no intention of leaving yet.

I tried to explain to her that I needed to get back home. My son in law was in the hospital and my daughter needed me. Jane told me, if I left her there she was going to make my life miserable. I stared at her in disbelief. What was she saying? Why couldn't she seem to understand? What had I seen in her, other than the obvious?

I started to turn away from her and suddenly she ran towards me, hitting me from behind and knocking me against the wall. I bashed my head into the mirror. When I managed to pull myself upright, I saw blood on the mirror and the wall. I ran my hand across my forehead and felt the gash in my head.

I turned around and looked at Jane as the blood ran down the side of my face. "What is wrong with you?" I screamed at her.

"No one walks out on me!" Jane yelled back at me. "I will not take a back seat to your daughters!"

"My daughters have never done anything to you. And I have news for you, I am going to be the first one to walk out on you." I told her, feeling much calmer now.

Jane walked up to me and punched me in the nose. Then she started to throw more punches at me, making contact anywhere she could. I didn't hit her, but I did raise my hands trying to ward off the blows. I tried to talk to her, but she didn't seem to hear me.

Finally she must have gotten exhausted, because she stopped hitting me and she slumped down onto the bed. I looked down at her, then I picked up my jacket from the chair. I started to reach for the door, but before I opened it I turned back to Jane.

"We are through, I don't want you to contact me or my daughters again." I said to her firmly, as I opened the door and left.

I didn't look back as I walked out of the motel room. I left Jane in Cancun and I never saw her again.

After getting back, I spent much of my time at the hospital with my daughter and son in law. He was a very lucky young man indeed, his car had been hit by a drunk driver, which caused eight cars to pile up on the highway. The accident ended up killing six people and injuring eleven. I am very grateful that my son in law is okay now and that my family is back together again.

In the last few months, both of my daughters have come forward to tell me about the many things that Jane had said and done to them. I was furious with Jane. I was furious with myself for not seeing Jane for what she really was. I had been so blind! I was so flattered that someone like her wanted to be with me, I didn't think clearly. I hope that Alice didn't see what I allowed to happen to me and the girls, from my stupidity.

MORE OF OUR STORIES

These are stories about women in abusive relationships. They tell about what actually went on inside their homes. Some have survived by going into hiding, finding that our legal system doesn't work and some didn't make it out alive. A few have been helped through the legal system.

These stories are all too real for a lot of women, seeing these as 'their stories.'

But they all share a common goal, they want the abuse to stop. Many feel trapped for a number of reasons, but mainly because their financial situation makes it next to impossible to be able to leave, thereby forcing them to stay.

Things need to change for women and their children. The abuse needs to stop. The abuser needs to be punished, not just slapped on the wrist.

DEANA

My name is Deana and I was married to a very abusive man. His name was Todd. Todd started out being so sweet and nice, so attentive and caring. Then I don't know what happened, I guess that gradually he changed. I mean, it seemed like all of a sudden that he changed, but I guess that it really happened a little bit at a time.

He started out verbally abusing me and then he started slapping me. Finally it ended up with him punching and kicking me. Then I became terrified of him, I really thought that he was going to kill me.

It got to the point where I had to leave, so I went to a shelter and they helped me to get away. They helped me to leave and to stay away. Now I am safe and I have a whole new life. I have a new name and I am finally away from Todd.

CARRIE

Carrie was a waitress in a popular restaurant. She was dating a guy who worked in a law office. Craig was a jealous man. He didn't trust Carrie, he didn't trust anyone.

She eventually got sick of his angry, violent outbursts and split up with him. He didn't take the break up very well at all.

One night when she left the restaurant, she was run down in the parking lot. A co-worker saw the car leaving and had gotten the license plate number.

Carrie died later that night in the hospital. Craig is in prison for her murder.

DANIELLE

My name is Danielle and I killed my husband. It was in self defense. My husband beat on me many times. I was admitted to the hospital numerous times, because of him. I had a broken jaw, had lost some teeth, I even had broken ribs and my arm was broken on three different occasions. I was only married for three years!

When I got out of the hospital the last time, I'd received stitches above my eye. As soon as I got home, Jack went after me again. This time he had a hunting knife. As I ran through the house trying to avoid him, I grabbed a kitchen knife. I hid in the closet and after he had passed by, I quietly slipped out. I snuck up behind him and I stabbed him in the back.

He dropped to his knees and told me that he was going to kill me. I pulled the knife out and stabbed him with it again. I knew he was dead when he fell forward.

I ran from the room and I called the cops. When they came I told them what had happened. They called an ambulance to take my husband's body away. Finally most of the cops left, but one of them stayed behind and told me that it would most likely be ruled as self defense. It was ruled as self defense.

TERESA

Teresa worked in a women's clothing store in the mall. A man came in a few times a week and just hung around. He made her feel uncomfortable, but he was a potential customer.

She was pleasant to him and at the same time she made sure that she did nothing to lead him on. He would keep asking her to go out for coffee or drinks with him, but she always refused.

When the individual stores would start to close down at night, the man would hang out in the food court, just watching her. Teresa's manager also noticed this and she called security.

Unfortunately, the man was doing nothing wrong. All they could do was watch him, which they did, for a while, but they had other things to do.

One night when Teresa left the mall she didn't see 'the man.' 'Maybe he had gotten tired of being rejected,' she thought to herself. She didn't notice the man sitting in one of the cars in the parking lot.

Teresa climbed into her car and drove away from the mall. She drove straight home to her apartment, not noticing the man that was following her.

She got out of her car and unlocked the door to her apartment. As she was about to shut the door someone slammed into her, pushing her into the livingroom and away from the door. She looked up and saw the same man from the mall. He shut the door and he grabbed her by the throat.

"Go out with me," he told her.

"No." Teresa said to him.

Slowly he put more pressure on her throat, he squeezed until she stopped struggling and slid to the floor.

She was unconscious, but he thought that she was dead, so he left her there in her apartment. When she came to, she called the police. They took her statement and brought her to the hospital to be checked over. The cops told her that they didn't have much hope of finding the guy.

Teresa decided to quit her job and move away, since the man knew where she lived. She couldn't be sure that he would never come back.

KATHLEEN

Kathleen had been dated Roger for a few weeks, when she discovered that he had a terrible temper. She had him over for dinner and had cooked the pot roast too long, causing it to dry out. Roger was very upset and he threw his plate of food onto the floor.

"I can't eat this crap." Roger yelled at her.

"It's just a little dried out, but it's still good." Kathleen said to him.

"Don't ever serve me something like this again." He told her, before he slapped her across the face.

Kathleen stared at him in disbelief. Roger stormed out of the door, leaving her to clean up the mess on the floor.

Later that night, Roger came back to her apartment. His knocking soon turned to banging when she refused to answer the door. Then her phone started ringing, it rang and rang.

Finally after about an hour, he seemed to grow bored and he stopped.

Kathleen did answer the phone the next day and it was Roger. She told him to leave her alone and he did. Kathleen thought the whole situation was very strange.

BRENDA

Brenda shared an apartment with her older sister. Brenda went to college and worked part time in a bakery. Her older sister, Sue, was a model.

Brenda started dating Donny, who she found out was not very pleasant to be around when he had been drinking or was drunk. He became a totally different person.

One night Brenda told him that things just weren't working out between them and that they really needed to see other people. He seemed to accept it and Brenda left him to go home.

From the time that Brenda had left Donny, until the time that Sue got home, it is still unclear as to what actually happened that night. Somehow Brenda had made it back home, because her sister found her under the bed, with her throat slit. No one saw or heard anything. Donny had no alibi, but there wasn't enough evidence to convict him.

RAMONA

Ramona met Dan at the laundry mat. They talked while each of them did their laundry. Then they went out to have a cup of coffee together. Things were going pretty well, so they agreed to see each other the next day. They dated casually for a few months.

Ramona told all of her friends that she and Dan were in love. You always saw the two of them together. Everything looked great on the outside, but Ramona kept a lot of secrets.

Dan was very abusive and Ramona was too ashamed to tell anyone. She blamed herself for her situation. But she wasn't sure how to get herself out of it.

Things steadily got worse for her as Dan became much more violent. A few months later, Ramona told her friends that she was going to break up with Dan. She said it was because things just weren't working out, so she was going to tell him that weekend.

Saturday night on the news, one of Ramona's friends heard about a fire near Ramona's house. Quickly she called Ramona, but no one answered.

On Sunday she decided to go visit her friend. When she got closer to the house, she realized that the fire had been at Ramona's. She pulled up to the side of the street and saw a detective walking around with the fire marshal.

Ramona's friend got out of her car and she ran over to the two men.

"Where is Ramona? Is she okay?" she asked, concerned about her friend.

"I'm sorry ma'am. There was a female found in the house. Her body is being autopsied now." The detective told her, writing something down in his notebook.

"How did the fire start?" her friend asked.

"It was set with gasoline." The fire marshal told her. "Someone set it."

"Oh my god, where is Dan?" she asked them.

"There was only one female found, no male." The detective said, turning his attention back to her. "Is that her husband?"

"No, but Dan did it." Ramona's friend told the men.

They all walked over to the detective's car and they listened to what she had to say. When she'd finished, the detective told her that they would be investigating what they were now calling, 'the murder.'

Ramona's friend left, she was terribly upset about losing her friend.

A few days later, the detective knocked at her friends door. He told her that they believed the fire had been set to try to hide the fact that Ramona had been murdered. She had died from a blow to the head by a blunt object. They also told her that Dan had been arrested, but so far he had not been cooperating with them.

EMILY

I'm Emily, well, at least that was my name before I'd been forced to leave. My husband used to abuse me. I'm not talking a slap here and there. I'm talking broken bones, busted lips and lots of stitches. I even had to have a bridge put in my mouth, because some of my teeth had been punched out.

Each time the beatings got worse and they lasted for a longer period of time. If the house wasn't vacuumed every day, if items were out of place in the cupboards or if the sheets had just one wrinkle on them, I'd be beaten. It really was ridiculous. You would think, that a lawyer would have other things on his mind, besides being such a perfectionist.

He wanted me to take pride in our home, my appearance, our yard and my cooking. He said that all of these things reflected back on him, which I guess it did. He was wrong though, I did take pride in all of those things, but I also felt that you should be able to take a little break once in a while. Did the house really need to be dusted everyday? Maybe once a week, but not every day.

I called the shelter numerous times, but I never actually went there. I was afraid of my husband. He told me that he would kill me if I ever left him. I honestly thought that he would. Besides, I had no money to go anywhere.

I found out that I was pregnant and he beat me up really bad. He kicked me and punched me in the stomach. Three days later I started bleeding. After being examined, the doctor told me that I'd had a miscarriage. I was heart broken. My husband was happy. He laughed, then he told me he could preform an abortion. He kept telling me that and each time he'd laugh at the pain he was causing me.

A week later, after another horrific beating, I called the shelter again. I was still recuperating from my miscarriage. One of the volunteers at the shelter came to pick me up. I had already packed a couple of bags and that day I walked out of my house, for the last time.

I was afraid of what my future might bring, but I was terrified of what my present held.

Two days later I boarded a bus, looking forward to the new life that was waiting for me. I was excited about it, but also very frightened at the thought of leaving everything that was familiar to me. I knew that I would always have to be careful and watch out for my husband.

ROBIN

My name is Robin now and I am finally safe. Ken was a very abusive man, who seemed to get real pleasure in causing me pain and discomfort. He used to love to torture and torment me. Ken used to burn me with his cigarettes, take pins and stab me with them, as well as punch, kick and slap me.

This torture and abuse went on for two years, I was so afraid of him. I had no doubt that one day he would kill me. I was always being threatened with death by him. During some of the abuse, I had actually wished and prayed for death. I felt like I couldn't endure anymore abuse.

He would do these awful things to me for stupid reasons. Like I didn't do the laundry one day or there were some spots on our drinking glasses. Yeah, those are some really good reasons to abuse someone.

One day he even grabbed my hand and held it on top of the stove...because there was a wrinkle on his shirt. He used to hold his lit cigarettes up to my arm or on my back and burn me with them.

Ken had a very good job, he was a broker. So why did he do the things that he did to me? Who knows.

I was afraid to tell anyone, until the day he took the iron and held it to the side of my face. The sheets weren't smoothed out and I just happened to be ironing his shirts for work. He absolutely hated wrinkles, anywhere. My face burned so bad. To this day, I still pull my hair over the side of my face to try to cover up the burn.

After he left for work, I called the shelter. A woman from the shelter came and picked me up. I stayed at the shelter for less than two days, then I was put onto a bus. They wanted to get me away from him as soon as possible.

I was on my way to a new life and a safe life. I was so excited and really looking forward to the move.

Today it has been three years since I left and I feel much better about myself and everything. I still worry that Ken may find me, but I pray every night that he doesn't.

I have a job, my own place and a whole new life, thanks to the women at the shelter. A little makeup covers the awful red mark left on the side of my face by the iron, eventually I hope it will fade. The burn scars from the cigarettes have faded, somewhat.

It'll be a long time before I can ever trust another man.

JUDY

Judy was my old name, I used to live in a big beautiful house. I drove a brand new car and had tons of clothes. But with all of those things came a terribly high price. I was abused by my husband, at least once a week.

Every Monday when he came home, after the weekly sales meeting at work, he'd be in a miserable mood. He almost always had a late lunch and it just built up from there. By the time he drove home, he'd be in a real ugly mood.

My husband owned his own business. I realize that he was under a great deal of stress, but I also felt it was unfair that he take things out on me. It wasn't my fault things weren't going well at work. My husband owned a good size advertising agency and he had quite a few employees.

He used to tell people that he'd never hit me with a closed fist. He actually bragged about the abuse he inflicted on me! But my husband was right, he never did hit me with a closed fist. It was usually a backhand swing or a slap. Occasionally, he'd hit me with his belt, the dog's leash or whatever else he happened to grab.

I put up with the abuse for five years. I can't explain why I left when I did and not before, but I will admit, when I left him I was terrified. I knew that I would get nothing or have nothing when I left him. He always told me if I left, he'd hunt me down and kill me. I honestly was afraid he would.

One Monday night he came home in a real ugly mood. He said that he was going to have to fire some of his employees. He grabbed a coat hanger and he hit me on the back and legs with it, that really hurt.

When I got up the next morning I was pretty stiff. I decided that I'd endured enough abuse and I called the shelter. I gathered up a few things and I drove to the shelter.

The women were so nice and helpful. They took my car and parked it at the mall, so he wouldn't be able to find me at the shelter. They told me what I needed to do to stay safe. The next day I left and I have never gone back.

Today I have about ten outfits, I live in a small dingy apartment and I drive an old junk of a car. But I am happier now, than I ever was with all of that 'stuff.' I don't wake up stiff, sore or bruised anymore. I haven't gone to bed afraid or in pain!

I feel much more relaxed and at ease. Although I do keep a watchful eye out for any sign of my husband. Other than that, life is pretty good. I have a job and I make my own money. Who would have thought that by having so little, I have actually gained so much?

JILL

My name is Jill and my husband is in prison for murder. When we were separated, he was allowed visitation rights with our small son. I still can't figure out why a judge would allow it, especially after all of the documentation we had proving his abusive behavior. But the judges do not look at each case individually, I know that now. They should, but unfortunately, they don't.

My husband used to beat on me and our little son Anthony. We had doctor's letters, police records, you name it. I finally left him and some stupid judge allowed visitation. The worst part is, that the judge can not be held accountable for what happens during visitations. Where is the justice?

My husband got our three-year-old son on Saturday afternoon and he was supposed to bring him back on Sunday. This was the first visit since I'd left him. That stupid judge decided it was in my son's best interest to have a relationship with his father. Little Anthony was terrified of him!

I spent a very nervous night at our new apartment and on Sunday when he didn't return Anthony, I was beside myself. I called the cops and being familiar with my case, they got right on it. They started looking for them, for my Anthony.

When they arrived at my old house, they caught my husband digging a hole in the backyard. One of the cops stayed with him and the other one went into the house.

The first thing he saw when he entered the house, he thought, was just a pile of blankets. The cop walked over to the small pile and lifted a few of them up. That was when he discovered my son's small, lifeless body.

My husband had killed my son. My son had over one hundred and twenty stab wounds in his little body.

The cops arrested my husband and now he is in prison. No matter what punishment they give him, it will never be enough for what he'd done to my baby.

I think that the judge should be serving a sentence alongside my husband, for allowing this to happen! After all the documentation I presented to him and he still allowed the visits, it isn't right. How many other people does this happen to?

KELLY

My name is Kelly and my husband was very abusive towards me, for the entire year that we were together. On the day we got married, he said to me 'so, now your mine.' I thought it was an odd comment to make. During the three years we dated, he had never even raised a finger to me.

His father died two months after we'd gotten married. My husband worked for his dad's trucking company, so now all of the responsibility was his. He didn't know how to run the business and he used to get very frustrated.

When he would come home, he'd be in a real ugly mood. I figured that once he got used to it he'd be fine. But he wasn't, he just couldn't seem to grasp the idea of how to run a business. Slowly the business started to lose money and within six months, he was threatened with repossession.

That's when he started to hit me. I realized that he was upset about failing at the business that his father had spent his entire life building.

First he slapped me and then he started punching me. After about the third time, I figured that it was just going to get worse, before it ever got better. So I left him. I walked out, filed for a divorce and I now live in a small apartment alone.

I knew that if he hit me once, he most certainly would do it again. I didn't want to become another statistic.

EMMA

My name is Emma. I used to be married to the meanest man alive. Even the kids were afraid of him, we have three daughters. We had never been blessed with sons, which my husband has always blamed me for. That's what Carl was mad about, he always wanted sons to take over the farm one day. The girls didn't want anything to do with it. They also didn't want anything to do with their father.

He used to beat on me and the girls. We all had to wait on him hand and foot. That man thought that he had four slaves.

The occasional beatings I could handle, but when he started touching my girls…that's where I drew the line. I wouldn't stand for that.

First he started to molest our oldest daughter and then he went right down the line. What would cause a man to do something like that? The girls talked about it with each other and then they decided to come to me. They were afraid, because he told them if they told me or anyone he'd kill them.

I called the shelter and someone was at our house to pick us up within half an hour. My husband had gone into town for some supplies, so I knew that we didn't have much time. We had some of our things ready and we were waiting for them.

Sandy, from the shelter helped us to leave. We are now far away from my husband and we don't have to worry about getting hit by him anymore. The best part is, that he will never again molest my girls.

JOSIE

My name is Josie and my daughter killed her father, while he was abusing me. Right before she had killed him, he'd been beating on her.

You see, Jack drank a lot and I suspected that he was involved with drugs, although I wasn't positive. But every Friday night he'd come home drunk and he would wake me and our daughter up. He always wanted something to eat, so that's what we did, we'd cook for him.

As we were making his food he would insult and ridicule us. Of course we didn't say anything, because he would just start hitting us that much sooner. We knew that would come soon enough!

After he ate he would just start picking on everything, the house was dusty, the dishes weren't done or why was there a pile of clothes not put away? No matter what, he'd get mad. Sometimes even the most stupid thing would set him off.

Jack would come after us and we tried to avoid getting hit with his hand, fist, his belt or whatever else he felt like hitting us with.

A few times he had even thrown boiling water or hot grease at us, almost always splattering us with the hot liquid. Both of us had lots of tiny scars on our faces and arms from him.

Jack was miserable to be around, that was for sure. Sometimes he would remember something that happened months before and it would set him off again.

One time when my daughter and I went grocery shopping, a woman had backed up into us in the parking lot. We only had a small dent in the bumper, but you could have sworn the car had been totaled by the way Jack acted when he saw it! He threw a major fit and ushered us into the house, where he then proceeded to hit us. The accident wasn't even my fault.

Jack used to reach out and hit us as we walked by him, for no reason. My daughter and I were both terribly afraid of him. There was nowhere we could go and no one who we could turn to. A few times I had gone to my parents house, but they were old. Jack would come over and bang on their door in the middle of the night, which upset the both of them. I didn't want to keep putting them through that, so I stayed at home and I dealt with it. My dad used to say to me 'Josie, you made your bed, so now you've got to lay in it.'

The night that my daughter killed her father, he'd been drinking a lot. He'd already beat us both up earlier and he was now getting ready for round two.

Jack yelled for my daughter, but she was in her room trying to avoid him.

She was doing her school work and listening to the radio. She told me that she hadn't heard him calling to her. He stomped in there to get her.

When I went into the bedroom to see why it was so quiet, I was shocked. My daughter was standing against the wall and Jack had his hands around her throat, he was forcing her to kiss him. I yelled at him and he quickly let her go. I could see that my daughter was upset and crying.

Jack said something about 'his two women' and I started to yell at him. He turned, pushed me and I fell to the floor. Suddenly he was on top of me, slapping and punching me.

My daughter jumped on his back and started to punch him. This really angered him, because we had never fought back before. He somehow managed to get her off of him, just before he punched me in the nose.

Jack started to choke our daughter again and I could see that she was having a hard time breathing. I hit him in the back with the broom, which made him let go of her and come after me again.

Our daughter saw this and grabbed my cast iron pan, she clubbed her father on the side of his head. He fell to the floor and blood started to form a puddle around his head. That's when I noticed, that he wasn't breathing.

I dialed 911 and soon the paramedics came. They told me that my husband had no pulse or respiration, he was dead.

After we talked to the cops, no charges were placed against my daughter. The cops passed the file over to the District Attorney's office and they decided not to press any charges.

JASMINE

My name is Jasmine and I was married to Mark for six months. When we had been married for about three months, he started to show his true colors. He became very violent. One night when we had gone out to a club, a guy came over to talk to me, after Mark had gone to the rest room. When Mark came back he saw the guy. He walked right up to us and hit the guy. Then he slapped me in the face, telling me that I had embarrassed him.

A few weeks later, we went bowling with a couple and Mark started again. We lost the game and he got very upset with me, again he slapped me. We never went out with that couple again.

It kept getting worse, it got to the point were no matter what I did he would get mad at me. He would almost always slap me or he'd punch me.

I'd put up with it for six months and then I decided that I'd had enough. He wasn't going to change at all. I could tell by the way the beatings were becoming more frequent. I knew that eventually he would hurt me again, so I left him. We got a divorce. Actually I filed for a divorce. He tried to fight it, but the judge let me have the divorce.

Today I pretend that it never happened.

ANNIE

Annie attended dance class every Monday night, she also stayed a little late to practice after her class. She'd known her teacher for ten years and Ms. Todd let her lock up when she was through. She always wanted to be a professional dancer and she dreamed that someday she would make it to Broadway.

One Monday before class, a man was standing out in the parking lot, she'd seen him there before. She assumed that he was a father. Although, a while later she remembered that he was the same man who had followed her through the mall. She started to walk towards the door and he asked her for some money. She told him no and quickly walked away.

When she got inside the dance school, she looked out the window. He was following her! He opened the door and he asked her to go back outside.

"No!" she told him, turning away.

He reached out his hand and slapped her across the face. Annie was caught off guard and she was very surprised.

"I'm going to call the police, if you don't leave, now." Annie told him, as she tried to hold back the tears.

He walked out the door and Annie went into the classroom. She lined up with the other girls and started to do some of the stretches.

By the end of the class she'd almost forgotten about the man. She stayed and practiced for about an hour after the class had ended.

When she was through, she locked up the door and went out to her car. Suddenly a hand reached out from under her car and grabbed her by the ankle. Annie tripped and fell onto the ground, scraping her elbow and both of her hands.

Annie saw the 'homeless' man crawling out from under her car. Before she could stand up, the man grabbed her by the hair and pulled her up, then he stabbed her with his pocket knife. Over and over again, that tiny two inch blade penetrated into Annie. She had never felt such pain before. Slowly she fell back onto the ground and she lay there, until the light faded completely from her eyes. She thought about Broadway and how she would never make it there now.

KERI

My name is Keri and Samantha and I lived together for nearly eight years, we even bought a house together. I thought things were going great between us and they were, for the first seven years. Then everything started to fall apart.

Sam lost her job due to downsizing, then she became depressed. Shortly after that, she was involved in a car wreck, which injured her back. Once a week Sam went to a chiropractor and she was given pain pills, which she became addicted to. It was a pretty rough time for us.

At about the same time I got a promotion at work, not only did I get more pay, but I also had a lot more responsibility. The job caused me to be away from home longer during the day. This angered Sam, especially because of the promotion that I got. It really bothered her, I think because she had lost her job.

Sam started to verbally abuse me. She would say such mean and hurtful things to me. This went on for months. One day I came home and found a woman's jacket hanging from the doorknob in the bedroom. I asked Sam about it and she told me that a neighbor of our's had stopped by. Okay, but why was her jacket in our bedroom? When I asked Sam that question she became violent, she slapped me across the face and started yelling at me. Sam told me that I ignored her. I put my job first, I never spent any time with her and that our neighbor was very attentive towards her. She was even teaching Sam how to play golf.

I was totally devastated. I was working so hard to keep up with all of the house payments since Sam had been laid up. Not only was I paying my portion of the bills, but I was also paying her portion as well. The accident had been Sam's fault, so she wasn't collecting anything from it. We got stuck with all of the bills.

I told her that I didn't think she was being fair, I was busting my tail to support the both of us. Not only was I making the house payments, but I was paying the utilities, the credit card bills, her doctor bills, her prescriptions and buying the food. I was so upset with her.

"Sam I am not going to continue to pay for everything, while you sit in this house and entertain our neighbor!" I told her. I admit that I was more than a little bit jealous.

"Are you accusing me of something?" Sam asked, coming closer to me.

"No, not really. But if your okay enough to play golf, then you probably ought to think about, maybe finding a job. At least a part time job." I said.

"I'll go back to work when I feel like I'm ready to go back to work!" Sam yelled at me.

"All I'm saying, is that I need some help with the bills. I didn't create all of these bills myself. Besides the credit card bills are yours, not mine." I tried to explain to her where I was coming from.

Sam made a fist and punched me in the face, causing me to fall back against the wall.

"What is wrong with you?" I asked her, in total surprise.

"Don't tell me what to do. I still don't feel well enough to work, so get off my back!" Sam yelled at me. She grabbed me by the hair, yanking hard. "Do you understand?" she asked me.

"Yes." I whispered.

Sam had never acted like this before. There was no way that I was going to sit here and take this.

That night when Sam was taking a shower, I put a bunch of my clothes inside the washer, but I didn't turn it on. After Sam had taken her pills she went in to bed. I put the clothes from the washer into a bag and I quietly brought it out to my car.

I went through all of our papers and made copies on our copy machine. Insurance papers, bank account numbers, anything that I thought I might need. Then I made another trip out to my car with those.

When I was done I lay down on the couch and I fell asleep. I woke up at three in the morning to see Sam staring down at me. I had purposely left the TV on, so it didn't look like I stayed out there intentionally. Sam was furious with me for falling asleep on the couch.

"Get in bed." Sam yelled at me.

I slowly got up from the couch and I followed her into the bedroom, where we made love. I didn't really want to do it, but I didn't want her to somehow figure out what I had planned for the next day.

I woke up at six thirty and I took a shower. As I got ready for work I tried to think if there was anything that I had forgotten to get together.

I jumped when Sam walked into the room. We talked for a few minutes and then I left for work.

Once I got to work I called the shelter. 'We only deal with traditional couples.' I was told by the woman on the phone. 'Traditional couples?' I was still a woman in desperate need.

I wasn't sure who to call or where to go for help, since 'we weren't a traditional couple.' I called a lawyer and she advised me not to go home. I went to a motel that night and met with the lawyer in the morning.

She was really great, her name is Angel and she turned out to be an angel.

She helped me to get my name off the house, the utilities out of my name and we took out most of the money in the accounts, because it was mostly mine. I did take a loss on the house. We had a contract drawn up which read, when and if the house went up for sale, I would get half of the money.

Angel really watched out for me and made sure everything was pretty fair. I did take a loss, but it was worth it to me to get out of that situation.

Sam still lives in the house, but I also live in a nice house. You see, Angel and I have gotten together. I am very happy and so much in love! We are planning on starting a family together later this year.

GWEN

My name was Gwen and now I have a new name. It's kind of weird, because everything is so different now. My baby has just turned two and she is doing really well. I actually left when I was pregnant. Now I live in a whole new place, just the two of us. I don't know anyone and no one knows about my past.

The worst part is, that my parents have never seen their granddaughter. Vanessa will never be able to know her grandparents, because of Bob.

Bob and I got married when I was four months pregnant. We had lots of problems before we got married, but I hoped that things would get better between us, they didn't.

I stayed with Bob for three months before I left him, he treated me so badly. He would spit at me, hit me, pull my hair and even burn me with his cigarettes. He would get mad over the stupidest things, like because the laundry was still out hanging on the line or my nail polish was chipped.

After putting up with this for about three months I went into a shelter. I knew that things would get even worse after the baby was born. He kept telling me that he didn't want 'it.'

I went to the shelter and they helped me to leave Bob. They told me where to go and what to do once I got there. They understood what I was going through. They also gave me some money and a bus ticket.

They even found me a midwife, who delivered my baby so I didn't have to go to the hospital. I had my daughter while I was staying in another shelter. The women there were great and they helped me out a lot. After my daughter was born, they helped me to find an apartment. That way it would be next to impossible for Bob to find us.

My daughter and I are both doing great.

HARRIET

My name is Harriet and I am in prison for the murder of my husband. Yes, I killed my husband, but for years he abused me. But because he was a cop they really stuck it to me. They said that they wanted to make an example out of me.

For years Troy would hit me or punch me. Sometimes he would pull out his gun and threaten to shoot me with it. I was so afraid of him.

On the night that I killed him, he had come home drunk and started in on me. I threatened to leave him, which I had never done before. Oh, this got him very upset and he started hitting me more. I ran out into the kitchen, but he followed me. Troy picked up a knife and grabbed me by the waist. As he held the knife up to my throat, I honestly thought I was going to die.

I reached around and grabbed for his gun. Somehow I managed to get it into my hand. He kept screaming at me, unaware that I was holding his gun in my hand. Suddenly he pushed me away and that's when he saw me holding the gun, my hands were both shaking. Troy laughed at me, then he started to walk towards me.

"I'll shoot you Troy! You'd better stop right there." I told him, as calmly as I could.

"Don't you ever threaten me." Troy said, as he came closer to me.

I clicked off the safety and fired his gun, afraid of what he was going to do to me. Suddenly I was afraid of what I had done to him.

I had shot him in the chest, Troy's eyes widened as he stared at me in disbelief. He made some little croaking noises and then he fell to the floor. I knelt down beside him and called out his name, but he didn't move at all.

I ran over to the phone and quickly dialed 911. Within minutes my house was full of cops. One of them came over to me and asked me what had happened. I told him and then he walked back over to the others. I watched them talking quietly together, then he came back over to me and roughly put handcuffs on my wrists. A few of the others came over, they told me that I was being arrested for murder.

"But I was defending myself!" I screamed at them.

"There is no physical evidence on you to make me to believe that you have been abused. I can see no bruises or marks of any kind. Therefore, until you go to trial, I am forced to treat you as I would any other suspect in a murder case." The cop told me, sounding mean.

"What?" I asked, completely confused.

"As far as I know, there is no documented proof to support your claims of abuse. Is there?" the same cop asked me.

I didn't know how to respond, besides there was nothing that I could do. They brought me to jail and a few days later I went into court, where my attorney entered my 'not guilty' plea. I was held on such a high bail, that I couldn't possibly make it out of jail.

At the trial, my lawyer tried to help me, but I had no evidence to support anything that I tried to tell them. All the times that I had called the police station for help were either destroyed or never even entered into their log book.

I had never been to the hospital or had any pictures taken of my injuries. Some of his fellow officers testified that on the occasions they had seen us together, he was nothing but loving and attentive towards me. They made me out to be an attention seeking, lying wife.

What? I know I had called the station at least twenty times. I had even talked to Rachel, the dispatcher, about the abuse at some of their baseball games. But when Rachel got up to testify, she never made eye contact with me. When my lawyer questioned her about those times, she said that she couldn't recall our conversations. They were all protecting him and at the same time they were ruining my life!

At more than one policeman's ball, Troy had been abusive towards me in front of many of them. They were all lying and there was nothing I could do about it.

The judge sentenced me to life in prison for the murder of my husband. I couldn't believe the ruling! So now it has been over a year and I am sitting here in jail. I am waiting for my appeal which keeps getting bumped back. I was abused by my husband and yes, I did shoot him, but I was only trying to protect myself.

GRETA

My name used to be Greta, but now I have a new name, a new place to live and a whole new life. Randy, my four-year-old and I have had a really rough start. I finally got us out and away from an abusive relationship and now we are safe.

Todd was my boyfriend, he's not Randy's father, but we did start dating while I was pregnant. He pretty much ignored Randy, except when he'd hit him or chase him around with a belt.

Randy started to wet himself again, he had been doing so well before that. But once the abuse started he began to wet his pants. He'd wet himself during the day and he'd also wet the bed at night.

Todd would get so angry at Randy. He would hit him with his belt and when I would try to stop him, he'd hit me with the belt. He rarely hit Randy or me with his hands. He seemed to prefer a belt or a stick, both of which really hurt.

Randy and I were both so afraid of Todd. Sometimes for no reason Todd would just start hitting us. This went on for nearly two years, at first Todd was fairly decent to us, he just yelled a lot.

When I saw what it was doing to my Randy, I decided that we had to get out. Randy started to whine a lot and he became petrified of the dark, which he never had been before. He started to wet the bed almost every night and he even started to 'baby talk.'

I left our apartment and went to stay with friends of mine, but that didn't keep Todd away. He found out where we were and he threatened to kill us if we didn't come home.

I took Randy and went into a shelter. They helped us to get away and start a whole new life. I am so grateful to them for everything. They gave me a whole new start, a whole new beginning.

Randy still sleeps with me, but he's getting much better.

GRETCHEN

My name is Gretchen and I am now divorced from my abusive husband. Although my four daughters seem to be siding with my ex, which I can't figure out why. Maybe they feel bad for him, because I left him.

They will never know how many times they slipped by without getting beaten, because I took it for them. When he was upset and going to go after one of the girls, I stood up for them. He'd look at me and ask 'Are you gonna take it for her?' to which I'd always answer 'yes.' Don't get me wrong, I didn't enjoy the beatings, but I didn't want my girls to be hurt. Especially when most of the times that he wanted to go after them, it was because of something stupid that they could have just been asked about. They never knew what I did for them.

Since the divorce Ted has told them that I lied about everything. He said that I had cheated on him and that I was emotionally unstable. They aren't even civil to me anymore, because they blame me for splitting up our family.

It is killing me inside, but there is nothing that I can do about it. Maybe someday they will listen to my side of things.

LUCY

My name is Lucy and my husband used to hurt me quite a bit. I always hoped that things would get better, but they never did, it only got steadily worse. I had wanted kids, but now I am thankful that we never had any. Floyd was a very mean person and I'm not sure how he would have treated a child. I do know that he was awfully mean to animals.

My sister had given me a puppy for my birthday one year, which Floyd ended up killing less than two weeks later. I watched in horror as he kicked that puppy, it lay whimpering and trying to crawl away from him. He kicked it and kicked it, until that poor thing didn't move anymore. The whole time I screamed for him to stop and when I tried to stop him, he slapped me and pushed me away. When he was done I picked up the lifeless little body and cried as I held onto it. I kept telling the puppy how sorry I was.

Floyd got worse and I didn't know what to do. He wouldn't let me talk to my sister anymore and I couldn't do anything outside of the house either. He took away my car, disconnected the phone and he would lock me inside the house, while he was at work.

One day after having endured a terrible beating the night before, we had an electrical fire inside the house. I couldn't call for help and I had to get out of the burning house, so I broke out a window. I knew that Floyd was going to be really mad at me when he got home, but I didn't want to burn to death.

The firemen and police both showed up. There was so much commotion going on, that I blended right in with the crowd that had formed in the street. I shrank back farther into the crowd, when I saw Floyd's car coming up the street.

'Oh god.' I said softly to myself. I watched Floyd get out of the car and run up to the house. Two cops quickly pulled him back, before he could get too close to the burning building.

"Lucy!" He yelled out, trying to break free of the hands that were holding him back.

I looked around to see if anyone recognized me and to my relief no one did. I quickly slipped away from the crowd and headed down the street. I ducked behind bushes every time a car drove by, fearing that it would be Floyd. I was so afraid that Floyd would catch me.

I somehow managed to make it to the convenience store at the end of the street. They let me call my sister. Annie brought me to a shelter, where they helped me.

I hoped that Floyd would think that I'd died in the fire, but the women at the shelter told me they wouldn't find a body, so he would most definitely be looking for me. I thought about just taking off, but that would mean I couldn't keep in contact with my sister.

The women at the shelter found out that Floyd was being questioned by the police. They wanted to know why the doors to the house were all locked from the outside. They also asked him why I was still missing. Together, the women at the shelter, my sister and I came up with a plan and we went forward to the police.

Later Floyd was arrested, tried and he is now in jail. I was basically kept a prisoner in our home. We are divorced and I live in a pretty nice apartment. The house had burned almost completely, but we did have insurance on it. The district court judge ended up giving me most of the insurance money. He told Floyd that it was to cover my pain and suffering. Floyd was so mad about the courts decision, he yelled out, ' that he was going to kill me,' as the police led him away.

I don't know what I'll do when Floyd is released from jail. I do know that he will come after me, which really scares me, but I will deal with it when the time comes.

JENNA

My name is Jenna, I'm twenty-two-years-old and I will never be able to walk again. I wanted to be a dancer, all of my life I have dreamed of becoming a dancer. I started taking ballet lessons when I was eight and have had lessons ever since, at least three classes a week.

I met a guy named Jake at the mall and we went out for a few months, but it was never serious. He wanted more from me than I was able or willing to give. I had a dream and I didn't want to give that up. I told him right from the start that I could only be serious about my dancing. I never mislead him and I was always up front and honest with him.

After dating for only a few months, Jake asked me to marry him and he got very angry when I told him no. Actually he had started talking about marriage after our first week together. He also started to get upset with me because I spent so much of my time at the dance studio. I always had done that, so nothing had changed.

I couldn't figure out why he started to get so upset about my dancing. One night, he practically begged me to marry him and I told him no. Jake slapped me and then he punched me in the stomach. I didn't know how to react. I had never been hit before, nor had I ever seen anyone else get hit.

"You are going to marry me or you'll be sorry." Jake yelled at me.

I was still trying to catch my breath, but I did manage to whisper that I didn't want to get married. Jake grabbed me by my hair and he pulled me up.

"You are going to change your mind." He told me, his face only inches from mine. "Or I'll kill you."

I began to shake uncontrollably, then I heard my roommate Kathi unlocking the front door to our apartment. Jake heard her and let go of me.

"Is anyone home?" Kathi called out.

Jake looked down at me. "I'll be back later, we aren't finished yet," he said to me.

"Hey you guys." Kathi said, walking into the livingroom. She quickly took in the scene before her. "Is everything okay?"

Jake turned and walked out of the room. I waited until I heard the front door shut, before I told Kathi what happened. Kathi went out to the kitchen and locked the front door. When she came back into the room, we decided that if Jake called again, she was going to tell him that I wasn't home. That's what she did when he called. For almost a week, Jake followed me and continuously called the apartment. I told him that I didn't want to see him anymore, which seemed to really anger him.

One day as I was crossing through the parking lot, heading from my car to the dance studio, I heard a car revving it's engine. When looked up I saw Jake behind the wheel of his car. His car started to drive straight towards me. I tried to get out of the way, but it seemed like whichever way I went Jake followed me.

Suddenly I felt a sharp pain in my hips and legs as the car struck me. I heard a loud cracking sound and the pain that I had originally felt, turned to a numbness. I know I fell, but I don't remember falling down.

I heard Jake yell. "That'll teach you," before he drove off.

People started to crowd around me and I think that once I knew I wasn't alone, that's when I passed out. When I came to, I was laying in a hospital bed. One of my first visitors was Ms. Derby, my ballet instructor. She was holding onto my hand and crying softly. When she realized that I was awake, she looked up at me.

"I'm so sorry," she whispered to me, I saw the tears rolling down her cheek.

"Why? My legs…oh god, I can't feel my legs. Are they still there?" I asked her, trying to pull myself up.

"Yes, your legs are still there. But…" she said, in almost a whisper as her voice cracked.

"Please don't tell me that I'll never walk again." I begged her.

"I'm sorry." Ms. Darby said quietly, as she wiped her eyes.

"No!" I yelled out, feeling like had just been stabbed in the heart. All my dreams of dancing were gone. This was more than I could handle and I fell into a very deep depression.

I don't remember anything else that Ms. Darby said to me. I can remember Kathi coming to the hospital and the doctors talking to me, but I can't recall the conversations. I know that my parents were by my bedside the entire time. What I do remember, is being told that I will never be able to walk again, even with physical therapy. I've had too many operations to count, but the doctors have always been very careful not to sound too hopeful.

My parents are devastated by what has happened to me, but they also want me to be thankful that I am still here. Should I be? For what reason? I can't walk or stand and I certainly can't ever dance again. What is there to be thankful for? I'll be in a wheelchair for the rest of my life, I'll never be able to have kids and I'll always be a burden to my parents.

I have had to move back home to my parent's house and every day I have to force myself to think about reasons why I shouldn't commit suicide. I just don't feel like life is worth living anymore.

Jake is in prison, but that doesn't really matter to me, what good does that do?

Do you have any idea what my days are like? I sleep. I sleep all of the time, because that's the only way that I don't think. My mother wakes me up to eat, which I don't care if I do or not. I force myself to eat, but I'd really rather be dead. My dreams, my whole reason for living, are dead.

PAM

My name is Pam and I was left for dead by my abuser. My boyfriend at the time was Jeff and he was a real jerk. My best friend Cassie and I shared an apartment, I swear everyday that she tried to persuade me to leave Jeff. I finally did come to my senses and I called it off with Jeff. I was pretty scared after that because he threatened to kill me, he told me that no one ever breaks up with him!

Cassie witnessed the abuse I suffered on many occasions. After I broke up with him, she told me that she was very happy. But shortly after that the phone calls started and he would bang on our door during the night. He would even stand across the street and stare at our front door, it was all very creepy.

One Saturday morning, Cassie and I were going to go do our laundry together. We left the front door of our apartment opened, as we brought a couple of loads of laundry and the soap out to the car. I waited in the car for Cassie to come out. After waiting a few minutes for her to come out, I went back inside. That's when I saw Jeff. He was standing behind Cassie with his arm around her throat.

"Get in and shut the door." Jeff told me. "Do it now or I'll kill her."

I was so afraid that I wanted to turn and run out the door, but I did as he said. Once the door was closed, he seemed to relax his arm around Cassie's neck.

"Let's all go into the livingroom." he told me, waiting for me to go first. He followed me, still holding onto Cassie. "We are not over until I say that we are. You broke the rules and I am going to kill you for that."

"Please, let Cassie go, she doesn't have anything to do with this. Please, just let her go." I begged Jeff.

"No, you wouldn't have left me if Cassie hadn't pushed you. I know that Cassie hates me. Now you are going to watch her die and then I am going to kill you. You have no one to blame, but yourselves." Jeff said to us.

"You're right, I do hate you." Cassie yelled at him. She tried to pry his arm from around her neck. "Pam is better off without you."

"You bitch." Jeff yelled, pulling something out of his pocket. He touched a button and a sharp looking blade came out of the top of what he was holding. I saw that it was a switch blade. Quickly, he moved it across Cassie's throat and I screamed. I watched as my best friend slid to the floor, her eyes wide open and blood was pouring from her neck.

"Oh my god." I whispered, putting my hand up to cover my mouth. I stood there staring down at Cassie, I couldn't move. I was afraid to.

"One down, one to go." Jeff said, as he wiped the blood from his knife off onto Cassie's back.

Hearing his voice seemed to bring me back to the present. I turned and started to run from the room. Suddenly, I felt Jeff grab me by the hair and jerk me back. I tripped over my own feet and fell to the floor. I tried to twist away from his grip. I managed to turn onto my stomach and that's when I felt the knife plunge into my back, buttocks and legs.

The pain was unbearable, I felt myself being turned over onto my back. Jeff took the knife and plunged it deep into my stomach and he slid it all the way over to my hip bone. I watched as Jeff got up off me and walked towards the door.

Slowly I pulled myself up, so that I could look down at my stomach. I saw that the carpet around me was very bloody. I looked down and slowly lifted up my shirt. When I did that, something fell out of the gaping hole. I saw my intestines hanging out and I tried to push them back inside. I kind of crawled over to the phone and I dialed 911, then I passed out.

I'm told, that I woke up three days later. I was in the hospital and ended up staying there for a few months. Cassie was dead by the time the ambulance got to our house.

Later the same day that he had attacked us, Jeff had been stopped by the police on a traffic violation. The cop let him go, after issuing a ticket. The information on him hadn't been processed yet. By the time I told them what he had done, he was long gone. He left me for dead that day and I have no idea where he is now…hopefully he's far away.

RONI

My name is Roni and I am living with people in a 'safe house.' None of the women here know each others real names, we aren't allowed to tell. It is for our own protection. I had to leave my husband, because I am sure that he would have eventually ended up killing me.

I got some help from the women at our local shelter, they helped me to leave. Since leaving I have been in a few different 'safe houses.' They keep moving us around to protect us, while we wait. Some women are patient, while others wait impatiently, for our 'papers.'

I can't wait to have a semi 'normal' life.

NICOLLETTE

My name is Nicollette. For years I had no idea that I was even in an abusive relationship. Tony never hit me, slapped me, punched me or kicked me. But he did call me names, throw things at me and he made me isolate myself from my friends and family.

I felt really bad about myself, I guess my self esteem was pretty low. One night after I'd watched a movie on tv, a special came on. The special had some women discussing the different signs of abuse. When they said name calling, isolation, etc., my mouth dropped open.

The next day I called a shelter and I asked some questions, actually I asked a lot of questions. I found out that it was wrong for Tony to treat me the way that he did.

Today, we are divorced and I am happily remarried. My husband Mark treats me with total love and respect.

ANTONIA

I was once called Antonia, but I have a different name now. I have a different life now, too. I am a waitress, it's not much for pay or glamour, but I am safe. I also have a tiny apartment, it's not the nicest place, but no one hurts me there. I can go to sleep and leave the dirty dishes in the sink until morning. I don't have to make my bed in the morning, if I choose not to.

My husband doesn't tell me what to do anymore. He also doesn't know where I am. I have to be careful when I do things. I always have to worry that he may be looking for me or that someday he may find me.

I used to have a good paying job and I never worried about money, but I worried about being hit. Today I worry about money, but I don't worry about being beaten.

Everyday when I wake up, I thank god for the shelter. Without their help, I am sure that I would be dead by now. I've even started to date again.

ANGEL

My name is Angel and Carlos was my husband for twenty six years. He was a good father and a nice man, at first. Actually he was okay, until his mother died four years ago. After his mom died, he had to listen to his father constantly degrade him. Carlos' mother used to keep the peace between Carlos and his dad, things like that rarely happened when his mother was alive.

Enrique, Carlos' father was terrible to my husband. Unfortunately, my husband would start to take things out on me. He started to slap me and punch me, because he felt frustrated. I didn't know what to do. Normally if something happened I would go to my mother in law, but I couldn't now.

I allowed it to happen for about three years. I tried to cover the bruises and the black eyes. I thought that I did a pretty good job of hiding them too, until one day my oldest daughter asked me why I let him hurt me.

I couldn't believe that she knew what was going on. She didn't even live at home anymore. She was married and had her own family. We talked about it for a while and then she called a hotline number for me.

My daughter brought me to the shelter the next day. I talked with some of the women there. I even sat in on a support group they were having. I was surprised to hear that other women were going through similar things.

For the next few months my daughter picked me up and we went to the support groups together. Thanks to my daughter and the group, I got the courage to leave my husband. We have been separated for six months now. Carlos did agree to go to counseling with me four months ago. He wants me to move back in, but I am going to take it very slowly. Things are going really well with the counseling and between us, but I am not ready to get back together yet. I want to be sure that he will never hurt me again.

I do love my husband and I miss him very much. Every week after we go to the counselor, we go out and have a nice dinner together. Next week we are going to go to a movie. We both know that we have to take things slow, but it is nice that we can talk to each other. He can express his feelings without using his fists.

CRYSTAL

Crystal was a good student in school, she didn't have a lot of friends, but she did have a couple of close ones. Every weekend Crystal and both of her friends would hang out at the mall. All three girls were attractive and a lot of boys noticed them, especially when they were at the mall.

They lived in a college town and there were a lot of twenty-year-old boys that hung out at the mall. One weekend Crystal and an older boy started talking to each other. They did some harmless flirting and then the girls went home, but not before he had gotten her phone number and her email address.

When she got home, there were four email messages waiting for her. They were all from 'Mark.' She quickly emailed him back and then she went into the bathroom to get ready for bed.

When she came out a few minutes later, there were two more emails from him. Feeling flattered, she sat down and spent the next two hours emailing back and forth with him.

He suggested that they get together the next weekend, which she agreed to do. She was so happy that their age difference didn't matter to him, because she thought that he was very cute. Mark was twenty one and Crystal was fifteen, but she was going to be sixteen in four months.

Crystal couldn't wait for the weekend, she and Mark emailed each other the entire week. Finally Saturday morning came and she asked her parents if she could stay at the mall longer, so that the girls could see a movie. Her parents agreed and told her they would pick her up at midnight. At four o'clock, Crystal's dad dropped her off at the mall's main entrance.

The three girls agreed to meet at the water fountain. Crystal was the first to arrive and as she stood there waiting for her friends, she was surprised to see that Mark was already there. He walked towards her and she smiled at him. They talked there by the fountain, while Crystal waited for her friends.

Once the others showed up they hung out together until the movie was about to start. As the four of them walked towards the theater Mark whispered to Crystal. He told her that he would rather grab something to eat and talk with her, than to go see a movie.

Standing outside the theater Crystal told her friends that she didn't want to go in. She told them that she would meet them after the movie. Reluctantly, Jeannie and Mandy went into the theater without her, leaving their friend standing outside the entrance, next to Mark.

Ninety minutes later, when the movie was over, the two girls waited by the fountain for Crystal. After about twenty minutes, they decided to walk around and look for her. All of the stores were closed as they walked through the mall. The only places that were opened, was the lounge and an arcade.

After circling through the mall twice, they decided to go out into the almost empty parking lot. They thought that maybe she was out there. Within a couple of minutes they saw Crystal's dad pull into the parking lot.

"Hey girls, how was the movie?" he asked them, looking around. "Where's Crystal?"

"We can't find her anywhere." Jeannie said, as she started to cry.

"Weren't you all in the movie theater together?" Crystal's dad asked them.

"Well, no. Crystal left with Mark, before the movie started. We thought that she would be back by now." Mandy said, wiping away the tears from her cheeks.

"Wait right here!" He told them, as he parked the car and got out. "Let's go inside." Crystal's dad said to them when he came back.

Together the three of them walked into the mall. They walked all through the mall and saw nothing. Crystal's dad went inside the lounge and a few minutes later he came back out.

"The bouncer said that you two can come inside with me and see if you can find Mark." he said, to the two girls.

Jeannie and Mandy looked closely at everyone inside the bar, but neither one of them saw Mark.

"Okay, let's drive through the parking lot, maybe they're outside talking in one of the cars." Crystal's dad suggested. Jeannie and Mandy looked at each other, realizing that he was desperately trying to think of everything. They both had noticed the tears welling up in his eyes and that really unnerved them.

Once they were in the car, they must have circled the parking lot at least three times. Mandy suggested that they try out in back of the mall. When they drove out there they saw nothing, but trash bins and empty boxes.

"I have to call the police and we need to call your parents, too." he told the girls, slowly putting his head down onto the steering wheel. It took him a couple of minutes to regain his composure.

They went back inside the mall and called the police. Two police officers came and listened to what the girls had to say. Then the police and the security guards began to search everywhere. A few minutes later, one of the cops came over to them carrying a purse. Yes, it was Crystal's and they noticed that the strap was broken. They said that it had been found near one of the trash bins in the back.

One of the cops brought the two girls home, because it was getting very late. Jeannie and Mandy each gave Crystal's dad a hug before they left. Unfortunately, nothing else was found and they continued to search throughout the night.

In the morning, the cops saw some blood near where they had found her purse. After he had been at the mall for more than seventeen hours, the cops told Crystal's father to go home.

Two weeks later they discovered a female body, almost three miles away from the mall. It was Crystal's, she had been raped and beaten to death. They never found Mark.

CASSIE

Cassie was my old name and now I have a new one. My son and daughter also have new names. We live in a different place and we are beginning to make some friends.

Every week I go to the support group at the shelter, which really helps me a lot. We talk about the abuse that we've suffered and how it has affected our lives. There are a lot of women who also have new names in the group. We don't talk about our old names, we were told to forget them.

My husband threatened to kill me and my kids, so we left. I put up with the abuse for many years. There were many emergency room visits for me and the kids. We used to have to avoid people, until the bruises faded. We all had stitches and broken bones on numerous occasions. One day he really busted me up pretty bad. I ended up with four cracked ribs, a black eye, split lip and I'd lost one of my teeth. That was enough!

We went to the shelter and they got us away from there. Legally I am still married to him, well Cassie is, I'm not. Today my kids and I can smile and laugh. We are not afraid to do something wrong for fear of being beaten. My family is so much happier now.

JENA

My husband never hit me, but he did yell at me and call me names. I thought that I was stupid and ugly. I was afraid to take a chance or to try anything new, I figured that I would just fail. I had no self esteem or confidence in myself at all.

My cousin pointed out that he wasn't treating me right. I went to a support group for battered women, I had myself convinced that I wasn't one of them. I found out that I was wrong. I had been beaten and abused verbally, emotionally and spiritually.

I am now divorced and much happier. I still go to the support group and I am in a healthy, loving relationship now.

PAT

My name is Pat and my boyfriend wouldn't let me see any of my friends or family. He always talked bad about them and he would call them names, not to their faces, but to me. When my sister would call, he'd be really rude to her and sometimes he'd even hang up the phone on her.

If I was gone when he called I'd get into trouble. He would call at different times, so I never knew when to expect his call. If the phone was busy when he tried to call, he'd be furious. I was afraid to go out to even get the mail, because I might miss his call. If I didn't answer the phone, he'd be miserable to me all night long.

Sometimes he'd yell at me and other times he wouldn't say a word. Sometimes he'd go for days and never say one word to me. He kept me so isolated from my friends and family. He didn't want me to be around anyone, but him. When his friends and family stopped by, he didn't like for me to talk with anyone, which was actually pretty awkward. I enjoyed talking to people and being around people, before I was with Jim.

Now I am enjoying the company of other people again. I was with Jim four years ago. I finally got tired of it and I left him. He threatened me and he kept calling me on the phone. Eventually, he got bored and he left me alone. I guess he got tired of talking to my answering machine.

MARLENE

My name is Marlene now, I used to have a different name, but that was a long time ago. Today I have two beautiful children and a wonderful husband. We have been married for five years and he has never once hit me or even yelled at me. My children are happy and healthy. I call them my little miracles, because I was told that I probably would never be able to have any children.

When I was married to my 'first husband' I got pregnant, which really got him upset. One day, after I refused to get an abortion, he took out a coat hanger and the vacuum cleaner, then he proceeded to give me an abortion.

I was admitted into the hospital because I was hemorrhaging, it was really awful and I was pretty messed up inside. The doctors tried to repair what they could, but they were also honest with me. They told me that I probably would never be able to conceive.

My husband got away with it, because he said that I begged him to get rid of it. It came down to my word against his and everyone assumed that because I was scared, I was blaming him. They thought that I had wanted an abortion and got scared because it was botched up.

After I healed as well as I was going to, I told him I was going to get a divorce. He reacted in his usual way and beat me up pretty badly. Each time I left him he found me, then he'd drag me back home and beat me for leaving. I was terrified of him. I knew that it was useless to leave him, because he always found me. Maybe not right away, but eventually he did. It was just a matter of time.

Finally I called a shelter and asked them for help. They came and picked me up, then they brought me to a 'safe house.' Once I had settled in, I went to bed, because I was so emotionally and mentally exhausted.

In the morning I was called into the offices, where they told me that they would be able to help me to get away. They also told me if I did what they told me to, they were pretty confident that he would never find me.

Within a few days, I had instructions on where to go, who to talk to when I got there and I also had a new name. That was hard to get used to, after twenty eight years I was supposed to answer to a different name. I was so afraid. Every time someone looked at me, I was afraid that my husband had sent them.

After a few months I began to relax a little and that was my mistake. I didn't get careless, but I did stop worrying so much. I stopped becoming aware of things around me. I wasn't aware of anything or anyone different.

I didn't notice that I was being followed. Now looking back, I can remember the car and even the man. Needless to say, my husband found me and beat me. Again, I was dragged back home.

The next day when my husband went to work, I called the shelter. They brought me back to the 'safe house.' They told me not to feel bad or blame myself. He had hired a private investigator. They also said that next time it would be easier, I would pay more attention.

Within a week, I had a new name and a new destination to go to. When I left I kept my guard up, I was aware of everything. I worked in a restaurant and met a wonderful man, who I gave the hardest time to for months. Finally after about six months of flowers and flirting, I agreed to go to dinner with him.

We dated for two years and he still wanted to be with me, even after I had told him about my husband. Jack is the most loving, tender and patient man I have ever met. I don't know what I did to deserve him, but I thank god every day for that man.

Jack and I talked to the pastor at our church and told him everything. He sympathized with us and told us that he would be willing to marry us, before the eyes of god. So we arranged a simple ceremony and invited a few of our friends. I am still unclear how my marriage is legal with my 'new name,' but the pastor assured me that everything was legal. The 'old' me no longer existed, Marlene and Jack were getting married.

After we had been married for about two years, I decided that I really wanted to have children. I had told Jack about what had happened to me before. We tried for months and when nothing happened, we again, turned to our pastor and church. Amazingly, within three months I conceived a child.

I was bedridden during my pregnancy, because of all the scar tissue. The doctors were very concerned. No one expected me to carry the baby to term, but I did. I even went two weeks over my due date! Andy was the most beautiful baby that I'd ever seen. Jack and I were so happy. Just when I decided that life couldn't get any better, I found out that I was pregnant again.

When Andy was eleven months old, I gave birth to Jessica. My husband and I were deliriously happy. These are my two miracle babies and my husband is so unbelievable.

Sometimes I have to pinch myself, to make sure that I am not dreaming. My life is so wonderful and full. I still keep an eye out for 'him' and I probably always will. Occasionally, I'll wake up in the middle of the night, crying and sweating. But Jack always rolls over and holds onto me, until I fall back to sleep. The nightmares don't happen as often now as they used to.

I didn't think that I would ever say, I love my life, but I do.

TESSA

My name is Tessa and I was once the Prom Queen. Now I am in a horrible marriage to a terrible man. Things weren't always like this, we were once very happy, at least at first. Then his brother moved in with us, after he lost his job and all he did was sit around and drink. I wanted him to move out, but my husband didn't. He said that he couldn't just throw him out. I didn't exactly want to throw him out, but I did want him to get a job. I wouldn't have just thrown him out, not without a job or a place to go.

His brother was the cause of many of our fights. I would fight with my husband and his brother would get involved in our arguements. He wouldn't stay out of our business. The worst part was, that he always stood up for his brother, whether he was right or wrong. There was so much friction inside our house.

One day my husband's brother slapped me across the face, during a fight. I punched him back. My husband then proceeded to hit me. The entire time, his brother kept egging him on. I threatened to leave and they both told me if I did they'd hunt me down and drag me back.

That all started a few months ago and I'm still here. I'm afraid to leave, I'm afraid of my husband and I'm afraid of his bother. His brother is still living here too. I'm so depressed.

JERRI

My name is Jerri and my husband used to hit me. He would get very angry at work and then he would come home and take it out on me. I didn't know what to do and I didn't know who to turn to.

One day I was fed up and I left him, I went to a shelter. My husband would call me at work all the time. First he threatened me, then he begged me to come back and finally he broke down and cried. We agreed to meet and he proceeded to tell me that he loved me. He said that he would do whatever it took to get me back.

I talked to the women at the shelter and they found us a wonderful counselor. We made an appointment and have been seeing the counselor ever since. After six months, I moved back in with him.

That was four years ago and things are going pretty good for us.

JESS

My name is Jess and my husband is in prison for the murder of our children. I left Randy and moved into a small apartment with our three kids, after receiving a very severe beating.

I had temporary custody given to me through the courts, while we waited for a divorce hearing. During that time Randy was given visitation rights. He never beat our kids, but he did discipline them rather harshly. I never thought that he would hurt them, but he did want to hurt me and apparently he found the best way to do that.

Our kids were one, three and five years old when they died. Randy kept begging me to come home and stop the divorce, but I wouldn't. I wish now that I had lied to him and told him whatever he'd wanted to hear. Maybe then my kids would still be with me.

He picked up the kids and asked me to come home, then he got angry when I told him no. I thought he acted strange after that, but I may be remembering things wrong. It was still summer and we were in the middle of a heat wave. I am not really clear about what happened that weekend, but I do know that our neighbor saw all three of my kids, floating in the pool.

The police came over to my apartment to tell me. I don't know for sure if my husband murdered them or if he just wasn't watching them. I find it hard to believe that all three of them drowning, was an 'accident.' Either way, my kids are gone and my husband is in jail.

I remember that weekend he kept calling me up on the phone. First, he'd invited me to have dinner with them, then he invited me to watch a movie. Each time that I told him no, he seemed to get more upset, but I didn't really think too much about it.

The courts put my husband away for negligence and child endangerment. None of my kids had bruises or any other marks on them that showed any signs of struggle. As far as I am concerned he killed my kids, whether it was an accident or not. I was told that murder could not be proven in this case.

We are divorced now, but I would go back to my awful marriage in a second, if I could just have my kids back.

UNKNOWN

I was married to Tom for two years and during that time he used to treat me very badly. He would call me names, tell me that I was worthless and constantly pick on me. He made fun of me and I felt like everything I did or every suggestion I made, was stupid.

I became very quiet and depressed. I felt like I didn't have anything worthwhile to say. The worst part was I didn't even realize I was being abused. I knew about physical abuse, but I never heard of emotional or verbal abuse, until I heard a couple of women talking in the supermarket.

Later that same day, I called the shelter in my hometown and talked to one of the women there. I was informed about emotional and verbal abuse.

I left my husband that weekend and never went back. Today I go to the shelter for group counseling and I am also taking an assertiveness class. I know that I have a long way to go, but I am feeling much better about myself now.

JACKI

My name is Jacki and I put up with my husband's abuse for about three years. It all began when I started to take some classes at the community college. I now think that he became threatened, by my trying to better myself.

I was pregnant when we got married and I stayed home with our daughter for the first four years. Then I decided that I wanted to do more than just stay home. I had decided that I wanted to be a nurse, I wanted to help people.

My husband set up the first obstacle by telling me that we couldn't afford for me to go to school. I filled out some papers and managed to get a grant, which paid for my classes and my books. Then he told me we couldn't afford to pay for a sitter, but I managed to enroll our daughter in the Early Childhood Education Program, which was free because it was run by the students. My husband then said, we didn't have any extra money for gas. So I got a bus pass and took the bus back and forth with our daughter. My husband tried to make everything as hard as he could for me.

I couldn't understand why he was working against me, instead of working with me. But I did manage to go to school, take care of our daughter and the house, despite what he had to say.

Things were going really well at school and okay at home, until one day my husband got mad at me. I was studying for a test and hadn't had the time to do the laundry. My husband blew up at me, screaming and yelling. He pulled my notebook out of my hands and tore it up. I begged for him to stop, but he just kept yelling at me. He said over and over again that I wasn't smart enough to take and pass the test.

I began to cry and I ran out of the room, after a while I heard the door shut and I went back out into the dining room. As I knelt down picking up my notes, I cried and I promised myself that no matter what, I was going to finish nursing school.

Things were pretty strained between us, but I was committed to finish my schooling. I did manage to pass my test, despite the torn notes.

I went to school for two years, while I lived with my husband. I put up with the verbal abuse and the emotional abuse, but never once did he physically abuse me. Believe me, the emotional and verbal abuse was more than enough. I finally left my husband.

My daughter and I moved into the garage apartment that my parents had converted for us. Today I am divorced and raising my daughter with my parents help. My ex husband doesn't have much to do with our daughter, ever since he got remarried.

I finally got my nursing degree. I am confident now and on the road to having a better, brighter future with my daughter.

My parents have been very supportive to us and have enabled me to finish school without having to worry about paying rent or finding a babysitter. My daughter spends most Saturday's with my mom, shopping or making cookies, which gave me the time to study. Every Wednesday afternoon my dad takes my daughter to the park, that gave me extra time to study.

RACHEL

My name was Rachel, but now I have a different name. I have two daughters who also have different names now. We were forced to leave, because of my ex husband. Rex used to beat on me and I found out that he molested our daughters. Unfortunately, the judge didn't believe me or my daughters.

I was insulted, when the judge accused me of coaching them to lie on the stand about their dad. He reprimanded me right there in front of them and in front of a full court room. What an ignorant judge he was. Arrogant and ignorant. How could he think anyone would have their daughters lie about something like that?

My lawyer was very upset, but like she said 'her hands were tied.' We tried to get the shelter to help us out, but they told me that all they could do was help us to leave. I thought about it and decided against it. I didn't want to take my daughters away from all of their friends, I couldn't do that to them. I had already taken them away from their home.

The next weekend my ex husband took the girls. I had a very uneasy feeling the entire time, no matter what I did I just couldn't shake it. I wasn't able to relax until my girls were finally back at home with me.

Once they were unpacked, I noticed that they were both very quiet and withdrawn. When I asked them about their weekend, they both began to cry and tell me their father had molested them. I couldn't believe it. After having this all just come out in court, he had the nerve to do it again? He must have felt safe, because the judge hadn't believed my girls.

Later, after the girls had gone to bed, I sat at the kitchen table and thought about our options, which weren't many. There was no way I was going to have my daughters go through another visit with their father. There was also no way I was going to make them have to endure testifying in front of that ignorant judge again.

That's when I decided I needed to call the shelter. I dialed the number and was put right through to a supervisor. We talked for quite a while and I explained everything that had happened to us. She told me the same thing as the other woman did. We agreed to meet the next day.

I was told to grab a bag for each one of us, something we could each carry on our own. So, the next morning I let the girls pack their own bags, just taking the things which were truly important to them.

About an hour later we walked into Sophia's office. I was face to face with the woman who I credit for giving me the strength and the courage to get away. We talked for hours and by the time the girls and I were led up to a room for the night, everything had been arranged.

We left the next day and have never gone back. That was seven years ago and today my daughters are doing great. My oldest just made me a grandmother and she and her husband have a wonderful marriage. My youngest is a cheerleader and enjoying her role as an aunt.

I live in fear everyday that my ex husband will find us and all of this will come to an end. Every night I pray that he will just leave us alone and stay away.

KATE

I was at one time such a happy person, at least until I met Ron. Don't get me wrong, at first he was great, but after a few months he turned into this horrible person.

We actually only dated for about four months and during that time he made my life a living hell. I lived at home with my parents and when Ron used to come over to my house, he not only treated me badly, but my parents as well.

He was so rude to the both of them and he was just plain miserable to me. He treated none of us with any respect. It got so I hated to hear the sound of his old pick up truck pulling up into the driveway. Neither one of my parents said too much, I think they were afraid if they downed him I might pull closer towards him. They didn't have to worry about that.

At about our fourth month together, I started to really begin to see clearly that he wasn't right for me. He made me feel stupid and ugly. I was embarrassed to go out in public with him, because he was even worse to me then.

I wanted to be treated with respect, I felt I deserved at least that much.

So, one night when he showed up at my house I told him I wanted to split up with him. He went absolutely crazy. He yelled, he screamed and then he hit me. Right there in front of my parents. I remember looking over at my father and seeing the look on his face.

"Call the cops." I told my mother.

She went over to the phone and that seemed to scare Ron. He ran from the room and out of our house. He never came back and never bothered me again.

PHOEBE

When I was in college I dated a guy who I thought was just wonderful, boy was I wrong. At first I was flattered by the attention he gave me, I was even flattered when he seemed to get jealous. I thought that he must have really loved me, in order to get that upset and jealous.

It started to get real bad though, he began following me everywhere I went. He said he did it because he couldn't trust any of the guys. I know that he did it because he was so obsessed with me and it was really unhealthy.

It took me a while to realize that this relationship was a very sick and destructive thing. Thankfully, I got out of it before it was too late.

ANGEL

Angel is my new name. I used to have a different name and a whole different life. I had a career and a big beautiful house, but I have none of those things now. I do have my sanity, I'm safe and I don't have to worry about being beaten anymore. To me, that's worth a whole lot more than all of my 'things.'

I have no children, which is probably a blessing. I would have loved to have had children, but the circumstances would have been horrible. You see, my husband used to beat me. Not just an occasional slap, oh no, I'm talking broken bones and lots of blood.

My husband was obsessed with having a clean and spotless house. I had a great job which demanded a lot from me, but he expected me to also keep a tidy house. A tidy house I could handle, except when he would actually check for dust in the most unusual spots.

He wanted the towels to be placed a certain way on the rack, he wanted everything in the cupboards to line up exactly right. The design on the dishes had to all be facing the same way, it was the same with everything. My husband wanted the house to be a spotless showplace. I found it impossible to keep up with his demands and to have a career. My job started to suffer and then I started to resent him and his craziness.

I found the beatings happening more and more often. I couldn't keep up with the demands at work and his crazy demands at home. I told him that he had to relax and lighten up a little or I was going to leave him. This sent him into a rage and he started busting me up. He ruined a lot of our things. When he had finally calmed down and stopped, he left. He always left after, where he went I don't know. At least he was gone and I could lick my wounds. Then clean up the mess he had made, like I always did.

Only this time I didn't. I grabbed my purse and a few of my things. I walked out of my big beautiful house and I left my demanding job. I registered in a motel a few towns away and then I got up enough nerve to call a shelter.

The next morning I found myself sitting in a strange room, talking to a few women, women who I had never met before. I was telling them all about my personal life and I must admit, I felt pretty uncomfortable doing it. I had never told anyone about what happened inside my house before. I was so embarrassed to admit the things my husband had done to me through the years. I was embarrassed to admit the things that I had allowed him to do to me through the years.

Yet, as I told these women the most intimate things about myself, they never once judged me or looked down on me, which I was convinced they would. They listened and talked to me about my options. It seemed as though they really cared and felt bad for me. I knew they must have heard these same things or similar things from other women and yet they still listened intently.

When I was through and mentally exhausted, that's when they told me I should leave the area. I was told to leave and never come back. I had no family to help me out and the only friends I had were at work. They knew nothing about what went on inside my home.

I stayed in the shelter for two weeks and during that time they kept receiving phone calls from my husband. He told them he knew I was there and if they didn't let me come home, he was going to burn the place down.

I was sure he would do something to all of us in that house. I was afraid to put all of those other women at risk. I decided I had to leave, I had to leave as much for me as for them.

Within a few days I had papers with my new name on them. I knew where to go. I also knew it was going to be a struggle for me, but I was up for it. I will admit that even without all of those 'things' I used to have, I am a much happier person today. It has been six years since I left and although it has been a struggle, it was worth it. I am finally free.

PAT

My husband Fred and I have been married for eleven years and have had our share of hard times. We went through a real difficult period about six years ago, where Fred started to feel frustrated and he hit me a few times. Well, it was more than a few times. He started to feel a lot of pressure from his job. He is the foreman down at the plant and he had to lay off a lot of employees right around the holidays.

Between Thanksgiving and Christmas, was always the worst possible time to be laying people off and unfortunately that job fell to my husband. He would come home so upset. People would cry or get very angry at him and there was nothing he could do. It was his job and he had to do what he was told.

It really got him when he had to lay off Scott, a good friend of ours. Scott had eight kids and had just discovered that his wife Rena had a brain tumor. He was laid off the day after Thanksgiving, it was terrible. Rena called me crying and I really felt bad for her. My husband was miserable.

He came home drunk that night and when I told him how I felt about Rena and Scott, he lashed out at me. Now, I love my husband, but I was not going to put up with that. I left him and went to stay at my mom's house.

The next day Fred was at my mom's door with a bouquet of the prettiest flowers and he apologized over and over to me. I, of course, went back home with him.

Less than a week later he hit me again. This time I had a bloody nose from it and he was completely sober. I left again, vowing that this would be the last time. I was wrong. I went back home with him the next day, after more flowers, another apology and more promises.

The last and final time this happened was two days later. Fred slapped me about three or four times. We just learned that Rena had died, because they had to cancel her medical treatment. Scott told us that the insurance company refused to pay for her continued medical expenses.

I told Fred that I was leaving him and I packed my bags. I understood his frustration. I felt such pain myself over the loss of my good friend. I felt terrible that the children would grow up with no mother. I felt such a loss, a loss for my friend and a loss for my marriage.

As I grabbed my suitcase Fred blocked the doorway. I didn't know what to expect.

"Please, don't go." Fred begged me.

"I can't keep living this way. I don't want to live like this. I love you, but this is more than I can bear." I told my husband.

"I want to get help. I want to go to a marriage counselor with you. Please, I need you. I am so sorry." Fred told me, as he reached for me.

I wanted to believe him, I loved him and I loved our life. I wanted to stay with him, but I didn't want to be slapped anymore.

"I will call a counselor right now. The first appointment you cancel…I am leaving." I told him, putting my bag down on the floor.

Fred scooped me up into his arms and we hugged. We made lots of promises to each other that day. I called and set up an appointment with a counselor for the both of us. We spent the rest of the afternoon in our robes, laying on the couch, holding each other and talking. We talked and talked. That day we got much closer to each other.

Today we still see the counselor, although we go only once a month now. Fred has given up being a foreman and is just an employee at the plant. It is less pay, but it is also less frustrating for Fred. We get along really great. We occasionally fight, but he hasn't raised a hand to me since that day.

TIFFANY

I was Tiffany, but today I have my sister's name. My husband used to hurt me a lot. I am a little slower than most people and I've always been told that people will take advantage of me. Reading, math and all those other things always came real hard for me.

I think that is why Joe wanted to be with me. I know he used to steal my money from me. I got a SSI check every month from the government and after I would cash my check, I'd always have money missing. He had his own money, but he wanted to control mine too.

He used to tell me that I should be grateful that he was with me, because no one else would want to be. I was too slow, I was too fat and I was too ugly. He told me that no one else would ever want me and he said that he was doing me a favor by being with me.

He married me, not because he loved me, but so I wouldn't be alone. I thought I loved him at the time. I know now he just married me because of my monthly check. I saw money was missing at first, but I never paid too much attention to it. He had me convinced that I must have somehow misplaced it.

This went on for a while and then I started to question the missing money. He would get very upset with me and he'd scream and yell. A few times he even hit and shoved me.

The last time he hurt me I had asked him where my money was, my entire check was missing. He grabbed me by the throat and started to choke me. He told me if I ever accused him of stealing my money, he was going to kill me.

I was afraid so I left the next day and went to my sisters house, where together we came up with a plan. I am using my sister's name now. I do not get my SSI check anymore and I don't make much money, but I really like the family that I take care of.

I babysit for my sister's friends, they have three little kids and I take care of the kids while they work. I have my own room at their house too, and if anyone asks, I tell them my name is Joy.

AMANDA

I attended a community college in the next town. My friends and I would go out on the weekends and usually stay out quite late. There was a group of us that had a habit of partying, well into the early morning hours.

One weekend I met Zack and he seemed like a real nice guy. We spent the whole weekend together and enjoyed each other's company very much. We made arrangements to see each other again on Monday night.

On Monday it was back to classes as usual. I found myself thinking about Zack all day, I couldn't wait to see him later on that night. I told my friends about him and they were real happy for me. Ever since Billy and I had broken up, I'd shown no interest in anyone, until I met Zack.

Zack wasn't like anyone I'd ever met before. He rode a big motorcycle and wore jeans and t-shirts. He was a mechanic and had to work hard for everything that he'd ever gotten. He even spoke differently and that is what I was looking for at the time. Someone completely different, completely different from Billy.

Billy had come from money and was spoiled. He took what he wanted and when he was done, he'd throw what he had away. Then he was out looking for something new, or someone new. He didn't care who he hurt along the way, as long as Billy was happy, that was all that mattered.

I had been hurt deeply by Billy, we had been engaged. We were going to be married next year. Billy and I had been seeing each other for three years and I had no clue that he was cheating on me the whole time. He broke off our engagement six months before I had met Zack.

When classes were over I went back to my dorm room and had six messages waiting for me, all from Zack. I had just walked into my room when the phone in the hallway rang, it was Zack. We talked for about a hour, he seemed upset when I told him that I had a lot of studying to do, so I wouldn't be able to see him that night.

That whole week, as soon as I got back from class Zack called and we would talk for a while. On Thursday, my friends and I went out for coffee before heading home. When I got back to my room, there were over twenty phone messages from Zack. When I finally talked to him he was very angry, he yelled at me and made me feel uncomfortable. But later, he apologized to me and said that he had gotten angry because he had been worried about me. We agreed to meet on Friday afternoon and spend the weekend together, again.

I had a great time with him that weekend. On Monday morning, I had a lot of thinking to do. All weekend he pressured me about moving in with him. He told me that he missed me when I was away from him. He pointed out that all the time we had spent on the phone, was time we could have spent being together. It made sense to me at the time, but I was still leery because we hardly knew each other and things seemed like they were progressing very fast.

I did enjoy being with Zack. I enjoyed doing things together and I was looking forward to getting to know him better. But I kept feeling pressure from him and I felt rushed. I was more comfortable to let things move more slowly, on a more natural level. I didn't want to feel rushed or pressured into making such a big decision.

I did feel like I could be happy with Zack, but on the other hand I didn't know him very well. He did treat me good, except on the couple of occasions that he'd gotten jealous. I figured he was jealous because his ex wife had cheated on him. I figured I couldn't really blame him for not trusting people right away. Zack was nine years older than I was, but it didn't really matter to me.

My friends tried to convince me to get to know him better before making such a big decision. The entire week my friends and I discussed this whole moving in with him idea. My friends were very persuasive. Together we decided that if he wanted me to move in and if he really cared about what I thought, he would respect my decision to hold off on my moving in with him, until I felt more comfortable. This was too big of a decision to make so quickly.

I decided to wait until we were together that weekend before telling him that I wasn't going to move in with him. I knew he'd be disappointed, so I thought it would be easier face to face. Now I wish that I had told him over the phone.

During the week he called me at the dorm as usual and he asked me everyday if I had thought about his offer. I told him that I had thought about it. When he asked me if I'd made a decision, I lied and told him not yet, but I would have one by the weekend.

On Wednesday night, he called to tell me that he loved me. He got a little upset when I didn't tell him the same.

Friday afternoon when I was walking to my dorm, I heard the roar of a motorcycle coming closer. As I turned I saw Zack. He had a big smile on his face as he pulled up next to me.

"It's Friday and officially the weekend." Zack said to me, climbing off his motorcycle.

"It isn't officially the weekend, until I drop off my books." I told him, smiling.

"Let's go drop off your books then," he said to me, as he got back onto his motorcycle. "I have a surprise for you."

I climbed onto the back of his bike. "I need to get some clothes for the weekend." I said, as I put on the extra helmet.

"We'll come back later, I need to show you something first." he said, starting the motorcycle.

"Why aren't you at work?" I yelled over the loud engine. I guess he didn't hear me, because he never answered.

We drove in and out of traffic, then finally stopped outside of his house. He lived on the top floor of a two story house. His apartment was small, but neat.

"Come on." Zack said, grabbing me by my hand.

Slowly he opened up the door to his apartment and I was surprised by what I saw. There were flowers everywhere and there were candles lit throughout the apartment. I looked around the room and then he led me into the bedroom.

The bedroom had vases full of flowers and the sheets were pulled back on the bed. On the pillow was a small box with a bow on it.

"Go open it." Zack told me, smiling.

"What is it?" I asked, curious.

"Go look." Zack said, gently pushing me into the room.

I walked over to the bed and picked up the box. I turned it over in my hand and I looked up at him.

"Open it," he told me, still smiling.

I opened up the box and saw a diamond ring inside.

"I want you to marry me." Zack said to me. "I want to do things right."

"Zack, I don't know. I just met you two weeks ago. We hardly know each other." I said.

"I love you." Zack told me. "You were going to move in anyway, right? So we'll just be engaged for a while, then we'll get married."

"Zack, I decided not to move in with you, yet. I don't feel like it's right, I feel as though we are moving way too fast." I told him.

Zack came over to me. "What do you mean you weren't going to move in? I thought everything was going good between us. I thought you loved me." He started to raise his voice, beads of sweat began to form on his forehead.

I backed away a step and gripped the tiny box in my hand.

"I never said I would move in with you. I never implied that I was in love with you or even falling in love with you. Things were going good between us, until you started to pressure me into moving in with you." I told him, trying to be gentle.

Zack slapped me across the face and the box fell from my hand. When it hit the floor he grabbed me by the throat. He slammed me into the wall and then he started to scream at me. He accused me of leading him on and how I had only used him. He told me that he was going to make me regret ever playing him for a fool.

I tried to plead with him and to explain why I didn't want to move in. Zack didn't want to hear what I had to say, he just kept yelling at me.

He bent down to pick up the box and that's when I decided to try to run past him, to the door. Zack was quicker than I was. He reached out and grabbed me by the ankle, which caused me to fall onto the floor.

As I lay on my stomach, I felt him grab me and flip me over onto my back. He climbed on top of me and continued to yell, while he held the box with the ring in front of my face.

"You mislead me," he screamed at me.

"No one mislead you. Please, let me leave." I begged him.

"Let you leave? Let you leave, me? No, I will not let you leave. You are going to move in and we are going to get married." Zack said, while he held me with one hand. He tried to take the diamond ring out of the box with the other hand. He grabbed my hand and put the ring on my finger.

"Please, let me go back to the dorm." I asked him, getting scared.

"Why?" Zack asked me.

"If I am going to move in with you, I'll need to get my stuff." I told him, trying to convince him into letting me leave.

"Okay." Zack said, after he had put the ring on my finger. "Let's go get your stuff."

He helped me to get up from off the floor and together we left his apartment. I was trying to think of a way to get out of this situation. I knew the dorm would be full of girls getting ready to go out, so maybe I could get some help once I got there.

We got on the motorcycle and drove to my dorm. Zack followed me inside and we went up to my room. Once inside, I slowly started to gather some of my things. I was trying to think of how to get myself out of this situation, but I kept drawing blanks.

"Come on, you are taking too long." Zack said to me, after a while.

"Look, Zack. I think maybe we need to take a couple of days to figure things out. I think we need to be sure that we both want this." I said, trying to convince him.

"I know that I want to be with you and that we are going to get married. We will be happy, I promise you." Zack told me.

"Try to understand. It's me, not you. I need to be sure I'm doing the right thing. I wouldn't want to end up hurting you." I said to him.

"Hurt me? How? Cheat on me? Leave me?" Zack asked me, as his voice grew hard.

"No. I would never cheat on you." I told him.

He grabbed me by both of my arms and squeezed tight. "We will be together, now and forever." Zack told me.

"I'm sorry. I can't be with you." I told him, deciding it was better to tell him here.

"What?" he yelled at me. Zack grabbed me and threw me onto my bed, then he started hitting me. "You are coming back to my apartment with me."

"No, I'm not. Things aren't going to work out between us. I think you need to leave." I yelled back at him.

Zack got real mad and I felt him start to punch me, as well as slap me. I tried to scream for help, but his hand was clamped down hard on my mouth. I kneed him in the crotch and he let go for a few seconds, long enough for me to scream out. I hoped that over the noise of the hair dryers, someone would hear me.

Zack grabbed me by the throat and started to choke me. I was so afraid, I thought I was going to die. Just when I started to see spots, I heard a banging in the distance. It sounded so far away, but it was really my door being busted down. The campus police came rushing into the room and pulled Zack off of me. I sat up gasping for breath.

The room seemed to fill with people and I saw my friends pushing past everyone to get over to me. We all hugged, while the police handcuffed Zack. I looked down at the ring on my finger and pulled it off.

"Zack…take this back." I told him, handing it to one of the campus cops.

Eventually my room cleared out and I found myself alone with two of my closest friends. We talked about what had happened and all jumped when there was a knock on my broken door.

It was one of the campus cops, he said that they were bringing Zack to the police station and more than likely he would end up in jail for a while. He told me that he felt I would be safe and if I needed anything to just call them.

Later that night, I heard the phone ring and I was told I had a call. Once I said 'hello' I heard Zack's voice, telling me that I was going to be sorry. He said that I never should have lied to him. He also told me that I'd better watch my back, because he was always going to know every move I ever made and one day he would find me.

I called the police and they assured me that they would let me know if and when he was released. Unfortunately, they didn't let the other shifts know this. Zack was released Monday, when he made bail and he showed up on campus.

"You bitch!" he yelled at me, as he ran through the parking lot towards me.

"Zack?" I whispered. Why hadn't the police notified me that he had been released? I looked around knowing he was about to make contact. "Help!" I screamed, as loudly as I could.

People turned to look and I saw two guys start to jog over towards us. But they didn't get there before I felt the knife that Zack was holding, plunge deep into my side. I stared up at him in disbelief, just a split second before he got tackled and thrown to the ground.

I was rushed to the hospital and stitched up. I don't know how it happened, but somehow he missed every major organ and artery. I survived, but I was in a lot of pain for quite some time.

I moved back home with my parents and now I am happily married. Joey and have been married for three years now and are planning on starting a family soon. It took me a long time to be able to trust someone, but Joey was patient with me. I am so happy that I didn't scare him off, like I tried to do in the beginning.

Zack is in prison now, the judge sentenced him to forty years for attempted murder. I hope that he stays in there at least that long.

The first step in ending the violence is recognition.

Domestic Violence is a systematic pattern of abusive behavior.

Does you partner:
Threaten to hurt you, your children or your family?
Isolate you from your family and friends?
Anger easily?
Control finances?
Exhibit extreme jealousy?
Humiliate you?
Destroy personal property?
Hit, punch, slap, kick or bite?

For more information you can contact: Domestic Violence Hotline

1-800-799-SAFE (7233)

If you have any questions or comments, you can email:

domesticwriter@yahoo.com

All messages will be forwarded to the author.

Other books by M. Webb

Domestic Abuse: Our Stories

Murder in New England & Closing the Circle